The Political Economy o
Cooperatives and Sociali

CW01507036

This book argues that capitalism cannot be said to be truly democratic and that a system of producer cooperatives, or democratically managed enterprises, is needed to give rise to a new mode of production that is genuinely socialist and fully consistent with the ultimate rationale underlying Marx's theoretical approach. The proposition that firms should be run by the workers on their own was endorsed by John Dewey, the greatest social thinker of the twentieth century, but is also shared by Marxists such as Anton Pannekoek, Karl Korsch, Angelo Tasca, Antonio Gramsci and Richard Wolff. This book explores the history of this argument, taking into account concepts from economic and political thought including historical materialism, cooperation, utopianism and economic democracy. The book will be of significant interest to scholars and students of political economy, Marxism, socialism, history of economic thought and political theory.

Bruno Jossa has held teaching posts at the Universities of Pescara, Messina, Venice and Naples. He is a co-founder of the Associazione Italiana Per Lo Studio Dei Sistemi Economici Comparati, an association which he chaired in 1992–1993.

Routledge Frontiers of Political Economy

259 **Nonviolent Political Economy**
Theory and Applications
Edited by Freddy Cante and Wanda Tatiana Torres

260 **Cognitive Capitalism, Welfare and Labour**
The Commonfare Hypothesis
Andrea Fumagalli, Alfonso Giuliani, Stefano Lucarelli and Carlo Vercellone

261 **Political Economy for Human Rights**
Manuel Couret Branco

262 **Alternative Approaches to Economic Theory**
Complexity, Post Keynesian and Ecological Economics
Edited by Victor A. Beker

263 **The Dark Side of Nudges**
Maria Alejandra Caporale Madi

264 **Inequality and Governance**
Andreas P. Kyriacou

265 **A New Approach to the Economics of Public Goods**
Thomas Laudal

266 **Marx's Capital after 150 Years**
Critique and Alternative to Capitalism
Edited by Marcello Musto

267 **The Political Economy of Cooperatives and Socialism**
Bruno Jossa

For more information about this series, please visit: www.routledge.com/books/series/SE0345

The Political Economy of Cooperatives and Socialism

Bruno Jossa

Routledge
Taylor & Francis Group

LONDON AND NEW YORK

First published 2020
by Routledge
2 Park Square, Milton Park, Abingdon, Oxon OX14 4RN

and by Routledge
52 Vanderbilt Avenue, New York, NY 10017

Routledge is an imprint of the Taylor & Francis Group, an informa business

First issued in paperback 2021

British Library Cataloguing-in-Publication Data
A catalogue record for this book is available from the British Library

Library of Congress Cataloging-in-Publication Data
A catalog record has been requested for this book

ISBN: 978-0-367-35987-4 (hbk)
ISBN: 978-1-03-208792-4 (pbk)
ISBN: 978-0-429-34307-0 (ebk)

Typeset in Bembo
by codeMantra

Contents

Introduction   1

1 A tentative assessment of the importance of the
   materialistic conception of history   14
   Introduction 14
   Alchian and Demsetz's theory of the firm 15
   Is Alchian and Demsetz's approach fully convincing? 17
   The transition to socialism and the power of capital 19
   Why is the materialistic conception of history so important? 22
   Does socialism still exist in today's world? 22
   Socialism from utopia to scientific producer cooperative economics 23

2 Is historical materialism a deterministic approach?
   The democratic firm and the transition to socialism   28
   Introduction 28
   *Does Marxism imply the assumption that history is heading in a
      given direction? 30*
   Further reflections on the notion of history in Marx and Marxism 33
   Possible transition scenarios against the backdrop of market socialism 37
   Is the capital-labour contradiction systematically escalating? 39
   Is the transition to socialism a certainty or a conjecture? 43
   Conclusion 45

3 Cooperation in the history of economic thought   49
   Marx's approach to producer cooperatives 49
   The cooperative movement in the estimation of Marshall 51
   Gramsci's theory of factory councils 52
   The separation of 'the economic' from 'the social' in Polanyi's approach 53
   Polanyi's theory of the influence of 'the economic' on human feelings 55
   Polanyi's model of socialism 57

4   Socialism today   60
    Introduction 60
    Is the rise of a new mode of production a realistic assumption? 62
    Producer cooperatives as a new production mode 64
    The scientific core of socialism 66
    Remote bankruptcy risks in democratic firms 68

5   Reform versus revolution: Struve's critique of Marx   73
    Introduction 73
    The transition to socialism 74
    Struve's idea of social evolution 76
    The roots of Marx's revolutionary vision 78
    *The basic contradiction of capitalism and the Hegelian
       matrix of Marxism 81*
    A comment on Struve's approach 82
    The notion of modes of production in Marx 86
    Further reflections on the notion of production modes 87
    Criticisms of reformism 89
    Conclusion 92

6   Competition in a democratic firm system: failures
    and constraints   96
    Introduction 96
    Solidarity in a system of democratic firms 97
    Marshall's idea of cooperation as a character-moulding agent 100
    Income distribution in market socialism 100
    Self-management and the 'challenge of Minerva' 103
    Conclusion 106

7   On dialectics and the basic contradiction in capitalism   107
    Introduction 107
    A few introductory notes on dialectics 108
    Dialectics as the analysis of a totality with real oppositions 110
    Dialectics as a method and a system of thought 112
    Defining the basic contradiction of capitalism 113
    *The basic contradiction of capitalism from the perspective
       of orthodox Marxists 115*
    Conclusion 117

8 Is socialism a utopian dream?   119

Introduction 119

The selfish gene 120

Marx and Engels on human nature 121

A materialistic analysis of human nature in different
   economic systems 123

The revolt of elites against the backdrop of self-management theory 125

A summary analysis of Social Darwinism 127

Additional notes on the relevance of the selfish gene theory to socialism 129

Conclusion 132

9 Schweickart's approach to economic democracy   135

Introduction 135

A workable form of socialism 135

Public investment funding 137

Investment control and publicly owned means of production 140

Is per capita allocation an efficient investment fund
   management method? 141

The unemployment issue 143

More criticisms of Schweickart's model 145

Conclusion 147

10 Richard Wolff's democracy at work; a cure for capitalism   150

Introduction 150

Wolff's WSDE 150

The way WSDEs work 151

Ownership rights, markets and planning 152

Conclusion 153

11 Critical perspectives on self-management theory   154

Introduction 154

Obstacles to the establishment of producer cooperatives 157

The funding difficulties of producer cooperatives 159

Possible solutions to the funding problems of LMFs 159

Equity financing 160

Non-distributable reserves 163

Risk diversification in democratically managed firms 163

Further reflections on the financing difficulties of LMFs 164

12 Marxist criticisms of democratic firm management   167
    Introduction 167
    Early Marxist criticisms of democratic firm management 169
    Further Marxist criticisms of democratic firm management 173
    Peter Marcuse's approach to producer cooperatives 177
    Conclusion 179

    Bibliography   187
    Index   223

Introduction

Two major ideas have been the preferential focus points of my speculation over the past forty and more years. One is my firm belief that capitalism is an evil, since it offers ample scope for the pursuit of personal interests and vests all power in the hands of a single class; the second is my conviction that the market, far from being an evil, is in many respects a beneficial mechanism. Based on the teachings of the known twentieth-century Scottish economists, it is a fact that just as we work towards advancing our individual interests, competition in the market simultaneously generates benefits for our fellow-beings as well.

However, for a market to produce its benefits, it must be organised in keeping with fully democratic criteria. Moreover, since man-made decisions will be prioritised over market-imposed processes, even in a system of democratic firms of the type suggested in this book, it is possible to argue that the benefit-generating potential of a democratic market is strictly dependent on the extent to which collective human will take precedence over the individual choices made in markets.

Crouch's statement that 'democracy thrives when there are major opportunities for the mass of ordinary people actively to participate, through discussion and autonomous organizations, in shaping the agenda of public life' (see Crouch 2003, p. 6) seems to foreshadow the situation that would arise following the creation of a system of worker-controlled firms.

According to Honneth (2015, pp. 77–78), 'the precondition for impressing fresh momentum on the socialist tradition is refuting Marx's definition of a market economy as a necessarily capitalistic model of society and fleshing out alternative hypotheses on the functions of markets.' Marx – he argues – adopted the conceptual strategy specific to Hegelian totalising thought in order to contend that all the multiple aspects of markets were inextricably associated with capitalism, and this may explain why the movement proved unable to frame a market-friendly socialist model even after his death (see *idem*, p. 77).[1]

Hence, Lasch is right in arguing that any philosophical speculations designed to define the twenty-first century-concept of 'public interest' should give priority to the demands of the community over the right of individuals to make their personal decisions, i.e. that emphasis should be laid on responsibilities, rather than rights (see Lasch 1995, pp. 115–16). The challenge before us, he argued, is shaping a community structure capable of outperforming the welfare state by reducing the role of markets and the power of corporations without replacing them with a centralised State bureaucracy.

In a 1935 paper weighing the benefits and shortcomings of Marxian political economy against those of mainstream economic theory, Oskar Lange argued that the former fell, admittedly, short of the latter in areas such as pricing and resource allocation but offered a variety of advantages: specifically, besides bringing to the foreground economic organisation patterns, class divisions in society and different modes of production, it was mainly designed to shed light on the laws governing the evolution of human society in a long-term perspective.

One major fault of Lange's approach is his failure to mention the tendency of mainstream economists (unlike Marx) not to rate markets as an evil solely because of its potential to leverage the private profit motive.

Time and again, Gramsci argued that it is not from scientific progress that we are to expect solutions to the problems traditionally explored by philosophers and economists. Philosophical and economics insights have rather come from notions such as 'social production relations' and can be summed up as follows: in that it highlights a sequence of different production modes in history (the mode of the ancients, feudalism, capitalism, etc.), it suggests that capitalism can hardly be the last link in this chain; furthermore, it makes clear that the mechanisms and evolution of each production mode obey specific laws and rules and that individual behaviour is greatly affected by the way production activities are organised. Weak points of Gramsci's approach are his endorsement of a Soviet-type centrally planned social model and little attention to the role of democratically organised markets.

Every theorist rating Marx's 'history-as-totality' conception as the true core of his theory of society must necessarily attach due importance to the concept of 'mode of production'. In Marxian theory, production, distribution, exchange and consumption are different links of a single chain, i.e. different facets of one and the same unit. Commenting on this point in a youthful work on historical evolution, Lukàcs[2] remarked that Marx, much like the German philosophers and chiefly Hegel, conceived of world history as a unitary process and an everlasting revolutionary avenue towards liberation, and that the uniqueness of his approach lay in the way he consistently prioritised a comprehensive global approach.

In the light of these reflections, the core point to be analysed in this book is whether the introduction of an all-cooperatives system can be considered a revolution that Marx would have been prepared to endorse.

2. In the *Inaugural Address* (1964), Marx wrote:

> But there was in store a still greater victory of the political economy of labour over the political economy of property. We speak of the co-operative movement, especially of the co-operative factories raised by the unassisted efforts of a few bold 'hands'. The value of these great social

experiments cannot be over-rated. By deed, instead of by argument, they have shown that production on a large scale, and in accord with the behest of modern science, may be carried on without the existence of a class of masters employing a class of hands; that to bear fruit, the means of labour need not be monopolised as a means of dominion over, and of extortion against, the labouring man himself; and that, like slave labour, like serf labour, hired labour is but a transitory and inferior form, destined to disappear before associated labour plying its toil with a willing hand, a ready mind, and a joyous heart.[3]

The *Inaugural Address* of 1864 has been described as the rough draft of a political economy of labour, and right upon its publication, some authors drew attention to Marx's argument that only a nation-wide system of producer cooperatives created with State aid could give rise to a socialist system.

The third volume of *Capital* includes the following, equally relevant argument:

> With the development of co-operatives on the workers' part, and joint-stock companies on the part of the bourgeoisie, the last pretext for confusing profit of enterprise with the wages of management was removed, and profit came to appear in practice as what is undeniably was in theory, mere surplus-value, value for which no equivalent was paid.[4]

These quotes are clear evidence that Marx looked upon an all-cooperatives system not only as feasible, but as bound to assert itself in history, as a new mode of production which would wipe out hired labour and a system where privately-owned means of production – capital – would cease being used to enslave workers. In such a system, he claimed, workers would no longer be exploited and, even more importantly, would be freely and willingly working for firms owned by themselves.

The system of producer cooperatives envisaged by Marx was a market system that made workers 'their own masters'[5] and deprived capital owners of the power to make decisions in matters of production. In Marx's opinion, this system was not only 'in accord with the behest of modern science', but even more efficient than capitalism because it was a new mode of production arising right within the older mode of production and supplanting it.

Both the equation of an all-cooperatives system with a new mode of production and its assumed potential for outperforming and superseding capitalism are underscored in other passages from *Capital*, vol. III. On pages 570–71, for instance, Marx describes joint-stock companies as firms which will lead to *the abolition of the capitalist mode of production* 'within the capitalist mode of production itself', and further on he also argues:

> The co-operative factories run by workers themselves are, within the old form, the first examples of the emergence of a new form, even though they naturally reproduce in all cases, in their present organization, all the

defects of the existing system, and must reproduce them. But the opposition between capital and labour is abolished there, even if at first only
in the form that the workers in association become their own capitalists,
i.e. they use the means of production to valorise their labour. These factories show how, at a certain stage of development of the material forces
of production, and of the social forms of production corresponding to
them, a new mode of production develops and is formed naturally out
of the old [...].

Capitalist joint-stock companies as much as cooperative factories
should be viewed as transition forms from the capitalist mode of production to the associated one, simply that in one case the opposition is
abolished in a negative way, and in the other in a positive way.[6]

One of the reasons why Marx forcefully endorsed cooperation and the abolition of hired labour even in a system remaining purely mercantile in nature is
that (from the perspective of a critic of capitalism) producer cooperatives realise such a basic component of political democracy as economic democracy.
Indeed, Marx, Marxists and other critics of the existing social order concordantly rate political democracy as merely formal when power remains firmly
in the hands of capitalists, in other words when capital is still the economic
power holding everything in its sway (see, for instance, Wolff 2012, p. 94).

The following excerpt from *Capital* is of similar relevance in this connection:

Capitalist production has itself brought it about that the work of supervision is readily available, quite independent of the ownership of capital.
It has therefore become superfluous for this work of supervision to be
performed by the capitalist. A musical conductor need in no way be the
owner of the instruments in his orchestra, nor does it form part of his
function as a conductor that he should have any part in paying the 'wages'
of other musicians. Cooperative factories provide the proof that the capitalist has become just as superfluous as a functionary in production as he
himself, from his superior vantage-point, finds the large landlord.[7]

Here Marx was clearly foreshadowing a market economy model that would
strip capitalists of all power.

3. The claim that socialism boils down to democratic firm management
was advanced, *inter alia*, by the elderly Lenin, who equated socialism with
cooperation, rather than centralised planning.

Lenin was one of the earliest political thinkers to set socialism against
communism and to contend that communism was to be built 'out of
non-communistic bricks'. In sync with Lenin on this point, Bukharin drew
a distinction between the transition from feudalism to capitalism and the
turn from capitalism to socialism. In feudal systems, he argued, the members
of the bourgeoisie were not exploited because they could, and did, use their
autonomous township status to achieve growth independently of and even

in opposition to the feudal lords. This is why they rose to the position of leading class even before seizing political power. Nothing of the kind applies to proletarians, he specified, since this class is the victim of exploitation through sheer want of an appreciable economic basis or independent status. For this reason, he concluded, proletarians are doomed to remain an under-developed class even at advanced stages of the society in which they live and are slow to secure the abilities needed to play a role in the process designed to build a new social order. As is well known, after the launch of the NEP, Lenin complained of the dramatic underdevelopment of the proletariat, but Bukharin objected that backwardness and immaturity, far from being specific to the proletariat in Russia, were specific traits of proletarians at every stage of a revolutionary movement. Just as communism is to be built out of non-communistic bricks, he argued, so socialism will have to be constructed using capitalistic bricks (for Bukharin's reflections on this point, see Cohen 1963, pp. 146–47).

Let me repeat that Lenin was the first politician to draw a clear-cut distinction between socialism and communism and to emphasise that the materials needed to build socialism were bourgeois bricks. Concerning the control issue, in *The Impending Catastrophe and How to Combat It* (1917c) he spelt out that the overall situation was much less complex than was usually assumed and that a 'very easy and quite practical method and way of control' could be fleshed out by 'uniting the population according to profession, purpose of work, branch of labour, etc.' (*idem*, p. 802).

> Bureaucracy – he wrote – must be abandoned for democracy, the initiative of the workers and of other employees must be drawn on; they must be immediately summoned to conferences and congresses; a certain proportion of the profits must be assigned to them, provided they institute overall control and increase production,

and further on, he recommended the abolition of commercial secrecy (*idem*, pp. 810–11).[8]

In matters of competition and incentives, before the outbreak of the revolution Lenin suggested that the public apparatus of a socialist State was to control and even organise competition.

> Far from extinguishing competition – he wrote – socialism for the first time creates the opportunity for employing it on a really wide... mass scale, for actually drawing the majority of working people into a field of labour in which they can display their abilities.
>
> (Lenin 1917a, p. 386)

In that same article, he also argued that 'competition must be carefully organised among practical operators, workmen and peasants' and that 'every attempt to establish stereotyped forms and to impose uniformity from above [...] must be combated ... All "communities" – factories, villages, consumers' societies and committees of suppliers – must compete with each other' (*idem*, p. 393).

Meyer's comment on this passage was that Lenin thought of emulation as 'a tool to oblige work-dodgers to work for the state' and that 'the finding that people had to be obliged to see to their duties in the workplace came as a hard blow to proletarian aspirations and the theses fleshed out by earlier socialist theorists' (see Meyer 1957, p. 220).

In another article written in 1917, Lenin made it clear that the radical re-organisation of the pre-revolution state apparatus by the victorious working class and the nationalisation of the economic apparatus were to be carried out in manners that would not 'deprive any "owner" of a single kopek' (Lenin 1917b, p. 804). Capitalists are to be deprived of all power, he wrote, but the institutions and organisational bodies of the older system are to be retained.

In the early post-revolutionary years, Lenin described Russian socialism as a tiny island surrounded by an ocean of state-capitalism but was criticised by Bukharin for an 'improper use of the word capitalism' (see Cohen 1973, p. 140). In an article entitled *On Cooperation*, which dates from 1923, the reflections reported above induced Lenin to argue that the immense and fundamental role of cooperation had been confirmed by the events of the early post-revolutionary years and that consequently the only, fairly simple and yet gigantic task lying before them was 'organizing the population in cooperative societies' and proclaiming that 'cooperation is socialism'. In other words, as the innovative political course launched in the framework of the NEP had shown that leveraging the private profit motive was the precondition for creating a socialist system, it is safe to conclude that Lenin was planning to further cooperation. In Lenin's view, cooperation offered the unique chance of reconciling the private profit motive with the principle of State regulation and welding together the ideal bricks out of which socialism could be built even in a system opting for the retention of markets. Concluding, he argued that a socialist system could be built by transferring corporate control powers to the working class within a state apparatus willing to further worker interests.

However, on reaching this conclusion he simultaneously realised that his understanding of the essence of socialism had radically changed. Now, he argued, 'we are entitled to say that the mere growth of cooperation... is identical with the growth of socialism' while, at the same time, admitting that 'there has been a radical modification of our whole outlook on socialism' (*idem*, p. 1802).[9]

Cooperation, he went on to argue, 'which we formerly ridiculed as huckstering', constitutes the social regime we have to support by any means. When power is conquered by a social class determined to further the transition to communism, 'cooperation under our conditions nearly always coincides fully with socialism' (see Lenin 1923, pp. 1797–1803).[10] In the mind of the older Lenin, therefore, the realisation that socialism could be achieved by introducing worker control of firms and had nothing to do with centralised planning necessitated redefining the traditional concept of socialism.[11]

In point of fact, shortly before his death, Lenin was won over to Bukharin's thesis that the true source of all exploitation was 'the relationship between organisers and organised' and that 'the administration of boundless capital... assigns at least as much power to the administrators as would possession of their own private property' (see Cohen 1973, pp. 148–49). In later years this idea induced several authors, with Bruno Rizzi and Gilas among them, to theorise that central planning breeds a new class that is inimical to the establishment of a truly socialist system.

In my opinion, Bukharin's and Lenin's arguments are cogent,[12] but as they were not widely circulated, socialism continued to be equated with centralised planning and the idea of socialism as democratic worker control of firms has failed to assert itself to this day. In a critical assessment of the work of an arch-enemy of socialism such as Friedrich von Hayek, Radnitzky wrote that throughout the 1940s the word socialism was used to designate a centrally planned system and that only from the 1970s onwards it came to describe a welfare state enforcing income distribution strategies through suitable fiscal measures (see Radnitzky 1999, pp. 23–24). What is sure is that Hayek did not think of socialism as worker control of firms and that most theorists of economic systems have traditionally been in full sync with him on this point.

4. Recent theoretical approaches which envision a new model of revolution tailored to the needs of our present-day world are evidence that Marx's theory of revolution has lost none of its topicality and confirm Sartre's argument that the reason why we cannot put Marxism behind us is that 'we have not gone beyond the circumstances which engendered it' (Sartre 1960, p. 19).[13]

> Marx's philosophy – Petrović argued (1975, p. 40) – is both speculation on the essence of being and speculation on revolution,[14] but not speculation on being plus revolution. On the contrary, thanks to its essence as speculation on being, it is at the same time (not 'additionally') speculation on revolution – and, consequently, on socialism.

The topicality of Marx is demonstrated by a 'Marx-Renaissance' of sorts, that is to say by a wealth of Marx studies that have recently appeared in the literature and bear witness to a continuing concern of scholars with Marxian theory.[15]

As is well known, economists hold that the term revolution (i.e. the break with the existing social model) is to be construed as the introduction of a new mode of production.[16] This was doubtless the view of Marx, the great theoretician of production modes and the way they arise, grow and pass away,[17] and of any theorist thinking that there are many possible modes of production and, specifically, that socialism is an organisational model which differs from capitalism and is consequently, a new production mode.[18]

The extent to which the notion of revolution as the establishment of a new production mode represents a dominant in Marx's thought necessitates the conclusion that Marxism is a theory of revolution (see Lukàcs 1922, p. 320). Hence, it follows (a) that the criterion against which we are to test the validity of Marxism is how far the establishment of a genuine socialist system will prove to be practicable; (b) that the qualification of 'Marxist' should be restricted to those who maintain that a socialist or communist order can be established in practice (and consistently with Marx's approach)[19] and (c) that those who do not believe in revolution cannot be characterised as Marxists.[20,21]

As Marxist thought draws nourishment from the prospect of social change, any attempt to deny its revolutionary essence will result in distorting its theoretical foundations. To the extent the twenty-first century proves to be an age of long-term social stability, all Marxist movements are likely to be perceived as irrelevant and to wither away; if, conversely, no stability should be achieved, social thought will necessarily be influenced by Marxist ideas or by any other ideas that should appear to be further developments of Marxism.[22]

5. To establish why Marx's worldview is so radically revolutionary, it is possible to refer to a well-reasoned 1961 book in which Tucker showed that Marx chose revolution and communism even before commencing work on his material conception of history.

The view that Marx's idea of revolution has its underpinning in historical materialism is generally traced to the following passage from the *Preface* to the *Contribution to the Critique of Political Economy*:

> In the real production of their existence men inevitably enter into definite relations, which are independent of their will, namely relations of production appropriate to a given stage in the development of their material forces of production. The totality of these relations of production constitutes the economic structure of society, the real foundation on which arises a legal and political superstructure, and to which correspond definite forms of social consciousness. At a certain stage of development, the material productive forces of society come into conflict with the existing relations of production or – this merely expresses the same thing in legal terms – with the property relations within the framework of which they have operated hitherto. From forms of development of the productive forces these relations turn into their fetters. Then begins an era of social revolution.
>
> (Marx 1859, p. 5)

The relevance of this passage is denied by Tucker, who traces the roots of Marx's communism back to about 1843, to the influence of Moses Hess and, specifically, to the realisation that alienation is principally caused by the way economic life is organised in civil society.

According to Tucker, Feuerbach had described 'productive activity' as a distinctive feature and attribute of the human species, but the Feuerbachian theorist Moses Hess had reached the conclusion that capitalistic society was in a state of 'perversion' because egotistic drives prevented man in the modern world from producing cooperatively. However – Tucker went on to argue – as Hess was a student of Proudhon, the originator of a form of 'philosophical communism' commingling the ideals of communism with Hegel's philosophy of history, it is from Proudhon that he took over the notion of property as theft, the founding stone of his Feuerbachian theory of alienation.

Based on these reflections, Tucker concluded that Marx grew into a communist when he embraced the philosophical communism of Hess and its Hegelian core idea of alienation, but that he wove into his view of communism the idea of the proletariat as the instigator of a new social order – a notion unknown to Hess. It was the idea of class struggle as the interpretative key of history – he wrote – that led Marx to distance himself from Hegel.

Sabine (1937, p. 588) holds that Marx took over from Hegel the idea of nations as the true actors in history (a notion which was actually but loosely connected to Hegel's overall system) and replaced the thesis of the struggle between antagonistic nations with the notion of a struggle between social classes. The end result of this process – he argued – was the transformation of Hegelianism into a powerful form of social radicalism through the erasure of its political overtones.

In Tucker's study, the notion of the proletariat as the instigator of a new social order is said to derive from a very influential book authored by Lorenz von Stein. In *Contribution to the Critique of Hegel's Philosophy of Right*, he argues, which was written at the end of 1843, Marx is seen to have undergone a major process of change that leads him to replace 'the image of self-alienated humanity' with that of the proletariat as the 'suffering expression of alienated man in revolt against his condition' within the existing economic system. Quoting Marx's saying that just 'as philosophy finds in the proletariat its *material* weapon', so 'the proletariat finds its *spiritual* weapon in philosophy', he emphasises that Marx developed 'this singular philosophical conception of the proletariat' under the influence of Lorenz von Stein's book.

In point of fact, von Stein was a conservative thinker whose primary aim was to refute the socialist and communist ideas circulating his day, but his book helped disseminate the idea that the proletariat, the new property-less class that had made its debut on the historical world scene, was, by its very nature, a revolutionary class engaged in a struggle against capital.

In the *Philosophy of Right*, Hegel had warned that a dangerous process resulting in the concentration of unheard-of wealth in just a few hands was threatening to unleash a rabble of paupers, though he added that poverty itself was not enough to generate a revolt of the masses. To create a rabble, he argued, it takes 'joined to poverty, a disposition of mind, an inner indignation against the rich'. The description of the proletariat as a rabble – Tucker argues – is also derived from von Stein's book, with which Marx's writings of the middle forties 'show a minute textual familiarity' (Tucker 1961, p. 115).

What marks out Marx's approach from that of Hess is his response to von Stein's characterisation of communism as the class ideology of the proletariat, in terms that Hess criticised von Stein for explaining communism as the reaction of a single class to its material deprivation, while Marx ascribed to the proletarian class the mission to free humanity from the evils of capitalistic alienation.

In conclusion, the initial step in Marx's progress towards communism was a Hegelian form of 'philosophical communism'[23] which had as its main, and probably permanent underpinning the idea of alienation,[24] and the acme of his development into a revolutionary coincided with the development of his materialist approach to history and the associated idea of modes of production.[25]

With the passing of time, however, he came to reconsider his one-time beliefs and spoke out for a peaceful transition to socialism.

With reference to the description of universal suffrage as one of the main goals the proletariat was to strive for, it has been pointed out that even in such an early work as the *Manifesto of the Communist Party* Marx described the takeover of the proletariat as a victory in the battle for democracy (see Avineri 1968) and that *Capital* includes passages underscoring the importance of Factory Acts and the fact that many British parliaments passed resolutions favourable to workers, rather than their employers (see Sidoti 1987, p. 280).

1867, the year when the Second Reform Act enfranchised British working men in the upper income brackets, marks a watershed of sorts, in terms that Marx began to envisage a peaceful transition to socialism.[26]

Although Lichtheim (1965, pp. 120–21) draws attention to the fact that *The Civil War in France*, written in 1871, includes passages which show Marx upholding ultra-democratic views that call to mind his traditional enemy Proudon, it is fair to say that due to the continuing influence of the educational background that made him a communist when still a young man, Marx never completely discarded the idea that the new order might have to be established by violent means.[27]

6. The prominence of production modes in Marx's overall approach offers clues to the identification of the correct scientific method of Marxism and, probably, of Marx himself.

Following the gigantic, yet incomplete effort to merge the high points of Western thought (Hegel + Ricardo + French Jacobinism) into a critically contrived synthesis – Tosel writes (1966, p. 147) – Marxism became an orthodox creed of sorts which doubtless helped socialise and politicise workers, but failed to teach them how to secure a hegemonic position in economic life.

Now that economic cooperative theorists have fleshed out an alternative option to capitalism which is sure to work at high levels of efficiency, it is possible to argue that Marx has happily survived a spell of near-hibernation since his name will no longer be associated with the oppressive bureaucratic system prevailing in the past century.

7. Chapter 2 reproduces, with some changes, the text of a paper published in the *Review of Political Economy* (2015, vol. 27, no. 4).

Chapter 4 is the slightly revised version of a paper which first appeared in the *Open Access Library Journal* (2015, vol. II, no. 5, May).

Chapter 6 reprints pages from a paper originally published in *Modern Economy* (2017, vol. 8, no.11).

Chapter 7 is the revised version of a paper published in *Open Access Library Journal* (2017, vol. 4, no.7).

Chapter 9 is the reprint of a paper first published in the *Review of Radical Political Economics* (Autumn 2004, vol. 36, no. 4).

The book includes occasional quotes from earlier studies, specifically *Producer cooperatives as a new mode of production* (Routledge, 2014) and *Labour managed firms and post-capitalism* (Routledge, 2017).

Notes

1 The idea that capitalism is not the only market economy model feasible today is the main thesis advanced in Arrighi's interesting 2007 book entitled *Adam Smith at Peking*.
2 Lukàcs G. 1968a, *Scritti politici giovanili, 1919–1928*, Laterza, Bari, p. 34.
3 Marx (1864, p. 11).
4 Marx 1894, *Capital*, vol. III, Harmondsworth, Penguin Books, 1981, pp. 513–14.
5 Mill 1871, *Priniples of Political Economy*, ed. by Ashley, Longmans, Green and Co., 1909, p. 739.
6 Marx 1894, *Capital*, vol. III, Harmondsworth, Penguin Books, 1981, pp. 513–14.
7 Marx 1894, *Capital*, vol. III, Harmondsworth, Penguin Books, 1981, p. 511.
8 In this connection, Mandel aptly described the elderly Lenin as literally obsessed with the need to combat bureaucracy (see Mandel & Johnstone 1970, p. 61).
9 This is clear evidence that, unlike Stalin, Lenin did not rate a bureaucratic system as infallible (see Lukàcs 1924, p. 166).
10 It is clear that the issue with which Lenin was striving to come to terms was not so much ownership of means of production, as the social relations of production. And this is why he looked upon a system of cooperatives as "the socialist regime".
    Hence, Tonini's argument that Lenin had but a vague idea of the way a non-capitalistic production system could work is, at best, applicable to the years before 1923 (see Tonini 1967, p. 31).
11 In *Antidühring* Engels spoke of cooperatives as "transition measures to the complete communistic organisation of society" (see Engels 1898, p. 281).
12 Tamburrano is one of many scholars who reject the idea that the older Lenin had come to equate socialism with worker control of firms (see Tamburrano 1959, p. 47).
13 Forty years later, Musto wrote that "thanks to Marx's unequalled critique of the capitalistic production mode, his approach will be a milestone in social science unless and until it is proved wrong" (2005b, p. 155). On this point (see, also, Kellner 1995, p. 26).
14 In a 2006 paper, Roberts refuted the view of Marx as a theoretician of capitalism (which he thought to be widely shared) and offered instead a – supposedly new – picture of Marx as the theoretician of the anti-capitalist revolution. In fact, this paper just shows its author forgetful of the fact that the characterisation of Marxism as a theory of revolution goes back to Lukàcs (1923, p. 320) and has been concordantly upheld by scholars ever since (see Jossa 2006).
    Agnes Heller, a disciple of Lukàcs, (1976, p. 135), has argued that identifying a codex of socialist morality in Marx (the codex of communism) is crucial if we

are to gain a correct appreciation of his approach and develop a form of 'living Marxism'.

Without denying Marx's status as a theoretician of revolution, Wallerstein, Przeworski and others have remarked that trade unionists chose capitalism just because they had realised that fighting their pro-worker battle within the system was the best option open to the working class (see, for instance, Przeworski 1995, p. 169).

In this connection, let me emphasise that purging Marxism of its revolutionary kernel might arguably lead to an academically correct picture of Marx, but would deprive his approach of its unmistakable sting.

15 The claim that Marxism is on the wane is widely shared. One of the first authors to challenge this view by close reference to contemporary events was Struve (1899).

16 Marx's definition of revolution is a clear and simple notion. In Kautsky 1902 (p. 168) we read that the main difference between reformism and revolution is not the use of violence in one case and its rejection in the other (to tell the truth, on occasion he did suggest the exact opposite – see, for instance, Kautsky 1892a, pp. 65–77). In Kautsky's opinion, the salient characteristic of a revolution was «the conquest of political power by a new class (*idem*, p. 169). Authors endorsing the opposite view, i.e. the idea of non-violence as passivity and of violence as an essential component of any revolution, include, by way of example, Settembrini (1973, p. vii), Geary (1974, pp. 92–93) and Roemer (2008, p. 14).

Notwithstanding the evidence that Marx and Kautsky proposed clear, simple and ultimately concordant definitions of revolution, Simone Weil argued that "among all those who still persist in talking about revolution, there are perhaps not two who attach the same content to the term" (see Weil 1955, p. 32). The definition of revolution discussed by Sartori in a 2015 study differs greatly from the one suggested in this paper (see Sartori 2015, pp. 15–35).

The view of revolution as the introduction of a new production mode and the clarification that revolution does not necessarily entail the use of violence go to explain that revolutionary aspirations have nothing to do with the 'lyric age' discussed by Milan Kundera in his charming book entitled *Life Is Elsewhere* (1973). According to Kundera, revolutionism is the typical attitude of the inexperienced young, is born of a 'lyric' disposition of mind and arises in people who are unable to act and give themselves up to dreams of a better life, seeking refuge in dreams, in lyric life, in poetry. The links between revolution and violence lead Kundera to claim that police action, poetry and revolution have in common much more than is generally assumed. On closer analysis, though, Kundera's reflections, for all their acumen, have no bearing on Marx's view of revolution as the replacement of the existing production mode with a different one.

17 "The scientific standing of Marxism – Gruppi argues (1970, p. 340) – rests entirely on the emphasis laid on the historically determined essence of economic laws, on the dynamic evolution of economic systems and the inextricable nexus between economic and political-sociological analysis."

18 The idea of Marxism as a theory of revolution and the belief that revolution is the mission of the proletariat back up Lukàcs's argument that Marxism is the expression of the class consciousness of the proletariat (Watnick 1962, p. 161).

19 In a speech delivered on Marx's grave, Engels said:

> Marx was before all else a revolutionist. His real mission in life was to contribute, in one way or another, to the overthrow of capitalist society and of the state institutions which it had brought into being; to contribute to the liberation of the modern proletariat, which he was the first to make conscious of the conditions of its emancipation.

(See Mehring 1918, p. 530).

20 Unlike myself, most theorists hold that only those who accept the labour theory of value can describe themselves as true Marxists (see, *inter alia*, Napoleoni 1972, p. 181).

21 In a well-known paper by Holloway, a disciple of Lukàcs and Adorno, we read that the problem with the traditional concept of revolution

> is perhaps not that it aims too high, but that it aims too low. The notion of capturing positions of power, whether it be governmental power or more dispersed positions of power, in society, misses the point that the aim of the revolution is to dissolve relations of power, to create a society based on the mutual recognition of people's dignity.
>
> (Holloway 2002, p. 20)

On closer analysis, Holloway's argument is to be rejected for two main reasons. Firstly, it fails to construe revolution as a change in the production mode; secondly, it fails to point out that a new production mode would amount to a proper revolution even where its effect should be, not to overthrow the existing power structure altogether, but just to bring about a more equitable distribution of power.

As Korsch put it, all the deformations that Marxism underwent at the time of the 2nd International can be summarised in "one all-inclusive formulation: a unified general theory of social revolution was changed into a critique of the bourgeois economic order, the bourgeois State" (see Korsch 1923, p. 59).

22 In the opinion of one of the founders of analytical Marxism, far from being a theory of revolution Marxism is actually a critical approach to the analysis of capitalistic society which offers no key to its transformation (see Elster 1985, pp. 513–31).

23 As far as Hegel's influence on Marx is concerned, I agree with Tucker and Berlin that this ascendancy was understated by Marx's immediate successors regardless of the fact that when Marx's theory is read from the perspective of his own perception of himself as an earnest investigator of truth, but without a concomitant focus on the unifying model that went into its making, his throretical edifice will, as it were, be splintered into a myriad loosely linked intuitions.

24 For a different description of Marx's road from liberalism to socialism (see Cornu 1955).

25 According to Tucker (1961, p. 172), "mature Marxism was the baby grown to adulthood" and it was therefore "perfectly proper to speak of the mature doctrine in terms applicable to Marxism".

26 The turn of British Marxists to reformism at the end of the nineteenth century has often been traced to a rapid pace of economic growth. According to Lichtheim, this explanation is barely convincing since due to a downward trend in Britain's overseas trade money wages hardly rose in those years and continued to stagnate even during the subsequent upswing of the economy (see Lichtheim 1965, pp. 207–8).

27 If revolution is understood as the transition, albeit non-violent, to a new mode of production which is set off under the impulse of the development of the forces of production, there is obviously no reason to think, with Pasolini (1968, p. 98), that "revolutionaries are necessarily angries". Every Marxist looks upon revolution as a development that will necessarily come about in history at some point in time.

1 A tentative assessment of the importance of the materialistic conception of history

Introduction

Authors who look upon the materialistic conception of history (or sociological materialism) as the true mainstay of Marxism include Bernstein (1899, p. 30) and Vygodskij, who described it as the 'brilliant formula' with which Marx and Engels made their debut in social science in the early 1840s, well before Marx developed his theory of value and surplus value[1] (see Vygodskij 1967, p. 5). Lenin rated it as 'one of the greatest achievements of scientific speculation' (Lenin 1913, p. 477) and Godelier explained its importance by highlighting a far-reaching difference between the approaches of pre-Marxian historians and Marx's method: whereas the formers' favourite focus points were political events or religious and philosophical ideas – he argued – the latter's innovative approach to political history (or the history of ideas) turned the spotlight on prime causes and the agents behind them, as well as on the interrelations between man, nature and a horde of actors grouped into castes, orders and classes (see Godelier 1982, p. 332).

Engels himself reckoned the materialistic conception of history as the true core of Marxism (see Engels 1859a, pp. 202–3), and Antonio Labriola went so far as to argue that Marxism ultimately boiled down to historical materialism (see Labriola 1902, p. 16). Aron, for his part (1970, p. 178), saw the gist of Marxism in the theory of modes of production, which he held to be inextricably intertwined with historical materialism (for a comparable view, see Rodinson 1969, pp. 13–18). The claim that the materialistic conception of history is the true cornerstone of Marxism was also advanced in a well-known book by Cohen (see Cohen 1978 and 2000).[2]

The core idea behind the materialistic conception of history is that the true underpinning of each social order is a specific mode of production. In this book, this issue will be analysed by reference to the contractual origin of the firm as theorised in Alchian and Demsetz (AD) 1972.

A historical materialist thinks of the socio-political structure of society, the ideals and policies of a nation and the distinctive facets of a civilization as *mainly* shaped by the structural conditions under which production is carried on (see Schumpeter 1941) and will consequently agree with Engels that "policy and its history are to be explained from the economic relations and their development, and not vice versa" (Engels 1885, p. 1086).

From my perspective, a system of employee-managed system is a new production mode with a distinctive potential for outperforming capitalism which contrary to AD's opinion has failed to materialise because of the predominance of economics over politics – in full accord with the core assumption behind the materialistic conception of history.

The importance of historical materialism is consequently twofold: on the one hand, it opens up a new perspective on history (see Croce 1896a); on the other, it tells us why the transition from capitalism to socialism is slow to become a reality. Specifically, the observation that developments that would be in the interests of society do not necessarily become a reality justifies both the argument that the real is not necessarily 'rational' and the resulting conclusion (which is not Croce's) that historical materialism is a new form of philosophy of history. As far as I can see, Croce's argument that "as soon as the materialistic conception of history is stripped of its teleological and providence-related overtones, it proves to be unable to further socialism or any practical purposes in life" (1896, p. 15) is unwarranted since the rationale behind historical materialism helps us understand why socialism has failed to take the place of capitalism down to this day.

A preliminary issue to be discussed at this point is the cultural roots of historical materialism.

According to Fromm, the first philosopher to develop a correct understanding of the unconscious was Spinoza, who described men as aware of their desires, but ignorant of the springs from which they originate. In other words, although men like to think of themselves as free individuals, they barely are since they are spurred on by unconscious drives. In all probability – Fromm argues – Marx was influenced by his in-depth study of Spinoza's *Ethic*.

There is general agreement that Marx was greatly influenced by Hegel, specifically by his argument that men are but puppets on the stage of history, that they advance the ends of history 'without their knowing', and that the strings of their actions are actually pulled by the Idea (or God). It was thanks to the dual influence of Spinoza and Hegel – Fromm concludes – that Marx proved able to offer a precise and correct idea of the function of conscience and the objective factors by which it is governed (see Fromm 1962, pp. 118–20).

This said, let me spell out that the importance of the materialistic conception of history lies in its ability to shed light on the reasons why the power wielded by capitalists in business firms is of hindrance to a democratic transition to socialism.[3]

Alchian and Demsetz's theory of the firm

AD's pioneer contribution is the theory of the contractual origin of the firm. In a 1972 article they wrote (p. 77): "It is common to see the firm characterized by the power to settle issues by fiat, by authority, or by disciplinary action superior to that available in the conventional market. This is a delusion".

According to AD, therefore, a firm draws its origin from contracts and its authority and disciplinary powers are strictly determined by the clauses of agreements which are freely negotiated between parties in the marketplace. An entrepreneur telling his employees what to do is comparable to an individual consumer who will order the commodities he needs from a grocer's as long as he deems it fit and will cease to buy his provisions from that supplier if his orders are not satisfactorily performed.[4] To look at the manager as continually engaged in organising, directing or assigning workers to individual tasks within the firm, they argue, is misleading because an entrepreneur's real task is to negotiate contracts on terms that will prove acceptable to both parties (see, also, Nozick 1974, pp. 160ff).[5]

If this is true, where does the difference between the employer/employee relationship and the corresponding customer/grocer relation lie? In the fact – AD answer – that a firm is (a) a team which carries on production activities and (b) an organisation in which one central agent enters into contracts with all of the remaining team partners.[6]

In an effort to discourage employee shirking, each firm establishes a specific corporate function responsible for supervising and monitoring the performance of individual team partners. This is the task of the entrepreneur, or monitor, the above-mentioned central agent who hires and dismisses team partners, enters into contractual agreements with them and sees that all of them perform their tasks to the best of their abilities. But who will monitor the monitor? In 'classical' capitalistic firms, this problem is solved by empowering the central agent to appropriate the balance between revenues and costs, since this creates an incentive for the entrepreneur to discipline team work at a high level of efficiency. As AD put it, the reason why the classical capitalistic entrepreneur is allowed to appropriate the firm's profit, i.e. the difference between revenues and costs, is not so much the greater risk proneness of those who go into business (as Knight argued in his celebrated 1921 contribution),[7] as the consideration that this is the most appropriate way of remunerating a person monitoring and measuring the commitment of the team partners to their tasks.[8]

In short, AD's central thesis is that the entrepreneur is he who takes upon himself the task of watching team partners at work and that a fair remuneration for this task is an income which increases in a direct proportion to the performance of the team.[9]

In their opinion, this explains why firms preferably organise themselves along capitalistic, rather than cooperative lines (see AD 1972, p. 786). If profit – they argue – were equally apportioned among the workers instead of being entirely appropriated by the person in charge of watching others at work, the former would be induced to work both harder and better, but the monitor would have a lesser incentive to perform his tasks properly.

As a result, productivity losses from a lower level of control would probably exceed the gains from the reduced benefits that individual workers would draw from working less or less hard.[10] Even more so, in a firm which apportions all profits among its workers (as is the rule in cooperatives) and does without a specialised monitoring function AD hold it reasonable to assume that productivity levels would slow down despite the greater interest of workers in the efficient functioning of their firm (see, also, Jensen & Meckling 1979, p. 485).[11]

Before I proceed to discuss AD's approach in greater detail, let me mention the opinion of some authors that the reduced incentive to work in cooperatives is actually unrelated to the control issue. Whereas the workers of capital-owned enterprises tend to work as hard as they can due to the awareness of a proportional link between their incomes and their individual marginal productivity rates, in cooperatives the partners' incomes are strictly determined by the way the firm's residual is apportioned among them (see, for instance, Williamson 1980).

Is Alchian and Demsetz's approach fully convincing?

Ever since its formulation by AD, the thesis of the contractual origin of the firm has gained wide currency. AD's agency theory describes the firm as a 'nexus of contracts' and agency as the relationship whereby one person, termed the principal, directs his agent to perform a task for his account (see AD 1976, 1979, pp. 470–71).[12] To reduce the inevitable divergence between his own interests and those of his agent and confine the resulting losses – AD argue – the entrepreneur uses the agency contract and the monitoring function. Agency costs include the costs of monitoring, those of co-interesting the agent in the proper performance of the contract and the resulting loss; and the agency contract and the monitoring function are the tools used to minimise such agency costs.

The idea that still needs to be critically explored is AD's claim that the firm exercises no true power.

AD's claim that the entrepreneur/employee relationship vests in the former just as much power as is wielded by a party entering into contracts in the marketplace has been called into question by theorists who look upon the firm as a hierarchical structure where specific investments are all-important. According to these, AD's view that firing an employee is, to a manager, tantamount to switching over to a different supplier (at least from the perspective that interests us here) is misleading since the costs involved in finding a new job are far higher than those required to secure fresh orders (see, for example, Dahl 1985, pp. 114–16; Gould 1985, pp. 206–8; Williamson 1986, pp. 67–70).

As argued by Ronald Coase (1960), AD's approach would be correct if no transaction costs were entailed; but in the absence of transaction costs there would be no firms at all and all business operations would be directly transacted in the marketplace.

This leads up to a very general argument: if transaction costs were nil, there would be no firms (as said before); but this amounts to saying that "in the absence of transaction costs" firms would become unnecessary and that "any enterprise will operate efficiently regardless of how rights to participate in its management decisions may be assigned" (McCain 1992, p. 206).

One additional criticism of the idea that the employer exercises no power over his workers is raised in studies concerned with showing that certain forms of monitoring associated with the division of labour and other organisational patterns are not only adopted for reasons of efficiency, but also in an effort to strengthen the employer's authority (Braverman 1974; Marglin 1974; Edwards 1979; Putterman 1982; Bowles 1985).[13]

> Wage-labour relationships – Howard & King argue (2001, p. 796) – are one area in which Marx discusses the role of coercion as a means of ensuring coordination in fully developed capitalistic systems. His argument hinges on the fact that employment contracts cannot be specified for all contingencies, so that the terms of exchange of labour services for wages are contestable and conflict is endemic.[14]

On closer analysis, though, none of these objections are strong enough to refute either the idea of the firm as a nexus of contracts or the resulting conclusion that workers must necessarily submit to the authority of their employers.

The reason why I start out from AD's contribution will appear palpably clear as soon as we raise the question if the transition to socialism recommended in this paper can be assumed to materialise 'spontaneously' in situations of corporate failure.

Preliminarily, let me specify that no defaulting enterprise can be turned into a cooperative unless and until its workers conceive the wish to run its operations on their own. To underscore this evident truth, Hobsbawm wrote that "the basic problem of the revolution is how to make a hitherto subaltern class capable of hegemony, believe in itself as a potential ruling class and be credible as such to other classes" (see Hobsbawm 2011, p. 325).

Setting out from Spinoza's and Freud's concordant belief that *intellectual* knowledge is conducive to change only if is, at the same time, *affective* knowledge, Fromm argued that inasmuch as this was true the factors preventing workers from running businesses on their own were an aversion to entrepreneurial risks and the fear to face pecuniary losses (see Fromm 1962, p. 110). Although workers are probably well aware that they are being exploited – he explained – they put up with their subjugation to capital due to the unconscious fear that entrepreneurial risks, once taken, may prove difficult to manage. To explain their plight, he reported a telling example.

> Your friend – he wrote (op. cit., pp. 111–12) – has to undertake a trip of which he is obviously afraid. You know that he is afraid, his wife knows it, everyone else knows it, but he does not know it. He claims one day

that he does not feel well, the next day that there is no need to make the trip, the day after that that there are better ways to achieve the same result without travelling, then the next day that your persistence in reminding him of the trip is an attempt to force him; and since he does not want to be forced, he just won't make the trip, and so on, until he will say that it is now too late to go on the trip, anyway, and that hence there is no use in thinking any further about it. ... What has happened? The real motivation for not wanting to go is fear, ... and this fear is unconscious.

And due to the attitudes of mind that that Freud terms 'resistances', it is difficult to find a cure that will bring the unconscious to the surface.

These reflections more than justify the assumption that the transition to socialism would be greatly expedited in a nation where the State apparatus should make it its task to ensure permanent conditions of full employment.

As far as the codetermination issue is concerned, in the opinion of Pejovich, "the fact that stockholders must be forced by law to accept codetermination is the best evidence that they are adversely affected by it" and "the fact that the law has to mandate the codetermining firm and protect it from competition by alternative organizational forms is evidence of its relative inefficiency" (see Pejovich 1982, vol. iv, pp. 242–43). This inefficiency, he clarified, is proof that the benefits workers draw from codetermination come short of the corresponding disadvantages for stockholders. While it is clear that Pejovich's line of reasoning can easily be extended from codetermination to worker management of firms, its cogency remains doubtful.

Considering that true Marxists look upon socialism as a new mode of production that will become a reality only after the collapse of capitalism, i.e. when society is ripe for such a development, the conclusion prompted by Pejovich's argument is merely the awareness that the general public have as yet failed to develop a correct appreciation of the benefits offered by conversion of capital-owned business firms into cooperatives. But is it reasonable to think that the aversion of workers to entrepreneurial risks will ebb away at the same pace that they secure higher incomes and educational qualifications?

Although the reflections developed in this section have probably helped put the role of the materialistic conception of history in its right perspective, this subject will be taken up again in the subsequent sections of this chapter.

The transition to socialism and the power of capital

The downsides of representative democracy are well known. In a survey of the 'perverse effects' of democracy, the Italian political theorist Norberto Bobbio argued that the feeling that promises have remained unfulfilled and a disillusionment with universal suffrage originate from the awareness that, "due to the ability of mass media to condition the minds of electors", universal suffrage fails to attain the goal for which it is ultimately intended – "keeping in check the power structure" (Bobbio 1989). Charles Wright Mills emphasised the tendency of the masses to cling to values that holders of vested interests had instilled into them by accident or on purpose (see Mills 1959, p. 194). Hence, I can hardly be accused of overstating the truth if I argue, with Raniero Panzieri, that obstacles to progress and risks of a downward spiral in democracy stem from the failure to extend democracy to the workplace, the very seedbed of totalitarian integralism.

> It is there that the power of the class of employers puts down roots before extending its range well beyond the factory and shaping the basics of economic and political action across the country, and it is there that the hostility of capitalists towards prospects of a positive evolution of society acts itself out in forms such as oppression and blackmail and ends up by breeding imbalance, unemployment and misery. The place where totalitarianism keeps society and its political institutions under constant check is the factory,

and it is there that workers will have to battle "for a new, genuinely democratic power structure capable of overthrowing the dominance of large capitalists" (Panzieri 1975, pp. 122–23; see, also, Vanek 1985, pp. 27–28); and the reason is that "until industry is changed from a feudalistic to a democratic social order based on workers' control, democratic forms may exist, but their substance will be limited" (Chomsky 2013, p. 143).

As the power of money is an obstacle to democracy in the workplace, the importance of disempowering capital should not be underrated. The media, press and television, would no longer be subservient to the interests of their owners nor would they be monopolised by anybody (at least not by a single individual). As mentioned by Marramao, this idea is reflected in Max Adler's distinction between 'political democracy' and 'social democracy'. Although the former is usually described as democratic, he argues, it is nothing but a dictatorship of sorts since the 'general will' it is said to express is in fact a compound of the specific interests of the dominant class (and its underlying rationale is the liberalistic principle of the atomisation of society into abstract individuals). As for the latter, Adler adds, it amounts to real democracy but can only become reality in a classless society (see Marramao 1980, p. 292). In years nearer to us, an advocate of industrial democracy such as Noam Chomsky argued that "of all the crises that afflict us, I believe this growing democratic deficit may be the most severe" (2009, p. 41).

Raising the question if capitalism really guarantees full freedom, Huberman asked himself: "Do we really tolerate all political and economic dissenting opinions?" And whereas he owned that in ordinary times we do not clap liberals or radicals in jail, he wondered what would happen in times of great tension. Isn't it also true – he continued – that jobs, power and prestige almost always go to those who do not dissent, those who are sound and safe? (see Huberman & Sweezy 1968, p. 74).

Capitalistic societies are typified by economic inequality, which results in political inequality. In political life, each of us does have the right to cast a vote, but the wealthy are nevertheless able to secure greater political power by bribing corrupt politicians and exercising control over the media.

One aspect of the unequal distribution of political power is that issues with which the more disadvantaged part of the population are most concerned will never enter the political agenda. The task of politics is problem-solving, but the power to draw up political agendas is in the hands of the power class. One relevant example is the issue of democracy in the firm. Why has it never been put to the vote or, if nothing else, earnestly discussed?

Hence, there is ground for concluding that the transition to socialism is slow to materialise because of the power that capitalists wield in business enterprises.

In abstract terms, stripping power from capitalists should be a major aim of the bourgeoisie, since decisions made in line with the 'one share, one vote' principle are at odds with the democratic principles to which this class is used to paying lip service. Concerning democracy, Lukàcs remarked that "the fact that a scientifically acceptable solution does exist is of no avail", because "to accept that solution, even in theory, would be tantamount to observing society from a class standpoint other than that of the bourgeoisie" and "no class can do that – unless it is willing to abdicate its power freely" (Lukàcs 1923, p. 70). The class consciousness of the bourgeoisie – he also wrote (*idem*, p. 80) – is

> cursed by its very nature with the tragic fate of developing an insoluble contradiction at the zenith of its powers. Due to this contradiction, it must annihilate itself. Historically, this tragedy of the bourgeoisie is reflected historically in the fact that even before it had defeated its predecessor, feudalism, its new enemy, the proletariat, had appeared on the scene. Politically – he went on to argue – "its strategy was to fight against the organisation of society into layers in the name of a 'freedom' which at the very moment of victory could not but generate a new kind of repression

that Lukàcs identified with capitalist exploitation but can also be explained as the exclusion of workers from the right to cast votes in their firms.

To explain why barring workers from corporate voting rights runs counter to the traditional principles of the bourgeoisie let me mention that when capitalism was in the ascendant the ideological exponents of the rising bourgeoisie looked upon the class struggle as a basic fact of history and that "in proportion as the theory and practice of the proletariat made society conscious of this unconscious revolutionary principle inherent in capitalism, the bourgeoisie was thrown back increasingly on to a conscious defensive" (Lukàcs 1923, p. 85).

The inability of the bourgeois to appraise the extent to which their power weighs on economic relationships explains the appearance of writings which come up with the entirely unwarranted idea that employers wield no power in the firm.

Why is the materialistic conception of history so important?

At this point, it is time to sum up the reflections based on which historical materialism, understood in non-rigorous terms, can with due caution be rated as a very important theoretical approach.

Emphasising the originality of Marx's approach to history, the Italian philosopher Giovanni Gentile defined it (1974, p. 10) as

> a new perspective for approaching history from an unprecedented angle of view and a new method and a new system dictating the need to take a step back and try to offer a different elucidation of human experience, a new perspective on the essence of life and, in short, a new philosophical approach.

Coming back to the starting point of this chapter, i.e. AD's contention that all such power as is wielded in firms originates from employer-employee contracts, to admit that the progress from capitalism to democratic firm management is impeded by the power position of employers in production one need not accept the labour theory of value (which equates capitalistic production with exploitation); this insight emerges clearly enough from the historical conception of history. Similarly, the unwarranted claim that a democratically organized society can be established by restricting the capitalist's power exclusively to firms is proved wrong by the rationale behind historical materialism – i.e. the teaching that the transition to a democratic firm system relieving workers from their subjection to capital is halted by the power of capital to control the media, have them circulate just those ideas that are in accord with the existing state of affairs and dictate political agendas that play into the hands of economic actors.

Concluding, the materialistic conception of history is important not only because it offers a new canon for historical research, as argued by Benedetto Croce, but also and primarily because it sheds light on the reasons why the transition from capitalism to socialism has failed to materialise to this day.

Does socialism still exist in today's world?

The question to be addressed at this point is whether socialism can be described as a new mode of production.

> The well-known Italian journalist Eugenio Scalfari put the matter in this way (see Scalfari 2008, p. 1224):Many people have been pinning their

hopes of liberation on communism. But now it is time to take off the bandages from their eyes and the plugs from their ears. The reification of individuals, the master-servant confrontation, the refusal to acknowledge the rights of others have been salient traits of our species for millennia and will continue to be so in future.

But while the truth of this can hardly be denied, there are reasons to believe that as soon as workers resolve to run firms by themselves and develop the requisite abilities, the master-servant confrontation will become a thing of the past.

In Marxist terms, it is possible to argue that the re-reversal of the currently capsized capital-labour relation that the establishment of a democratic firm system would set off helps solve the conflict between socialised production and private appropriation thanks to the fact that both production and distribution, being governed by the choices of the members' collective, become socialised activities. In a democratic firm system the workers' collective is sovereign, in terms that its decision powers in matters of production include authority to regulate distribution in manners that will appear most appropriate from time to time (see Jossa 2012a).

From my perspective, a feasible form of socialism today is worker management of firms (see Jossa 1998, 2015, 2018), i.e. the beacon of hope that Oskar Lange expected to rekindle the activism of the working class (see Lange 1957, p. 159). This is why I agree with Anweiler (1958, p. 472) that the original idea behind the movement for workers' councils – "the primary aim of Marxism" (see Garaudy undated, p. 187) – is "as topical as ever." According to Tawney (1918, p. 103), freedom will not be complete unless it brings with it not only absence of repression, but also opportunities for self-organisation – in short, unless it is attained by extending representative institutions to industry.[15]

Socialism from utopia to scientific producer cooperative economics

As argued by Bensaïd (2002, p. xi), after the collapse of the Soviet economy there was a strong temptation to return from 'scientific socialism' to 'utopian socialism'. From my perspective, instead, paraphrasing the title of Engels's well-known 1892 work[16] the evolution of socialism can be described as the progress from an illusory centrally planned regime without true markets to a system of producer cooperatives.[17] As Screpanti puts it (2007a, p. 145):

> Ever since 1850, Marx and Engels had been consistently advocating a revolutionary process entailing 'the most decisive centralization of power in the hands of the state authority' (Marx & Engels 1850, p. 1873) and they remained strong advocates of centralisation until the advent of the Commune.

It was the Commune that induced both Marx and Engels to rethink their previous position.

Roemer split the evolutionary process of socialism into four steps (see Roemer 1994a). At the first step, economists reached the conclusion that labour time is an inappropriate measure for rational economic calculus: even in socialism, they argued, the use of prices as scarcity indexes is doubtless the only way to prevent waste of resources, but – they made clear – such prices cannot be determined by exclusive reference to the labour-time needed to produce the commodities concerned.

The second step in the evolution of socialism started with the demonstration that general equilibrium theory can – viz. must – be the instrument for rational economic calculus even in socialist systems. This was the time when, more than a hundred years ago, Pareto and Barone showed that the prices to be applied by the planning board in an attempt to secure an efficient use of resources can only be determined by solving the complicated system of equations known as Walras's general economic equilibrium system.

The third step coincides with the 1930s, when a number of renowned economists including Marxists such as Lange (1936–1937) and Lerner (1938) concordantly reached the conclusion that the prerequisite for the proper functioning of a centrally planned system was a real and proper market – in terms that it was not enough to solve a system of equations in order to determine the prices that were to be used for the relevant calculations. In a much praised contribution, Lange formulated two general laws that the planner was supposed to observe in order to vouchsafe a properly functioning plan: the first of these laws, which Lange took over from the neoclassical marginalist approach, can be enunciated by saying that the planning board is expected to instruct firms to increase the output volumes of each commodity produced to the level where its marginal cost will equate the corresponding market price.

In the framework of the so-called 'Lange-Lerner model of socialism', the prices of commodities are determined by the market, whereas the prices of capital goods are fixed by the planning board. The planning board fixes the initial prices of the capital goods produced and waits for firms to submit their offers/orders at the prices thus set. If demand for a given capital good exceeds supply, this is held to be a sign that the price provisionally fixed by the planning board can be stepped up. The reverse will apply if the opposite is true, i.e. if supply exceeds demand. This process should be protracted until demand and supply are balanced out everywhere and for all the capital goods concerned. On closer analysis, however, the law which is being applied is nothing but the law of supply and demand that governs real markets and the planning board can be said to be ultimately acting in accordance with the laws of the market.

Let me specify that under the Lange-Lerner model the remuneration for any work done should be proportional to the relevant disutility level, i.e. to the effort required to do a job, which means that the pay rates for sweated jobs would be higher than those for softer and more pleasant jobs.[18]

The fourth step in the evolution of socialism was marked by the introduction of self-management in Tito's Yugoslavia, in Hungary in connection with the reform of the planning model, in the Soviet Union during the tenure of Gorbachev and in post-Mao China. Although these reforms were not fully compliant with the Lange-Lerner model, they were a sign that the socialist establishment had acknowledged the relevance of the economic debate conducted up to those years.

The fifth step of the process covers more recent years and is characterised by studies discussing market socialism models framed by a number of economists (including Roemer's own 1994 model).

Departing from Roemer, I hold that the fifth stage of the debate on socialism started with the publication of Ward's 1958 article and has been continuing to this date with a rich body of economic studies on producer cooperatives. Ward's paper was the first study explaining how a worker-controlled firm wishing to conduct business rationally should fix the prices of its products. The later stages of this debate made it clear that a system of producer cooperatives can be rated as a correct implementation of a Marxian version of socialism (see Lowit 1962; Jossa 2010a).[19]

The main objection to a model of socialism with markets – the conflict between the material incentives required for markets to work effectively and the Marxist idea that work should be undertaken for the sake of the pleasure, not the personal profit, that may flow from it – is barely convincing. Time and again, Lenin himself emphasised that a socialist system was expected to use to advantage the impulse to growth stemming and (as rightly remarked by Mészàros 1995, pp. 981–82) there is not much difference between the impulse stemming from the example of others and a material stimulus such as the profit motive.[20]

The core idea behind self-management theory is not an outworn ideal, as argued by some (see Hart & Moore 1996). Neither can it be described as abortive (see Chilosi 1992a, p. 159; Nuti 1992, p. 145),[21] inadmissible on account of its presentation of the market as a *locus artificialis* nor neutral (Amirante 2008, pp. XVII and 31–32). It is a crucial issue which is inextricably intertwined with the never-ending struggle between opposed classes,[22] "the primary goal of Marxism" (Garaudy undated, p. 187), and, as such, as topical as ever.[23]

Notes

1 It is widely held that the earliest systematic attempt at theorising a materialistic conception of history dates back to *The German Ideology*, i.e. to 1946 (see, *inter alia*, Buchanan 1982, p. 27).

2 Orfei (1970, p. 271) reports that Antonio Labriola described the materialistic conception of history as "an effective means of splitting the huge and extremely complex working mechanism of society into its simplest constituent parts". From the perspective of Kautsky, for instance, the key points of Marxism were the materialistic conception of history and the idea of the proletariat as the driving force behind the socialist revolution (see Geary 1974, p. 85). Conversely, in the opinion of Croce historical materialism was

neither a philosophy of history nor a philosophical approach proper, but rather an empirical interpretative canon, a recommendation to historians for them to focus on economic activity and give it the attention its major place in human life entitles it to.

(See Croce 1896, pp. 1–19; Labriola 1942, p. 292)

3 As mentioned by Bendix, unlike theorists of historical materialism Max Weber held that managers "frequently develop interests of their own, and in practice they often attempt to modify the policies they are supposed to execute" (see Bendix 1960, p. 485).

4 The idea that nothing obliges the employer or the employee to protract their contractual relationship indefinitely in time induced AD to argue that long-term employment contracts are not an essential attribute of the firm (see Alchian & Demsetz 1972, p. 777), but Williamson has shown that Alchian reconsidered this point in later years (see Alchian 1984, pp. 38–39; Williamson 1985, p. 53, note 11; Williamson 1986, pp. 241–42).

5 This is clearly a criticism aimed at Coase, whose theory of firm is supported by Hartt (see Hart 1989), but was dropped by Alchian in later years (see below).

According to Arienzo and Borrelli (2011, p. 58), in these past years "the employment contract has turned, from a relationship between unequals, into a relationship between individuals negotiating a commercial deal on equal terms".

6 Cooperatives have been described as hybrids blending market attributes with hierarchical mechanisms (see Menard 2007; Valentinov & Fritzsch 2007; Chaddad 2012), but while this view is probably relevant to farming cooperatives, it does not extend to producer cooperatives operating in industry.

7 Models vesting monitoring functions in tendentially risk-neutral individuals were theorised by Kihlstrom and Laffont (1979) and by Eswaran and Kotwal (1989).

8 Demsetz himself stated that the greater part of his own and Alchian's line of reasoning in the 1972 paper reflected suggestions drawn from Knight (Demsetz 1988b, pp. 163–64, note 6).

9 Demsez himself specified that the 1972 paper was mainly intended to suggest that different firm models require different monitoring strategies (see Demsetz 1988b, p. 153). Those holding that the 'who will monitor the monitor' issue is AD's main contribution suggest that the solution is appointing a residual claimant with a self-monitoring incentive, i.e. concerned with monitoring at a high level of efficiency (see Eswaran & Kotwal 1989, p. 162). The question if the appointment of a residual claimant is the only effective solution will be addressed below.

10 On the subject of the scant efficiency of shareholder control or control by a large group of persons (see Hart 1995, pp. 682–83).

11 Jensen and Meckling (1979) maintain that a democratic firm structure may weigh on efficiency in terms of weakening the authority of the managers over the partners by whom they are appointed. On closer analysis, this objection re-echoes Bernstein's argument that the abolition of the capitalistic ownership structure in the absence of concomitant organisational changes would interfere with the correct functioning of corporate firm governance bodies because of the loss of a common convergence point (see Bernstein 1899a, p. 159).

12 Rejecting the description of the firm as "a nexus of contracts", Screpanti (2004) and Zamagni (2005) rightly argued that the capitalistic firm is first and foremost "*a nexus of employment contracts*" and that theoreticians of the "nexus of contracts" hypothesis unduly equate employment contracts with the myriad other agreements entered into by firms, as if they were the same. This argument is perfectly in keeping with the reflections I have been developing in this book.

13 In this well-known essay Bowles argued that shirking is both congenital to human nature and greatly dependent on the way production is organised. To account for the greater efficiency of employee-managed firms, he claimed that workers who do not feel exploited have a lesser incentive to shirking than those of a capitalistic firm in which business is not carried on in the workers' interests.

14 The correct approach is that those who have no option but to do what is crucial to their subsistence or welfare cannot be rated as free (see, *inter alii*, Cohen 1978).

15 Some theorists hold that wage and salary work need not be done away because the working of the social ladder will create a classless society. In fact, there is general agreement that this does not hold true (on this point, see Lasch 1995, p. 78).

16 For detailed information on the complex drafting of *Socialism, Utopian and Scientific*, see Prestipino 1973, chap. I, footnote 3.

17 For an analysis of this celebrated work of Engels's (see MacPherson 2004).

18 The socialist calculation debate that took place in the 1930s is addressed in some depth in Jossa & Cuomo 1997, chaps 1–4.

19 According to Zamagni (2005, p. 3), "the twentieth century witnessed a head-on confrontation between two principal socio-economic organisation models: capitalism and the system which is generally described as 'state socialism'. As is well known, a far-reaching difference between these two systems is a different property regime of means of production, which are privately owned in the former and publicly (or collectively) owned in the latter. The past century ended with the victory of the capitalistic system. In this connection, F. Fukuyama much too hurriedly pontificated that this was the 'end of history'. In fact, the property issue is neither the only difference between different types of economic organisation, nor the most important one. And as I am firmly persuaded that an even more crucial factor is control – i.e. establishing who is in control of the production process – I daresay that the twenty-first century will be the scene of a dialectical confrontation between two major ways to exercise control within firms: control by providers of capital versus control by providers of labour.

20 Advocates of the abolition of markets and their mechanisms promptly upon the establishment of a socialist system include the most renowned Japanese economist, K. Uno, who holds markets to be absolutely incompatible with socialism (see Makoto 2006, pp. 22–24).

21 The market socialism model Chilosi and Nuti have in mind is a system that was launched in some countries in an abortive attempt to rectify the faults of the Soviet central planning model through the revival of markets.

22 According to Garson (1973, p. 469), in our generation the most convincing form of class struggle acts itself out within the movement for worker control of firms.

23 This is what Anweiler wrote in 1958 (p. 472); and in 1973, Trower remarked that the pendulum of democracy had stopped swinging the other way and was now swinging in the direction of the establishment of democracy in the firm (op. cit., p. 138).

2 Is historical materialism a deterministic approach?

The democratic firm and the transition to socialism

Introduction

Engels rated the materialistic conception of history as the true core of Marxism (Engels 1859a, pp. 202–3), Lenin esteemed it as "a great achievement in scientific thinking" (Lenin 1913, p. 477) and Aron (1970, p. 178) held that the gist of Marxism is the theory of the capitalistic mode, which is grounded in historical materialism (for a comparable view, see also Rodinson 1969, pp. 13–18).[1] Until the advent of Marx, historians had been preferably concerning themselves with political events, as well as religious and philosophical ideas; unlike them, Marx chose to investigate deeper motives that would shed light on political history, the history of ideas and the agents behind them, the relationship between humans and nature over time, as well as the actions of a horde of actors grouped into castes, orders and classes (see Godelier 1982, p. 332).

Considering the paramount place of historical materialism in Marx's overall theoretical framework, in this chapter I will try to establish if Marxism is a deterministic approach.

According to Plechanov (1895, p. 46), Marxists think of history as ultimately shaped by the dynamic of material production forces, rather than by human will. Bernstein, for his part (1899, p. 31), made it clear that "to be a materialist means first of all to trace all phenomena to the necessary movements of matter". And "as it is always the movement of matter which determines the form of ideas and the directions of the will", he argued, "these also (and with them everything that happens in human reality) are inevitable". Similarly, Merleau-Ponty (1948, p. 291) thought that Marx was fully aware of the important role of objective factors in historical evolution. "The beautiful parallel... between the realization of philosophy and the realization of socialism" that we observe in the young Marx, he argued, was destroyed by 'scientific socialism' to the benefit of the infrastructure".

Although these views have come in for severe criticism from more than one author, they are still widely shared and constantly resurgent, In more recent years, numerous orthodox Marxists, with G.A. Cohen the most prominent among them (see Cohen 1978 and 2000), have been advancing the so-called *fundamentalist thesis*, i.e. the claim that Marx's approach is to be categorised as a form of technological determinism.

In point of fact, it is long since the description of Marx's approach as 'techno-logical determinism' was first refuted by Kautsky (see Kautsky 1899, pp. 1–34), and modern theorists who appropriately rate Marx's dialectical method as an-tithetical to determinism include, among others, Acton (1955, pp. 159–68), Plamenatz (1963, pp. 274ff), Miller (1984) and Sowell (1985, pp. 30–31).

As a rule, determinism is described as the doctrine teaching that a particu-lar aspect or part of the social whole has a predominating influence on all the others. Several authors hold that economic determinism reflects the idea of a linear causality, i.e. of direct relations between a paramount economic cause and the effects that passively flow from it (see, for instance, Dunlap 1979, p. 313). Due to this linear notion of causality – they argue – the economic base is the necessary and, in itself, sufficient cause, whereas the superstructure is stripped of its autonomous role and production relations are the direct off-shoot of the prevailing state of technology. In fact, this conception is typical of mechanistic, rather than Marxian materialism, and as it tends to oblite-rate the role of superstructural factors, it is unable to account for the rise of existing forms of society and their different characteristics (see Karsz 1974, pp. 120–24). In Althusser's structuralist approach, causality is far from linear, since the political and ideological aspects of a mode of production are seen to act themselves out in a fairly autonomous manner.

The charge of determinism is usually pressed against Lenin's argument that the transition to socialism will follow upon the stage known as state monopoly capitalism. As is well known, in an attempt to provide an 'objec-tive' description of the development of capitalism, Lenin maintained that the growth of monopolies and ever more massive State intervention in the economy would pave the way for a centrally planned socialist system with large-size monopolistic concerns. In fairly advanced countries and, gener-ally, capitalistic economies – he wrote – the assumptions for the takeover of the capitalistic economic apparatus by the mass of workers had been cre-ated by such a genuinely socialist measure as the extension of compulsory schooling to all citizens, by the subjection of workers to the discipline of industrial work and, lastly, by greatly simplified governance and adminis-tration procedures.

At any rate, instead of expatiating on Althusser's far from consensus-based criticism, it is worth emphasising that when socialism is looked upon as a mode of production with worker-controlled firms, rather than a centrally planned system, the deterministic overtones of the materialistic conception of history will promptly appear in a more appropriate perspective.[2]

My claim that Marxism is not necessarily a deterministic approach is backed up by numerous quotes from Marx's own writing.

The principal aim of this chapter is to show that the slightly deterministic overtones of Marx's materialistic conception of history will appear acceptable if we think of socialism as a system of democratic firms.

My thesis can be summed up as follows. Against the background of the above-mentioned equation of socialism with democratic firm management,

- the only – fully acceptable – deterministic proposition in Marxism is the idea that socialism is bound to arise at some point in time,
- the deterministic overtones of Marx's approach are greatly dampened by the fact that the timing and location of such transition are not prevailingly related to the stage of development of the productive forces,
- the timing and location of the transition are prevailingly determined by political developments, i.e. by the dynamic of the *superstructure* in the country concerned from time to time.

In other words, on the one hand Marx's line of reasoning may sound deterministic in that it postulates a measure of necessity in historical development; on the other, it may sound teleological since it seems to suggest that history does tend towards a predetermined goal. On closer analysis, instead, in consequence of the emphasis on the role of superstructural elements Marx's propositions have but a slight deterministic colouring. The teleological hypothesis is ruled out by the fact that no superior goal is superimposed on historical evolution from outside.

At any rate, considering that Marxism tends to be associated with centralised planning even today, there is no denying that these ideas are slow to assert themselves. This conclusion is corroborated by the fact that until the 1950s people critical of the political experience and theoretical developments of communism in the Soviet Union could hardly dare to describe themselves as Marxists (see Pompeo Faracovi 1972, p. 129).

Does Marxism imply the assumption that history is heading in a given direction?

The prerequisite for answering the queries raised is clarifying if history is actually heading in a given direction and, if so, what this direction is.

For many years Marx described history as a process which is governed by laws and unfolds as an endless chain of changes in social interrelations. In *The German Ideology*, he wrote (see Marx & Engels 1845–1846, p. 27):

> History is nothing but the succession of the separate generations, each of which exploits the materials, the capital funds, the productive forces handed down to it by all preceding generations; and thus, on the one hand, continues the traditional activity in completely changed circumstances and, on the other, modifies the old circumstances with a completely changed activity.[3]

Further on, he and Engels specified (*supra*, p. 59) that it is "the history of the evolving productive forces taken over by each new generation, and is therefore the history of the development of the forces of the individuals themselves".[4]

This means that even a comparatively early work such as *The German Ideology* offers the demonstration that the main purpose behind historical materialism is

> expounding the real process of production – starting from the material production of life itself – and comprehending the form of intercourse connected with and created by this mode of production, i.e. civic society in its various stages as the basis of all history; describing it in its action as the state, and also explaining how all the different theoretical products and forms of consciousness, religion, philosophy, morality, etc., etc., arise from it.

As is well known, right to his maturity, Marx held on to the belief that the true foundation of the historical process was material production. In 1859, he wrote (Marx 1859, p. 5): "In the real production of their existence men inevitably enter into definite relations, which are independent of their will, namely relations of production appropriate to a given stage in the development of their material forces of production". In historical materialism – Elster argued (1985, p. 267) – productive forces hold the centre of the stage.[5]

In point of fact, Marx did not deny the importance man in history. "Men – he wrote – make their own history" (Marx 1852a, p. 103).[6]

Gramsci, for his part, held history to be the chronicle of the successful efforts of humankind to gain ever more freedom by dismantling and breaking up the ponderous repressive machinery put in place by the power structure (see Gramsci 1984, p. 601). According to Lukàcs (1968b, p. 34), Marx's conception of world history was 'as a unitary process and the highroad to liberation' and had much in common with the approaches of German philosophers and chiefly Hegel. This view goes as far back as Kant, who described history as steady progress (see Kant 1784, p. 174).

It is a fact that the long-term (not year-after-year) effect of the growth of productive forces is a rising trend in per capita incomes and that rising income levels are greatly dependent on an upward trend in access to education. In turn, scientific advancements and higher education levels help the population master their environment ever more effectively. Men and women are the only rational beings in the universe and it is thanks to reason that they are in a position to keep the environment in check. Provided it is true that the domain of knowledge is constantly widening and that people are ever better educated, there are grounds for believing that society will develop the ability to exercise ever tighter control over production activities as well. This leads us to argue, with Balibar, that any Marxist will "classify existing societies by reference to an intrinsic criterion: …, i.e. the extent to which individuals are collectively able to control the conditions of their existence" (Balibar 1993, p. 131).[7]

An additional point requiring further discussion is the tendency to absolute control that Marx extolled as the logic inherent in the economic process. Whereas Marx expected this tendency to impress momentum on the progress towards socialism, Horkheimer thought it to be fraught with danger. In Horkheimer's own words, it was this assumption that had induced him to distance himself from Marx. Far from paving the way for socialism, he argued, each piecemeal extension of control over economic activity by compact industrial groups organised in line with unitary criteria would rather entail a loss of freedom; and a society where all the existing factories obey the will of one and the same entity, though probably fairer and freed from the fear of the future, would doubtless stifle autonomy and free expression in its members. Marx was right, he added, in predicting the progress of human societies towards an ever more tightly regulated world, but due to his optimism he failed to realise that subterranean forces were stifling fantasy and inventiveness in human beings and that all such freedom as had been made possible by bourgeois society was to be protected against the dangers stemming from total control. This – he concluded – is why he was inimical to the very idea of centralisation (see Horkheimer 1972, pp. 30–31, 44–47 and 52).

Horkheimer's conclusion reveals his belief that socialism boils down to a Soviet-type centrally planned system – an idea that Marx would not have subscribed to.

From a different perspective, Marx's conception of history has been criticised for underrating the risks associated with prolonged processes of regression comparable to those recorded in the aftermath of the collapse of the Roman Empire or in the years immediately before Hitler's rise to power in Germany. When risks of regression are downplayed, Sowell argued, people may either come to think that nothing can be worse than their objectionable present or conceive the equally misleading assumption that revolution will not entail a period of prolonged misery for the masses. In fact, both these ideas are contradicted by the record of events in Russia and China (see Sowell 1985, pp. 205–9).

This objection can be countered by arguing that while it is true that Marx extolled the growing ability of humankind to keep the environment ever more effectively in check, he also specified that fully democratic forms of control would *only* become possible *in a socialist society*.

The idea that the ultimate goal of the historical process is the full emancipation of humankind has been called into question by numerous commentators. Among them are Lucio Colletti (in the 1977 interview printed in Colletti 1979) and Hodgson (2000, pp. 302–5). Both of them fault with a finalistic, i.e. teleological component they perceive in Marxist writings, but wrongly extend it from individual Marxists to Marxism overall. In point of fact, Engels and Marx made it absolutely clear that they had fleshed out a non-teleological approach (see Engels 1859a, p. 372;[8] Marx 1860, p. 131; Marx 1861, p. 578; Marx 1867b, p. 114; De Gregory 2003, pp. 19–20).

Let me re-emphasise that Marx did believe in the ability of mankind to master the environment ever more thoroughly in a long-term perspective, but never as much as suggested that the future of capitalism would entail piecemeal day-by-day gains in freedom. He rather thought that the ultimate effect of the evolution of the productive forces in capitalism would be the definitive subjection of workers to the oppressive power of capital. As he himself put it,

> at the same pace that mankind masters nature, man seems to become enslaved to other men or to his own infamy. Even the pure light of science seems unable to shine but on the dark background of ignorance. All our invention and progress seem to result in endowing material forces with intellectual life, and in stultifying human life into a material force.
> (Quoted in Ojzerman 1969, p. 270)

In the last years of his life – let this be clearly stated – Marx's view of history underwent radical change. From the letters to Vera Zasulich that Marx wrote in February–March 1881 it is possible to infer that the discovery of the grand Russian populist dream had induced Marx to abandon the Eurocentric view of growth and to modify the stringent laws he had until then assumed to govern development as mentioned above (see Cinnella 2014, pp. 119–74).

Further reflections on the notion of history in Marx and Marxism

Marx describes history as a process, governed by laws, which unfolds as an uninterrupted sequence of changes in the structure of social interrelations (see Fleischer 1969, p. 41). In an early work such as *The German Ideology* (Marx & Engels 1845–1846, p. 27), he and Engels wrote that

> history is nothing but the succession of the separate generations, each of which exploits the materials, the capital funds, the productive forces handed down to it by all preceding generations, and thus, on the one hand, continues the traditional activity with a completely changed activity.

Further on, they added (p. 59) that it was "the history of the evolving productive forces taken over by each new generation, and is, therefore, the history of the development of the forces of the individuals themselves". To Marx's thinking,

> production forces evolve from within on an impulse which is inherent in them and impress their imprint on the institutions of a society and its ideologies. Both in Marx and in Hegel, the strongest impulse was an expansive metaphysical element capable of shaping reality

Namely the factors of production.

Hence, even an early work such as *The German Ideology* (p. 53) is evidence that Marx's approach, historical materialism, is mainly aimed to

> expound the real process of production, starting out from the material production of life itself, and to comprehend the form of intercourse connected with this and created by this mode of production (i.e. civil society in its various stages), as the basis of all history; and to show it in its action as state, to explain all the different theoretical products and forms of consciousness, religion, philosophy, ethics, etc. etc., and trace their origin and growth from that basis; by which means, of course, the whole thing can be depicted in its totality (and therefore, too, the reciprocal action of these various sides on one another).

It is a well-known fact that right to his maturity Marx held on to the belief that the true foundation of the historical process was material production. In his own words:

> My inquiry led me to the conclusion that neither legal relations nor political forms could be comprehended whether by themselves or on the basis of the so-called general development of the human mind, but that on the contrary they originated in the material conditions of life, the totality of which Hegel, following the example of English and French thinkers of the eighteenth century, embraces within the term 'civil society'.
>
> (Marx 1859, p. 3)

Praising the sheer novelty of Marx's materialist approach to history, Althusser emphasised that the refusal to posit the essence of man as the basis of history enabled Marx to accomplish a radical theoretical revolution, i.e. to reject the "idealism of the essence" and replace "the old couple individuals/human essence in the theory of history by new concepts (forces of production, relations of production, etc.)" (Althusser 1965b, p. 204).

The teleological overtones that were still perceived in the *Economic-Philosophical Manuscripts of 1944* are absent from the conception of history of the mature Marx, who rejected the extension of Darwinism to the social sciences.[9]

In Althusser's view, thanks to the discovery of production modes, the way they arise, grow and die out, Marx made a major contribution to the advancement of scientific knowledge and laid the foundations for a theoretical edifice which is at the basis of all the sciences falling within the domain of history in the broadest possible meaning of this word (Althusser 1969, 1995, p. 23). In this connection, Therborn 1971 (p. 104) has argued that Althusser holds the notion of modes of production to be the very cornerstone of historical materialism.

In actual fact, dissenting from Althusser, I have to remark that Marx did not deny the importance of the subject, i.e. humankind, in history. "Men – he wrote

(Marx 1852a, p. 487) – make their own history." In the opinion of Marx, theory has to be combined with practice, but for this to happen "the emergence of consciousness must become the decisive step which the historical process must take towards its proper end – an end constituted by the wills of men but neither dependent on human whim nor the product of human invention" (Lukàcs 1923, p. 3).

The laws by which history is governed arise in connection with the fact that history is the record of the way productive forces evolve. Moreover – and this is what I wish to emphasise – all such movement as is observed within the historical process is sparked off by the contradictions within modes of production.

Hence, I fully agree with Pasolini (1964, p. 80) that "when history is looked upon as the chronicle of class struggle, the hoped-for communist dreamworld must ideally imply and posit the advent of an ahistorical phase", i.e. that Marx's theoretical approach implies a point in time, far ahead of the immediate future, when history comes to a stop and gives way to a metahistorical phase.

Coming back to the view of history that Marx held for several years in succession and that most Marxists took over from him, let me mention that Lukàcs divided the history of *Kultur* into a pre-capitalistic stage, a capitalistic stage and a third, classless stage. And whereas in capitalistic societies, where everything that is produced is turned into a commodity, he saw culture stripped of its autonomy and ultimately nullified, he predicted that thanks to the abolition of mercantilistic relationships communistic societies would provide fresh scope for meaningful work and help humankind wield "its inner mastery over the external reality", i.e. *Kultur* (see Lukàcs 1971 and the comment by Cases quoted there).

Hence, it is possible to conclude that the description of history as the record of successive steps toward ever more effective control of the environment and the argument that such control will only become democratic in a communist world are keystones of Marxism.[10]

A few explanatory notes concerning Marx's estimation of Darwin and Darwinism will help clarify the line of reasoning ascribed to Marx so far. The descriptions of reality respectively offered by Darwin and Marx are not only different, but antithetical. Darwin's is a deterministic process whose successive steps follow upon one another without the least scope for freedom; in contrast, Marx's is a process which, though entailing a measure of determinism (communism is held to be a necessary development), centres on the idea that human evolution is (in a long-term perspective, let this be repeated) the highroad to ever greater freedom.

This conclusion is backed up by two of Marx's letters.

In a letter written on 15 February 1869, Marx draws a clear-cut distinction between Darwin and Darwinism. Starting out from the struggle for life in English society (described as "the competition of all with all, *bellum omnium contra omnes*"), he writes, Darwin made the discovery that the struggle for life was "the dominating law of animal and plant life". In Darwinism, this is looked upon as "a conclusive reason for human society never to emancipate itself from its bestiality" (see Marx 1869).

Here Marx is evidently endorsing Darwin's approach, but not the tendency of Darwinism to extend the struggle for existence to human behaviour overall.

Similarly, in a letter dated November 1975, Marx rejected the tendency of Darwinism to extend the struggle for existence to sociology and reported scientific recommendations descending from the biological laws of animal and plant life (Marx 1975b).[11]

These reflections fit within the view of dialectics as a totality. The main effect of a totality-focused dialectical approach is indeed to magnify the impact of totality on the context, in terms that its individual components will be perceived as different depending on the specific totality they are part of from time to time. The end result is a compound of effects which impact on the elements constituting the system (Karsz 1974, p. 131).

The importance of a simultaneous focus on both the issue and the surrounding totality was underscored, among others, by Althusser (see Karsz 1974, p. 130). In Althusser's view, it was the only effective way to address and solve an issue dialectically, but he also claimed that this was only applicable to the method used by Marx. Hegel's, he argued, was antithetical to the non-contradiction principle and "completely dependent on the radical presupposition of a simple original unity which develops within itself by virtue of its negativity" and "only ever restores the original simplicity and unity in an ever-more 'concrete' totality" throughout its development (Althusser 1965, p. 175).

From this, it follows that no one sharing Althusser's view of dialectics as totality-focused should use a form of dialectical thinking that can be re-interpreted as economic determinism. In Althusser's approach, economic determinism descends from the idea of a linear causal chain implying direct cause–effect relations, i.e. relations between a single paramount cause and the effects that passively flow from it. The economic base is the necessary and, in itself, sufficient cause, whereas the superstructure, stripped of its autonomy, becomes ineffectual and production relations are seen to be shaped directly by the prevailing state of technology. As a result, the idea of a predetermined course of things, materialism, leads up to economic fatalism, i.e. determinism. On closer analysis, however, this conception is specific to mechanistic materialism, rather than Marx's approach, and as it tends to obliterate the part played by superstructural factors, it is unable to account for the rise of existing forms of society and their different characteristics (see Karsz 1974, pp. 120–24).

Like Althusser, Sowell also appropriately classifies Marx's dialectical method as antithetical to determinism (see Sowell 1985, pp. 30–31).

One possible objection, here, is that the reflections developed in this section have to do with teleology, rather than determinism proper. As far as I can see, the belief that history is heading in a precise direction is closely intertwined with the issue of determinism since only those who perceive a distinct long-term direction in history are supposed to ask themselves if theirs is, or is not, a deterministic view. In other words, before a given approach can be characterised as deterministic it is necessary to establish if it has a teleological colouring of sorts because anyone thinking of the historical course as more or less pre-fixed and nonetheless denying the deterministic overtones of such an assumption is expected to make plain his line of reasoning. Pending further clarifications that will be offered further on, at this point it is worth spelling out that the deterministic colouring of Marx's approach is acceptable (a) since it is merely a reflection of his belief that history must head towards socialism and (b) due to an emphasis on the decisive role of the decisions of economic actors in determining the timing and mode of the transition to socialism.

Possible transition scenarios against the backdrop of market socialism

Before attempting a final word on the deterministic essence of Marx's thought and the kind of control that will be possible under socialism, it is necessary to define the new mode of production that will arise from the ashes of capitalism and to ask ourselves in what way the transition to socialism might be followed through in practice.

As is well known, in the 1930s a group of eminent economists reached the conclusion that reconciling planning with markets was far from easy, if not altogether impossible. The belief that central planning is no comforting prospect for the future has been making headway ever since and has been confirmed by the sensational collapse of the regimes that had opted for this system.

Hence, the question arises whether socialism still exists.

This is why I agree with Anweiler (1958, p. 472) that the original idea behind the movement for workers' councils – "the primary aim of Marxism" – is "as topical as ever" (see Garaudy undated, p. 187). Back in 1917, R. Tawney emphasised that freedom can never be complete unless it brings with it both absence of repression and opportunities for self-organisation – in short, unless it is attained by extending representative institutions to industry.

It is necessary now to raise the question if a system of democratic firms operating in markets would actually generate a new mode of production.

As is well known, while capital-owned enterprises strive to maximise profit in the interests of capitalists, the self-managed firm theorised by Vanek (1970) aims to maximise average worker income or, even more correctly, benefits for its workers (in point of fact, for those majority workers who have authority to pass resolutions). Hence, if economic activity is made to pursue a different goal, the system also will change as a matter of course and will become a new mode of production. In the words of the well-known Italian philosopher Emanuele Severino (2012, p. 94),

> within a logic (prevailing over the course of human history) that postulates the existence of goals and means, there can be little doubt (though

the consequence is less dominant than the starting assumption) that whenever an action – in this case the capitalistic mode of operation – is made to deflect from its original goal to a different one, this same logic determines that the action itself will turn into something different in content, rhythm, intensity, relevance and configuration.

From a Marxist perspective, it is possible to argue that the reversed capital-labour relation specific to democratic firm control solves the conflict between socialised production and private appropriation thanks to the fact that production and distribution, being governed by the choices of the members' collective, become socialised activities. In a democratic firm system, the workers' collective is sovereign, in terms that its decision powers in matters of production include authority to regulate distribution in manners that will appear most appropriate from time to time (see Jossa 2012a).[12]

The next question to be raised is why democratic firm management should be rated as a major stride forward in the evolution of humankind.

The answer is, quite naturally, that the suppression of hired labour in a labour-managed firm system results in a gain in democracy since it puts an end to the coercion of workers by their employers. And coercion, Hayek wrote (1960, p. 21), is an evil which turns useful thinking individuals into lifeless tools for the attainment of another's ends.

One major aspect of this issue is that growth is usually enough to confer legitimacy on a going concern (see Carroll 1984; Carroll & Hannan 1989).

Coming to the way the transition from capitalism to a system of democratic firms can be implemented in practice, one possible scenario, though not the most important one, is converting down-run capitalistic enterprises into cooperative firms. Several countries have a considerable track record of insolvent capitalistic firms which were turned into cooperatives. In capitalistic systems, Vanek wrote (1977b, p. 46), a corporate insolvency case may be an excellent opportunity for setting up a self-managed firm (see, *inter alia*, Ben-Ner 1988). Unlike workers in capitalistic enterprises, the partners of a cooperative will seldom, if ever, oppose cuts on their wages in times of crises; they will put up with lower incomes whenever they feel that this sacrifice will keep their firm going. In other words, capitalistic business enterprises often face insolvency because rigid payroll expenses prevent them from boosting revenues, whereas the personnel costs of cooperatives are flexible by definition.

This can explain why the growth process of the cooperative movement is usually counter-cyclical, in terms that the creation of new cooperatives responds to increasing risks of job loss rather than prospects of higher bottomline results.

Based on the reflections developed so far, a revolution of the type envisioned in this book can be implemented by degrees and by democratic means, in line with the process suggested by Gramsci when he drew a distinction between revolutions feasible in the West and the Russian Revolution. A gradual transition process is what Rosa Luxembourg had in mind when she wrote:

> The conquest of power will not be effected with one blow. It will be a progression; we will progressively occupy all the positions of the capitalist state and defend them tooth and nail ... It is a question of fighting step by step, hand-to-hand, in every province, in every city, in every village, in every municipality, in order to take and transfer all the powers of the state bit by bit from the bourgeoisie to the workers' and soldiers' councils.
>
> (Luxemburg 1918, p. 629)

A different – and even more effective – way to establish the *new order* is to secure the passing of an Act of Parliament to convert the shares of existing companies into bonds of equal value and outlaw hired labour to the extent and in manners deemed appropriate. Thanks to the enforcement of such an Act, capitalists would be disempowered and capitalistic companies would be changed into worker-controlled firms. As the precondition for such a move is, quite obviously, a parliamentary majority of representatives of the working class, this scenario is probably no option in a country such as the United States, but might be a viable solution in a considerable number of countries other than the United States.[13]

Concluding, let me once again emphasise by firm belief that provided socialism is equated with democratic firm control and imagined to be implemented in one of the manners mentioned above, the deterministic overtones in Marx's materialistic conception of history are likely to appear acceptable.[14] Considering that a major step towards freedom such as the liberation of workers from the wage yoke is, in the long run, a realistic prospect, the deterministic overtones of the claim that history heads towards ever fuller freedom can be categorised as acceptable thanks to the clarification that the timing and mode of the transition to the new mode of production will be exclusively determined by the free wills of the workers themselves.

Is the capital–labour contradiction systematically escalating?

At this stage of history, the fact that technical evolution is moving in the opposite direction to Fordism makes it impossible to claim that the advent of economic democracy is being expedited in response to the degradation of human labour caused by Fordism and Taylorism.

Does this validate the opposite assumption that the higher educational levels and greater skills required by modern technology are hastening the transition to democratic firm management and thereby restoring momentum to labour management theory?

In a well-reasoned 1999 study, Hodgson contended that self-management was actually headway, though, admittedly, at a very slow pace. Advancements in knowledge and education, he argued, make people aware of their rights, and this will help them fine-tune and implement autonomous firm management modes and, inevitably, reduce the role of hired work in society (see Hodgson 1999).

The need to raise the educational levels of the working class was spelt out by Lenin in clear letters. Lefebvre reports (1968, p. 120) that around 1920, shortly after he had come to power, Lenin strongly recommended a real and proper cultural revolution designed to enable the working class to administer a huge country, manage industry, master technological resources and markets and assimilate – as well as instantly put behind – capitalistic rationality. His conclusion was that the revolutionary forces had to work towards raising the educational levels of the population. Today, this view is concordantly endorsed by all those who advocate a transition to socialism.

Consequently, I agree with Zamagni (2006, p. 60) that the moment we gain a correct understanding of the strategic role of human and social capital, "we will also have a correct appreciation of the overriding importance of democratic governance modes even on a strictly economic plain". Indeed, the more workers manage to raise their educational levels and qualifications, the more they will strive to acquire the skills and expertise required to run firms first-hand.

A great many authors (including Ben-Ner 1987, 1988, pp. 295–96; Bowles & Gintis 1996, p. 82) hold that the living standards of the working classes are a major determinant of the benefits granted to labour-managed firms and the difficulties they are likely to come up against. At the same pace that wages and salaries increase, workers are likely to become less risk-averse, recognise the opportunities associated with self-managing firms and endeavour to acquire the requisite entrepreneurial skills. Very often, workers in self-managed firms have the feeling that their incomes may be at risk and that they may fail to provide decent standards of living to their families, but this fear tends to recede in proportion to rises in income.[15]

Thanks to advancements in communication and knowledge economics, workers are likely to interiorise the conceptual dimensions of their jobs, join with others in carrying on business independently of capitalists and develop ever more socialised collective working modes.

The capital-labour conflict, i.e. the mismatch between ever-changing productive forces and production relations, is escalating under the pressure of two antithetical trends: whereas workers, i.e. the productive forces, are developing better entrepreneurial skills, production relations have remained unaltered and business firms continue to be run by capital.

It is interesting to mention that even in the years immediately after the October Revolution, when Lenin had not yet been won over to the idea of allowing workers to run their firms on their own, he never as much as suggested that the reason for postponing employee management was lack of entrepreneurial competencies. Neither do Marxist historians or, generally, modern Marxists. An example in point is the Althusserian Saul Karsz (1974, p. 188), who argues that no technical requirements whatsoever impose the need that the users of means of production should be propertyless individuals without power to make decisions concerning the use of labour power.

Whereas this suggests the preliminary conclusion that labour management will be implemented as a matter of course at the same pace that manual labour loses weight and workers hone their educational and professional qualifications (see, for example, Mandel 1973, p. 349), it is worth repeating that a belief in the ultimate advent of democracy at some point in time should not be categorised as a deterministic conception. In the words of Adler, it is not inconsistent to speak of a necessary historical course and, at the same time, to assume an ideal purpose behind it. As long as we speak of evolution as governed by necessity, he explained, we are arguing from a purely scientific angle of view, but the moment we assume an ideal goal behind it, we are plunged into the stream of the will and of historical action, which so far had been viewed objectively (see Adler 1904, p. 1989).[16]

My confidence in the ultimate success of worker control stems from the firm conviction that the preconditions for individuals to realise their humanity to the full are freedom, securing scope for autonomous action and the pursuit of self-conceived goals, as well as ceasing to serve as lifeless tools for the attainment of other people's aims. A well-known saying by Marx (1867a, p. 284) runs that "what distinguishes the worst architect from the best of bees is that the architect builds the cell in his mind before he constructs it in wax". This means that the human work process is characterised by the fact that the result "already existed, i.e. was ideally present, in the imagination of the labourer at its commencement" (*ibid.*) and that the working mode of a hired labourer passively obeying third-party commands can barely be described as genuinely human. Insofar as it is true that history is the record of the stepwise acquisition of ever tighter control over the environment, it is according to reason that workers should be free to pursue the aims they have in view.

One more question to be raised at this point is whether the class that is pressing most forcefully for the transition from capitalism to a system of democratic firms is actually the proletariat. As argued by Petruccioli (1972, p. 51), in an effort to define the true revolutionary agent – the social group potentially most committed to revolutionary action – Marxists have alternatively adopted the viewpoints of two different, though complementary ideologies, labourism versus proletarianism. As a result, he remarks, at times they have restricted this group to proletarians only and, at times, they have included other classes by extending its limits in accordance with the proletarisation formula.

From my perspective, it is clear that the basic distinction is between individuals who welcome change and those tending to oppose it, i.e. between hired and self-employed workers. And as statistics show that the former group (blue collars and lower-level clerical workers) has been steadily increasing,[17] there are grounds for assuming that the transition would be supported by the majority of the population.

With reference to Italy, Petruccioli reports that the most noticeable change in the social composition of the population has been a steady drop in self-employment levels and a rising trend in the number of hired workers (*idem*, pp. 47–48).[18] As far as the United States are concedrned, Stiglitz (2012, p. 13) has commented that the middle class has become "'eviscerated' as the 'good' middle-class jobs – requiring a moderate level of skills, like autoworkers' jobs – seemed to be disappearing, relative to those at the bottom, requiring few skills, and those at the top, requiring greater skill levels".

Concluding, it is evident that many obstacles stand in the way of the establishment of a system of cooperative firms and that it is far from easy to anticipate when such a revolution will come about.

Although Marx and Hegel held that the times were ripe and that revolution was at hand, it is a fact that "Engels waited for the fulfilment of his gloomy prophecy" for years, and that "for years he waited in vain" (see Henderson 1977, p. 21). Concerning the present-day situation, it is probably worth adding that following the failure of the revolutions in Eastern European countries there is no way of predicting if the transition will be a short- or long-term process.

In the light of these reflections I will attempt a critique of Lenin's claim that the class consciousness that workers develop *from within* is solely economic and trade-unionist in nature and that true class consciousness can come to workers only *from without*. At meetings and conferences attended by workers, he argued, debates are usually focused on economic issue, but seldom if ever on issues such as the living conditions of individual social classes, the history of the revolutionary movement or economic trends under way in the country overall. In Lenin's view, it was this unsatisfactory state of affairs that prevented the proletariat from taking the lead of the movement, raising general issues associated with democracy and working towards a change of the existing mode of production.

Dissenting from Lenin on these points, I firmly hold that where the establishment of a new production mode is made to coincide with the transfer of firm control to workers, class consciousness will arguably develop spontaneously from within the working class. Considering the economic benefits associated with self-management, there is a material chance that the workers may resolve to start a revolution, bring home the message that firm control by profit-seeking capitalists is an obstacle to the growth of democracy and the general good and, hence, win over the middle class to their cause.[19]

In this connection, let me specify that Marx and Engels divided each mode of production into two distinct phases. At the earlier stage of the capitalistic mode of production – they argued – most workers do not seek revolution since an awareness of the rational relational criteria behind capitalism induces them to accept the system. In due time – they concluded – as soon as they realise that these relations are the chains that fetter their progress, they will endeavour to join forces with the middle class in an attempt to revolutionise the existing mode of production.

Is the transition to socialism a certainty or a conjecture?

Scholars sharing Bernstein's view that Marxism is inextricably bound up with the idea of the collapse of capitalism are likely to argue that the transition scenarios discussed in this book are at odds with Marx's actual thought.

In point of fact, they are compatible with Marx's approach for at least two reasons. On the one hand, they postulate an escalating worker–capitalist conflict; on the other, they take it for granted that free access to education will enable workers to educate themselves, take their lives into their own hands and, consequently, experience the existing contradictions as ever more unbearable.

Both these assumptions are in full accord with Marx's claim that the prerequisite for a successful transitional process is a scientific vision of socialism with specific focus on the laws of motion and inherent contradictions of capitalism. According to Lukàcs (1923, p. 60), the core idea behind scientific Marxism is the belief that the real driving forces behind history are independent of the degree to which people are aware of them.

For my part, I think it unreasonable to assume that workers should not gain an awareness that the capitalist–worker opposition is specific to capitalism only.

In this connection, Lukàcs quotes a passage from *Capital*:

> Reflection on the forms of human life, hence also scientific analysis of these forms, takes a course directly opposite to their real development. Reflection begins *post festum*, and therefore with the results of the process of development ready to hand. The forms ... already possess the fixed quantity of natural forms of social life before man seeks to give an account, not of their historical character, for in his eyes they are immutable, but of their content and meaning.
>
> (Marx 1867a, p. 168)

This passage (which reflects the gist of Marx's historical materialism) tells us clearly that conscience is framed by being, and not vice versa, i.e. that the contrasting views held by men are the effect of real contradictions. "The contradictions of the capitalist system of production – Lukàcs wrote (1923, p. 63) – are reflected in these mutually incompatible accounts of the same object".

Marx's argument that the collapse of a production mode is caused by its inherent contradictions runs counter to the typical worldview of the bourgeoisie, which conceives of the organisational forms of the present as obeying natural and, hence, eternal laws. According to Burke (1981, p. 95), in Marx's writings specific elements of the revolutionary process are seen to prepare the working class for its task of self-managing society and exercising social control over means of production and the revolutionary process itself appears to be triggered by certain tendencies perceived in capitalistic societies.

On closer analysis, Balibar's observation that Marx postulated "a progressive line of evolution of modes of production" which "classifies all societies in terms of an intrinsic criterion, *socialisation*, i.e. the capacity of individuals collectively to control their own conditions of existence" (Balibar 1993, p. 131) go to strengthen the case of scholars who postulate the compatibility cooperation theory with Marx's approach.

With reference to the above, let me argue, with Rosa Luxemburg, that here we have, in brief, "the explanation of the socialist programme by means of 'pure reason'; or, to use simpler language, an idealist explanation of socialism"; and conclude that "the objective necessity of socialism, the explanation of socialism as the result of the material development of society, falls to the ground" (Luxemburg 1913, p. 151).

In an analysis of the transition van Parijs and van der Veen (1986, p. 159) argued that

> Marx did not offer any arguments in support of his claim that the growth of the productive forces (as distinct from their use) is fettered by capitalism and that – in line with the rationale behind historical materialism – the substitution of socialism for capitalism is necessitated by this fettering.

In other words, these authors hold that Marx offered no proof of the transition to socialism as a necessary development, but this criticism can be refuted by emphasising that the idea of the transition as an unavoidable necessity is a corollary of Marx's claim that capitalism will ultimately collapse in consequence of the inevitable escalation of its distinctive contradictions.[20]

In point of fact, some authors hold that the view of a steadily escalating capital-labour conflict is contradicted by the awareness that the determination of workers to rebel against capitalistic exploitation tends to ebb away in direct proportion to the increases in income that workers can realistically be assumed to secure even in capitalistic economies, but from my perspective there can be little doubt that the more workers educate themselves and acquire the ability to take their lives into their own hands, the more will they experience the capital-labour opposition as an unbearable condition.

In the words of van Parijs and van der Veen, "what is politically feasible depends largely on what has been shown to make economic and ethical sense" (1986, p. 156); and it is reasonable to assume that what makes economic and ethical sense will sooner or later come true.[21]

"Causation in Marx ed Engels – Sowell writes (1985, p. 34) – is a matter of interaction, rather than a one-way mechanism. And this, he argues, determines that there is neither pure determinism nor pure change, but a stream of events which reflect both 'accidental' factors and underlying forces whose necessary relationships shape the general tendency of these events as a whole.[22]

One point of Marx's approach which is difficult to reconcile with the transition scenarios reported above is the view of the state as the 'lobbying group' of the bourgeoisie.

In the awareness that the capitalistic state does allow workers scope for gaining strength and ultimately seizing power, I have abstained from describing it as a tool for ensuring class rule; neither have I characterised the socialist state as subservient to the aims of workers. In my opinion, such a line of reasoning would be an orthodox Kautskian approach of sorts and, as such, frustrate any attempt at a truly critical analysis of Marxist theory. For the same reason, I have avoided to describe the capitalistic state as a tool in the hands of capitalists.

Provided it is true that historical development is spurred on by ideas, it is possible to argue that nothing can stop worker control of firms (a typical offshoot of ideas such as democracy and progress) from asserting itself at some point in time. Since battles of ideas are of uncertain outcome, the time needed for this to happen is, admittedly, hard to predict, but Gramsci made it absolutely clear that it lay with intellectuals to make a consistent contribution to such an advancement.[23]

Although I do not doubt that the sway of capital over labour will sooner or later be dismantled, I agree with Napoleoni that capitalism will neither collapse mechanically nor escalate to a level where it must change into something different (see Napoleoni 1970, p. lxx). The well-known Italian journalist Eugenio Scalfari put the matter in this way (see Scalfari 2008, p. 1224):

> Many people have been pinning their hopes of liberation on communism. But now it is time to take off the bandages from their eyes and the plugs from their ears. The reification of individuals, the master-servant confrontation, the refusal to acknowledge the rights of others have been salient traits of our species for millennia and will continue to be so in future.

But while the truth of this can hardly be denied, there are reasons to believe that as soon as workers resolve to run firms by themselves and develop the requisite abilities, the master-servant confrontation will become a thing of the past.

Conclusion

Does my analysis necessitate the conclusion that Marxism is a deterministic approach? As far as I can see, the answer is a flat 'no' since the only deterministic detail I can detect in Marx's approach to history is the claim that socialism is bound to arise at some point in time. And as structural elements are paramount in a short-term perspective, there can be little doubt that the dynamic of historical development may move down, instead of up, the ladder towards full freedom.

My answer to the question if Marx's view of history has a teleological colouring is again a blunt 'no', because the idea of a goal assigned to history from outside is nowhere perceived in his approach. The direction in which history is seen to head in the long run is determined by the forces by which historical events are spurred on from time to time.

On closer analysis, the deterministic overtones in Marx's works are comparable to those perceived in every thinker, including Benedetto Croce or Acton, who assigns a given direction to history. Is this determinism or teleology? Croce held history to be the chronicle of man's progress towards freedom; Acton predicted that universal suffrage would sooner or later be achieved in all nations across the world. On the one hand, the claims of these authors may be described as deterministic in that they postulate a measure of necessity in history; on the other, they may sound teleological in that they appear to suggest that history tends towards a predetermined goal.

A unilinear view of history does not necessitate denying the role that human will can play in determining its course. Far from being the demiurges of history, relations of production are nothing but the backdrop against which the true driving force of progress, that is to say humankind, acts itself out.

Although Rosselli was right in arguing that theories postulating the inevitable fall of rates of profit or the stepwise impoverishment of people were not only objectionable, but in contrast with historical reality (see Rosselli op. cit., p. 372), as the workers' wish to become their own masters and fight for the abolition of hired labour is in the nature of things, it is highly likely that capitalism will eventually be supplanted by socialism. At the same pace that history advances towards ever greater freedom, hired workers will become ever more strongly averse to what Mazzini termed 'the slavery of wages' and will make themselves independent. Why should we take it for granted that the cars that workers manufacture for the account of Fiat must necessarily be the property of the Agnelli family? Centuries ago, Locke argued that those who produce goods become the owners of such goods. Inasmuch as it is true that the precondition for the transition to socialism was persuading workers to accept the risks association with production, there are reasons to think that this prospect will materialist at some point in time.

Notes

1 Unlike them, Croce categorised historical materialism as "neither a philosophy of history nor a philosophical approach proper, but rather as an empirical interpretative canon, a recommendation to historians for them to focus on economic activity and give it the attention its major place in human life entitles it to" (see Croce 1896a, pp. 1–19; Labriola 1942, p. 292).
2 The idea that a socialist revolution may come in two different ways is in conflict with a celebrated saying by Bernstein (1901, p. 234): "I am singularly uninterested in understanding what people commonly mean by 'the final goal of socialism'. This goal, whatever it may be, means nothing to me; it is the movement itself which is everything."

3 In *An Idea for a Universal History from a Cosmopolitan Perspective*, written in 1784, Kant himself described history as a process governed by laws. "Whatever concept of the *freedom of the will* one may develop in the context of metaphysics – he wrote – the *appearances* of the will, human actions, are determined, like every other natural event, in accordance with universal natural laws" (see Kant 1784, p. 123). The "grandiose ideas constituting Kant's philosophy of history – so Adler wrote (1904, p. 196) – show an extraordinary, at first glance surprising affinity with the basic ideas of the materialistic conception of history". And Kant's conception of history is an integral part of his overall conception – as is Marx's (see Adler 1904, p. 190).

4 From the social sciences, and particularly economics, Hicks thinks it reasonable to draw some general concepts that can be used "as a means of ordering their material" (see Hicks 1969, p. 2).

5 This quote would suggest that the materialistic conception of history is a socialist or proletarian notion. According to Kautsky, the progress and discoveries made in the nineteen-forties were in line with the basic tenets of the materialistic conception of history, but Engels and Marx,

> despite their genius and despite the preparatory work which the new sciences had achieved, would not have been able, even in the time of the forties in the 19th century, to discover it, if they had not stood on the standpoint of the proletariat, and were thus socialists.
>
> (See Kautsky 1906, p. 97).

6 According to Agnes Heller, although history in Marx is presented as the record of the earliest acquisition and gradual extension of freedom, it is fair to say that men have, admittedly, taken great strides in an effort to counteract fatality, but have failed to extirpate it completely (see Heller 1969, p. 325). Marx saw revolution as the upshot of evolving work processes. In *Capital* – Burke remarks (1981, p. 93) – Marx

> shows how revolution can come about in practical life, i.e. in work processes and revolutionary activities, as well in the self-managed firms that carry on business in post-capitalistic societies. The driving forces behind evolution are not only the ever greater skills developed by humankind over the ages, but also certain traits of capitalism which go to expedite this evolution. Put squarely, this is tantamount to saying that in capitalistic societies the working class is trained in revolution and communism right on the job.

7 Actually, there is general agreement that history is far from the record of piecemeal gains in freedom. Fukuyama, for instance, has written (1992, p. 13) that that advances in industrialisation levels far from generate political liberty as a matter of course. In the words of Buchanan (1982 p. 14), the idea that history is the record of long-term strides towards freedom can be traced to the interpretation of communism as the liberation from alienation in every form.

8 In a letter to Marx dated 12 December 1859 wrote: "Darwin, by the way, whom I'm just reading now, is absolutely splendid. There was one aspect of teleology that had not yet been demolished, and that has now been done" (Engels 1959b).C

9 Among Marxists, let me mention especially Kautsky, whose opinions on links between Darwin and socialism changed with the passing of years. At the time he was editing the *NeueZeit*, he used to emphasise such links, but starting from 1890 ever more often denied them.

10 Until the 1850s, Proudhon himself looked upon revolution as the 'fatal' offshoot of social evolution. Conversely, in the years of his maturity he came to believe that history, far from evolving in accordance with strict laws, was actually shaped by human initiative (see Ansart 1967, pp. 24ff).

11 For my line of reasoning in this paragraph, see Ureña (1977).

12 For Marx's approach to cooperative firms, see Jossa (2005a).

13 Pérotin (2006, pp. 296–97) reports that many cooperatives were established during period of social unrest or political change, for instance during the 1930 and 1848 revolutions, after the establishment of the Paris Commune, during the strikes proclaimed in the years 1893–1894 and 1905–1906, by Popular Front governments in 1936 and in the aftermaths of the two great wars.

14 The socialism = democratic firm management equation is also in contrast with the link between democracy and reformism that Galasso theorised when he wrote (2013, p. 35) that the distinctive characteristic of liberal democracies and all the political forces which accept libertarian practices is the belief that there is just one road to reform.

15 Ben-Ner (1988, p. 297) suggests that skilled and well-educated individuals will find it easier to pool their abilities and establish a firm of their own than to find an external entrepreneur.

16 Marx wrote that men tend to raise only those issues that they feel able to solve, but that this (as Merleau-Ponty appropriately remarks) does not mean that society pursues a pre-fixed goal or that human problems always have one and only one solution.

17 Concerning Italy's debated class composition, the reader is referred to the revised edition of Sylos Labini's book (Sylos Labini 1984), but also to Carboni (1986), Bagnasco (2008) and Pugliese (2008).

18 The fact that the proportion of the population prepared to welcome an end to capitalism increases as soon as the 'hired workers' are substituted for 'working class' has also been highlighted by other authors, including Catephores (1989, pp. 221–26).

19 For critical approaches of the views of Kautsky and Lenin just reported.

20 At some points in Marx's work, revolution and the rise of a new production mode are made to coincide with the point in time when the older production mode inhibits growth altogether; at others with the time when it is found to stand in the way of an *optimal* model of growth (for two antithetical opinions on this point, see Elster 1984, pp. 42–42; Miller 1984).

21 The 'Praxis Group' of Marxists in Yugoslavia advocated a form of humanistic socialism and self-management. While rejecting determinism, its members were confident that most socialist principles would be materially implemented at some points in time (see Crocker 1981).

22 The hypothesis of a one-directional approach to historical materialism is endorsed by Abbagnano (2006, vol. 9, appendix), who argues that the technique of causal explanation is the very foundation of this doctrine.

23 The query whether Marx ever formulated a theory of the collapse of capitalism was answered by Bernstein in the negative in a well-known book (Bernstein 1899, chap. XV) and by Cunow (1899) in the positive. In later years, the idea that Marx did enunciate a collapse theory was widely shared. With reference to the fall in rates of profit – which he held to be the main cause of the assumed collapse – Marx argued that "this process would entail the rapid breakdown of capitalistic production, if counteracting tendencies were not constantly at work alongside this centripetal force, in direction of decentralization" (Marx 1894, p. 355).

3 Cooperation in the history of economic thought

Marx's approach to producer cooperatives

An excerpt from Marx (1864) runs as follows:

> But there was in store a still greater victory of the political economy of labour over the political economy of property. We speak of the co-operative movement, especially of the co-operative factories raised by the unassisted efforts of a few bold 'hands'. The value of these great social experiments cannot be over-rated. By deed, instead of by argument, they have shown that production on a large scale, and in accord with the behest of modern science, may be carried on without the existence of a class of masters employing a class of hands; that to bear fruit, the means of labour need not be monopolised as a means of dominion over, and of extortion against, the labouring man himself; and that, like slave labour, like serf labour, hired labour is but a transitory and inferior form, destined to disappear before associated labour–plying its toil with a willing hand, a ready mind, and a joyous heart.[1]
>
> (Marx 1864, p. 11)

And in the third volume of *Capital* Marx argues:

> With the development of co-operatives on the workers' part, and joint-stock companies on the part of the bourgeoisie, the last pretext for confusing profit of enterprise with the wages of management was removed, and profit came to appear in practice as what it undeniably was in theory, mere surplus-value, value for which no equivalent was paid.
>
> (Marx 1894, pp. 513–14)

These quotes are clear evidence of Marx's belief that a system of cooperative firms is not only feasible but bound to assert itself in history and that it gives rise to a new production mode in which wage labour is swept away and the means of production – what economists term capital – would no longer be used to enslave workers. In such a system, workers would not only cease being exploited; they would feel free and happy to work for firms owned by them.

The system of producer cooperatives envisaged by Marx is a market system where workers become 'their own masters' (Mill 1871, p. 739) and where capital owners are deprived of decision powers concerning production activity. This system is 'in accord with the behest of modern science' and, at the same time, efficient – even more efficient than capitalism – because it entails a new production mode arising spontaneously within the older production mode and improving on it.

This thesis is confirmed by additional well-known passages from *Capital*, which clearly reveal how Marx looked upon a system based on producer co-operatives as a new production mode superior to that of capitalism. One of these, which completes Marx's description of joint- stock companies as a first step towards 'the abolition of capitalist private industry', though 'within the capitalist system itself' (Marx 1894, pp. 570–71), runs as follows:

> The co-operative factories run by workers themselves are, within the old form, the first examples of the emergence of a new form, even though they naturally reproduce in all cases, in their present organization, all the defects of the existing system, and must reproduce them. But the opposition between capital and labour is abolished there, even if at first only in the form that the workers in association become their own capitalists, i.e. they use the means of production to valorise their labour. These factories show how, at a certain stage of development of the material forces of production, and of the social forms of production corresponding to them, a new mode of production develops and is formed naturally out of the old… Capitalist joint-stock companies as much as cooperative factories should be viewed as transition forms from the capitalist mode of production to the associated one, simply that in one case the opposition is abolished in a negative way, and in the other in a positive way.
>
> (Marx 1894, pp. 571–72)

To understand why Marx emphasised the need to abolish wage labour even in a production system remaining purely mercantile in nature, it is worth bearing in mind that one main advantage of producer cooperatives (from the perspective of a critic of capitalism) is to realise economic democracy as an essential component of political democracy. Marx, Marxists and, generally, critics of society think of present-day political democracy as merely formal because all power is still firmly in the hands of capitalists; in other words, because capital is still the economic power holding everything in its sway.

The following quote from *Capital* is no less relevant:

> Capitalist production has itself brought it about that the work of supervision is readily available quite independent of the ownership of capital. It has therefore become superfluous for this work of supervision to be performed by the capitalist. A musical conductor need in no way be the owner of the instruments in his orchestra, nor does it form part of his

function as a conductor that he should have any part in paying the 'wages' of the other musicians. Cooperative factories provide the proof that the capitalist has become just as superfluous as a functionary in production as he himself, from his superior vantage-point, finds the large landlord.

(Marx 1894, p. 511)

Here Marx was clearly thinking of a form of market economy in which cap-italists would be deprived of their power.

The cooperative movement in the estimation of Marshall

Much like Marx himself, Altred Marshall too was favourable to the coop-erative movement. In his opinion, cooperation "undoubtedly does rest in great measure on ethical motives", "has a special charm for those in whose tempers the social elements are stronger" (Marshall 1890, p. 306), "combines high aspirations with calm and strenous action" and "sets itself to develop the spontaneous energies of the individual while training him to collective action by the aid of collective resources and for the attainment of collective ends." Marshall owns that cooperation "has points of affinity with many other movements", but thinks that these do not have in common with coop-eration the "direct aim to improve the quality of man itself" (*idem*, p. 227). In an earlier study (Marshall 1889, p. 228), enumerating the core ideas and objectives of the movement he puts 'the production of fine human beings' at the top of the list.[2,3]

An additional advantage of cooperatives according to Marshall is a poten-tial to use to advantage the human capacity to work which is wasted under capitalism. Cooperatives, he writes, make labourers feel that they are the masters and that the factory is their responsibility; they create an incentive to work and produce in a better way. In them, workers do not produce for others but for themselves, and this releases an enormous capacity for scrupulous and higher-quality work which in capitalism is bound to remain unused. "In the world's history there has been one waste product, so much more important than all others that it has a right to be called the waste product. It is the higher abilities of many of the working classes" (*idem*, p. 229).

In practice, he observes, the precondition for cooperatives to develop in line with their founding ideal is an improvement of human nature, in the absence of which cooperatives must necessarily come up against a wealth of obstacles, Concluding his analysis of cooperation, Marshall argues that "the world is only just beginning to be ready for the higher work of the coopera-tive movement" (Marshall 1890, p. 307), and that it is only to be hoped (even if with well-founded reasons) that in future it will have more fortune than it had in the past (*ibid.*).

In the *Principles* Marshall wrote: "whatever be the origin of our moral in-stincts, their indications are borne out by a verdict of the experience of man-kind to the effect that true happiness is not to be had without self-respect", and that "self-respect is to be had only on the condition of endeavouring so to live as to promote the progress of the human race" (Marshall 1920, p. 18). This is probably Marshall's clearest statement of the rationale behind his unconditional support for the cooperative movement: his firm belief that cooperation improves character and that the precondition for mankind to attain happiness is choosing ways of life that will further the progress of the human race.

Gramsci's theory of factory councils

Gramsci is one of many authors who emphasised the corrupting power of capitalism. In the imperialistic phase of capitalism, he wrote, "industrialists sabotage production" or, as a minimum, prove incapable of managing the production apparatus (Gramsci 1919–1920, pp. 49–50). Factories prove unable to carry on business autonomously and many of their functions are transferred from individual firms to system of enterprises owned by a single holding company. Enterprises are pooled under the control of a bank or system of banks. Factory owners are seen hanging about in banks and fashionable salons or lobbying in ministries or parliament, and capital owners lose their power by transferring their 'rights' into the hands of the government in exchange for iron-hearted actions designed to protect them (Gramsci 1919–1920, pp. 50–51).

Elsewhere Gramsci remarked that the traditional functions of the class of capitalists were in due time taken over by irresponsible members of the middle class who were neither set on furthering production nor culturally prepared to do so: a bureaucracy composed of State officials living from day to day, petty people driven on by greed and mercenary instincts, gourmands of sort bent on satisfying mean whims: securing the resources needed to buy the services of high-priced escorts in night clubs and exercising their power by harassing their subordinates (Gramsci 1919–1920, pp. 324–25).

As the capitalistic class distanced itself more and more from work – he wrote – it broke apart and lost conscience of its original unity, a dialectical kind of unity which originally resulted from the individualistic efforts of its members to become front-runners in the race for profit. And as they resolved to rely on a single State function, the government, and to suffer a gang of adventurers and shady mercenary politicians to carry on their struggle in their place, they gave in to the pressure of their worst instincts and reverted to a primordial brutish state (see Gramsci 1920, p. 325).

These reflections show Gramsci theorising a puritan workerism of sorts which vests in the working class the mission to rescue mankind from its moral degradation (see Tomasetta 1972, p. 143).

Under capitalism – Gramsci wrote –

> society is cut loose from any kind of collective bonds and reduced to its primordial element, the citizen-individual. Society begins to dissolve,

eaten way by the corrosive acids of competition: dragon's teeth are sown among people and frenetic passions, unquencheable hatreds, implacable enmities spring up, enormous, amongst them. Every citizen is a gladiator who sees, in other people, enemies to vanquish or to subjugate to one's own interests. All the higher bonds of love and solidarity are dissolved: from the bonds of craftsmen's guilds and social castes to those of religion and the family.[4]

(See Gramsci 1919–1920, p. 4)

Concluding, he argued that the socialist ideal emerged right within the capitalistic context as the response of history to the obstacles slowing down the evolution of society (*ibid.*). The socialist revolution, he added, is "the spiritual revolt of mankind against the new and pitiless feudal lords of capitalism. It is the reaction of a society which is striving to remake itself as a harmonious organism, living in solidarity, governed by love and compassion". Thanks to it,

the 'citizen' is displaced by the 'comrade'; social atomism by social organization. The cells of the new order spring up spontaneously, they adhere to one another and lay out the foundations for greater stratification of solidarity. The baleful power of 'freedom' is circumscribed and controlled; and limits are placed on the sway of capitalism in the workplace. The worker wins a degree of autonomy for himself, a degree of real, effectual freedom. He is no longer one individual standing against the world: he is a member of collectivities which mesh together into other, ever greater and more powerful collectivities. [5]

(Gramsci 1919–1920, p. 5)

A system of cooperative firms reverses the social atomisation process by joining workers into production units in which they are no longer solitary individuals pitted against their competitors, but members of communities in which the sway of capitalists has become a thing of the past and labour has wrested itself free from the need to obey the commands of capital.

In self-managed firms, producers cooperate because the surpluses earned are apportioned among all the partners in ways that will help them become 'solidarity-minded'.

The separation of 'the economic' from 'the social' in Polanyi's approach

In more recent years, Karl Polanyi chose to explore the influence of economic organisation on the human mind.

Like Aristotle in his day, Polanyi thinks of man as a social being, rather than as *homo oeconomicus*. In his opinion, both in archaic and in modern societies the main goal pursued by humans is not so much accumulating wealth, as creating the assumptions for brisk consumption, for gaining prestige in society and building a welfare state. In pre-capitalistic societies, he argues, work was not undertaken for the purpose of earning money and the profit motive was not the main driving force of economic action.

To expect being paid for a job accomplished – Polanyi writes – is far from 'natural' to a human being. In support of this claim he mentions Malinowski's thesis that under the original conditions gain never acts as an impulse to work. One of Polanyi's central theses is that an analysis of primitive and, generally, pre-capitalistic societies will provide evidence that the economy was *embedded* in social relations and the 'principle of working for remuneration' played a minor role.

The rise of liberal capitalism and the ensuing separation of the economic and political spheres – he went on to argue – came to the economically advanced world as a severe blow. Liberal capitalism created the earliest form of market economy, an institutionally distinct and self-standing economic system where even work, land and money were embedded in the economic sphere and were treated as commodities comparable to all the others. Due to the separation of the economic from the political, these two spheres lost autonomy and proved incapable of continuing to exercise their functions. Following this split, the political sphere became more and more irrelevant while the economic sphere gained in importance. To account to this, he argued, suffice it to think that one of the principal tasks of political action is to regulate economic activity by redressing imbalances and the resulting dysfunctions. An economic system which is left to get on by itself is, as it were, a system where the economy is the horse and politics is the cart: the cart will necessarily go the way of the horse (see Marquand 1994, p. 24). The institutional split of society into an economic and political sphere – he added – was achieved by invalidating the political sphere, i.e. by equating the economy with contractual relationships and categorising these as the only true expression of the domain of freedom. The rest is sanctimonious twaddle.

In Polanyi's mind, the rise of capitalism was the world's response to the need to meet the requirements of a technological society founded on the use of machinery. Due to the need to create ever more powerful and complex machines, the economy was changed into a system of self-regulated markets, and we suffered innovation to be at the top of our minds as our paramount value. With this aim in mind, the legislative systems in force in those days ceased exercising control over the labour market, the uses of land and money, changed the factors of production themselves into commodities and, hence, subordinated "the substance of society itself to the laws of the market".

The separation of the economic from the political, the distinctive trait of liberal capitalism, he wrote, impacted upon the fragile orders of human society with the violence of a cyclone and changed them from within. From Polanyi's perspective, the impact of technology on international relations in the present machine-oriented era is so strong as to threaten the destruction of mankind and the ferociousness of the market-oriented twentieth-century society must necessarily arouse implacable hatred (see Duczyska Polanyi 1970, p. XV). Like Owen, Marshall and other scholars, he thought that the tendency of liberal capitalism to leverage the private profit motive had a destructive impact on human character (see Stanfield 1986, pp. 11–14).

And he shared Marx's belief that all such interpersonal relations as are entertained in a market-oriented society are not immediate, but indirect because commodities exchange actions as a medium transforming direct and immediate cooperation into indirect cooperation. In a liberal capitalistic society, the fact that individuals produce for their mutual benefit is obfuscated by commodities exchange, and the relations between individuals, indirect as they are, become impersonal, objective and reified. Like Marx, Polanyi principally spoke out against the capitalistic market mechanism as the true cause of alienation and social disintegration. This is why he was particularly impressed by Marx's earlier works, i.e. those in which Marx fleshed out the notions of commodities fetishism, reification and alienation whose implications Polany' himself had made the main focus points of his work and whose evolution in time he was to analyse in depth in *The Great Transformation*.[6]

This, he argued, is one of the reasons why the true nature of man revolts against capitalism. Human relations are the reality of society and must be immediate, that is to say personal, even in a context structured in line with the principle of the division of labour. Production means must be kept in check by the community.

Polanyi's theory of the influence of 'the economic' on human feelings

Hence, liberal capitalism tends to incite violent opposition. According to Polanyi, the rise of *laissez faire* came as a traumatic blow to the self-esteem of the more civilised part of the population and its effects have never been fully stamped out. Laissez-fare marked a break in centuries old practices, i.e. it replaced the original embeddedness of economic relations in the social context with the inverse situation and hence, in the words of Tönnies, created the assumptions for 'society' to take the place of 'community'. Everything was accommodated within the economic sphere and made subservient to the requirements of the market mechanism (*idem*, pp. 68–69).

The traumatic realisation that capitalism causes degradation is vividly described in *The Great Transformation*, where we read that after the rise of liberal capitalism,

> huge masses of the laboring population resembled more the spectres that might haunt a nightmare than human beings. But if the workers were

physically dehumanized, the owning classes were morally degraded. The traditional unity of a Christian society was giving place to a denial of responsibility on the part of the well-to-do for the condition of their fellows. Two nations were taking shape. To the bewilderment of thinking minds, unheard-of wealth turned out to be inseparable from unheard-of poverty.

In *The Great Transformation* Polanyi traces degradation in a liberal capitalistic system not to economic exploitation, as is often assumed, but to the "disintegration of the cultural environment of the victim" (*idem*, p. 2002).

To understand Polanyi's train of reasoning to the full, it should be borne in mind that he held man to be basically the same in all ages. Mistrustful of psychologists claiming to have fleshed out theories capable of shedding light on the factors governing the formation of personality, he rather looked to Thurnwald and Malinowski, who stressed the similarity of men at all stages of their development. The essential oneness of human nature, he argued, makes the emergence of a basically unnatural production system all the more dramatic.

"Robert Owen's – Polanyi wrote – was a true insight: market economy, if left to evolve according to its own laws, would create great and permanent evils" (*idem*, p. 167).

These evils are, in the main,

> the exploitation of the physical strength of the worker, the destruction of family life, the devastation of neighbourhoods, the denudation of forests, the pollution of rivers, the deterioration of craft standards, the disruption of folkways, and the general degradation of existence.
>
> (*idem*, pp. 170–71)

Some of these evils have to do with the human psyche. The most obvious effect of the new institutional system that took a firm foothold in the nineteenth century was indeed "the destruction of the traditional character of settled populations and their transmutation into a new type of people, migratory, nomadic, lacking in self-respect and discipline – crude, callous beings of whom both labourer and capitalist were an example" (*idem*, p. 163). Time and again Polanyi made it clear that the worst aspects of liberal capitalism were not economic exploitation, but social and psychological factors such as loss of self-respect and basic values and the disintegration of the pre-existing cultural traditions (*idem*, pp. 6, 55–54, 130 and 202). For some seventy years, he argued, the horrors of the Industrial Revolution were stigmatised by poets and scholars in various disciplines, and more often than not they ascribed more weight to social and cultural factors, rather than to economic ones (*idem*, pp. 53 and 201).

> Scholars proclaimed in unison that a science had been discovered which put the laws governing man's world beyond any doubt It was at the behest of these laws that compassion was removed from the hearts, and a stoic

determination to renounce human solidarity in the name of the greatest happiness of the greatest number gained the dignity of a secular religion.

(idem, p. 130)

One crucial aspect of the issue is the irredeemable contrast between liberal capitalism and democracy. Liberal capitalistic systems are characterised by a conflict between the economic and the political because the distinctive traits of capitalism are allowed to act themselves to the full, in terms of placing control over production entirely in the hands of capital owners and preventing workers from exercising the influence to which a truly democratic system would entitle them. Under liberal capitalism "Democracy and Capitalism, i.e. the existing political and economic systems, have reached a deadlock because they have become the instruments of two different classes of opposing interests".

Polanyi's model of socialism

In due time, the ideas just discussed led Polanyi to support 'guild socialism', a system comparable to what today is termed 'self-management socialism'.

From Polanyi's perspective, a key function of socialism is helping the world revert to a type of social organisation in which relationships can once again be immediate, that is to say 'personal'. Like Rousseau, he thought that all human values are embodied in people and that a culture which is not the common heritage of the population, but the prerogative of just a few, is a contradiction in terms, that true freedom would only be achieved if people were given the right to shape their institutions in accordance with their wishes, and that the precondition for this to happen was an educational system tailored to the community's psychological characteristics and ethical values. Rousseau's innovative ideas – he argued – exercised a far-reaching influence on the subsequent evolution of political science and the idea of people as the custodians of culture became the germ of a movement whose importance can hardly be overrated.

The primary task of a socialist economy, he went on to argue, is to gain an awareness of the needs of people and their choices in the production sector, and no bureaucratic apparatus will ever succeed in accomplishing this task.

Specifically, these goals cannot be achieved by reverting to the separation of the economic from the political. What is needed is a social organisation model designed to embed the economy in the social structure or, at all events, to deprive it of its autonomy. Far from framing his approach to socialism against the background of an imaginary future – he concluded – a theorist has to monitor the movements under way in his day with open eyes, gain a full understanding of them and further develop them in the direction of socialism. The first theorist to draw a parallel between guild socialism and scientific socialism was a man of the calibre of G.D.H. Cole. Drawing a parallel between guild socialism and industrial self-management, Cole realised that "the seeds from which a future system of industrial self-management could sprout lay in present-day society".

The reason why a self-managed firm system has the potential to shape a production model capable of embedding the economy in the social structure or, at least, depriving its autonomy is that workers seizing corporate management powers will have the opportunity to tailor their working environment to their needs and reconcile the income maximisation criterion with pleasant conditions of life. An important characteristic of such a system is remote insolvency risks. Unlike capitalistic enterprises, worker-run enterprises hardly ever face insolvency. As they have no fixed payroll expenses, in terms of paying their members no fixed wages or salaries, they will not see their bottomline results eroded by escalating personnel costs and falling competitor prices. If the partners themselves resolve to do so, a self-managed enterprise can reduce the working week to three days, cut the partners' incomes accordingly and, hence, avert insolvency. This may explain why the economy of a self-managed firm system will again be *embedded* in society or, if nothing else, lose its autonomous role. A cooperative firm is a near proxy for a family organised in manners that will enable its members to see to their financial affairs while tackling any other problems they deem to be important.

In addition to this, from Polanyi's approach to guilds it follows that provided it is true that 'the State does not embody the essence of society', self-management creates a potential for reorganising political life and vesting political powers in the members of factory councils. In a socialist society structured in line with the principles of economic and industrial democracy, each individual is, at the same time, a member of a variety of different bodies making both economic and political decisions. As a result, what remains to be done is apportioning tasks among all these bodies on the assumption that their common task, i.e. representing those self-same individuals, will result in lesser conflict.

Hence there are grounds for arguing that a democratic firm system reverses the relationship between economics and society and once again embeds the economy in society. Needless to say, by restoring the original condition that was subverted upon the rise of liberal capitalism, this reversal creates a 'sound', i.e. more 'natural' relationship between economics, politics and society. A theorist has pointed out that "Polanyi's basic solution was to revive the notion of the economy as a material-providing sphere and to examine the different institutional frameworks in which that sphere operated in different societies".

An additional plus point of democratic firm management is the partial restoration of an organisational model making for immediate, i.e. personal, relations of production. As is well known, in Marxist theory the market is held to be responsible for the reification of human relations, i.e. the fact that the relations between individuals are mediated by things. And although the overall cogency of Marx's analysis can hardly be called into question, in a system of cooperative enterprises it would become irrelevant thanks to the potential of this system to further immediate, i.e. personal, relations between producers.

This finding is all the more important in that it goes to explain why cooperatives seldom, if ever, adopt destaffing policies. As shown by recent producer cooperative studies, in times of crises, especially cyclical ones, these firms tend to respond by cutting the incomes of all the partners, rather than ousting any of them.

Notes

1 The 'Inaugural Address' of 1864 has been described as an attempt at theorising a political economy of labour (see Balibar 1993).
2 Like Mill, Marshall held that economists were called upon to help improve the characters of the citizens, Specifically, he argued that they should strive to improve the living standards of humankind, help workers aspire to a nobler life capable of putting an end to poverty and, in short, hold out to them the prospect of an attainable utopian future, the 'fancied country'.
3 Back in the early twentieth century, the Italian economist Cabiati wrote:

> I saw one-time destroyers of machinery use to advantage formidable power-driven labour-saving devices; [and this simple fact is enough to make us] realise that the State's primary task is to do everything in its power to protect the sound and fecund parts of this generous cooperative movement.

4 In the *Critique of Political Economy* Marx describes individualism as a distinctive trait of capitalistic society. Concluding, he argued that the socialist ideal emerged right within the capitalist context as the response of history to the obstacles slowing down the progress of society (*ibid.*).
5 It is evident that Gramsci did not share Bernstein's view that class interests ebb down according as democracy gains strength (see Bernstein 1901, p. 335).

   At any rate, there is no denying that with the disappearance of proletarian class misery in developed capitalist countries, the problem of class consciousness has become an ever more urgent one (Fetscher 1973, p. 227, note 17).
6 Polanyi fully accepted the sociological distinction between community and society that Bobbio held to be the best-known of all dichotomies (see Bobbio 12970, pp. 138–39). In full agreement with Tönnies, he argued that society has always been and is still founded on impersonal markets and on pecuniary relations, the so-called *cash nexus* (phrases originally coined by Thomas Carlyle to describe the ties between people joined together solely by market relations.

4 Socialism today

Introduction

Simone Weil was one of the severest detractors of Marx. "As long as there is, on the surface of the globe, a struggle for power – she wrote (1955, pp. 15–17) – and as long as the decisive factor in victory is industrial production, the workers will be exploited" because "the power which the bourgeoisie has to exploit and oppress the workers lies at the very foundation of our social life and cannot be destroyed by any political and juridical transformation". "The very foundation of our culture, which is a culture of specialists – she concluded – implies the enslavement of those who execute to those who co-ordinate." Is this apodictic argument true?

Reviewing changes associated with the financiarisation of a globalised economy, the strong, though unexpressed need for community, as well as the "unfulfilled promises of democracy" (Bobbio), the Italian philosophical thinker Remo Bodei (2013, p. 175) suggested that the world was heading towards one of those radical shifts in historical perspective, which, due to various – as yet not univocally definable – factors may mark a turning point comparable to the breakaway of humanists from the culture of the Middle Ages or the triumph of the spirit of the Enlightenment over a conventional worldview. In a similar vein, the well-known Italian journalist Eugenio Scalfari remarked (2013, p. 23):

> the present era is fading out. Its agonies are sure to drag on for a fairly long period of time. As always happens in history, the changes in ways of thinking and living which are currently under way will remain unnoticed although they are not gradual, but radical and dramatic.

Concerning the direction of these changes, I daresay that the times are ripe for the transition of the economy to a form of self-management socialism, although the political system is as yet not prepared to work towards the attainment of this goal.[1] In *Theses on the Philosophy of History*, Walter Benjamin pressed the need to review the 'time of the now' from the vantage point of the losers, rather than the winners, and to keep memory of our oppressed ancestors.

A well-known work entitled *Socialism, Utopian and Scientific* (1882) offers Engels's brilliant outline of his own and Marx's basic contributions to political science. In Engels's words, both Marx and he offered ample evidence (a) that history is a sequence of different modes of production and (b) that a new mode of production, far from being preordained within the mind of a scholar and subsequently implemented in practice, is but the natural outgrowth of an earlier one. Can these propositions justify the claim that a socialist revolution is forthcoming?

Until the collapse of the Soviet system, Marxists used to endorse Engels's view that the post-capitalistic mode of production would be a centrally planned system designated as 'socialism'. This necessitates raising the question if centralised planning can be described as a new mode of production aimed to promote the interests of the working class.

As workers in centrally planned systems are denied any say in decision-making, they have no incentive to increase their work inputs in manners that will raise productivity levels. And as no economic system can function effectively unless it is driven on by the private interest motive, I daresay that the call for a centrally planned system is but an exercise in utopian thinking. From my perspective, it is much more realistic to assume that the new production mode to rise from the ashes of capitalism will be a system of worker-controlled firms, viz. a system in which production will be controlled by a conscious will, but where workers will find it worthwhile to engage in production with utmost dedication. In the words of Laibman, "the enterprise is the most significant (not the only) site for the progressive enhancement of socialist democracy: the world-historic reversal of the capitalist subsumption of labor to its conditions of existence" (Laibman 2013, p. 503).

According to Norberto Bobbio (1984, p. 136), the 'goalposts' of modern democracy are majority rule and the underlying principle that each head is entitled to one vote, and it is hard to see why a principle that holds good for politics should not hold good for economic processes as well. In Bobbio's view, the precondition for extending the scope of democracy today is progressing from the political domain, the context where people are reckoned with as individuals, to the social sphere, where they are reckoned with by reference to the multiple roles they play in society (Bobbio 1985, p. 147). And steps in this direction will be taken as soon as society starts working towards the establishment of a system of worker-controlled firms.

In the words of Gibson and Graham (2003, *mimeo*),

> once it was the vision of socialism or communism and the experiments of the soviets in the Eastern Bloc and the communes in East Asia that configured the foreground of the Left's economic imaginary. Today, at least for some, it is the original 'third way' communitarianism or a revitalized social democracy that occupies this otherwise vacated space.

Paraphrasing Engels, it is consequently possible to argue that the concept of socialism has been evolving from its utopian stage – its equation with

centralised planning – to the stage of the modern economic theory of producer cooperatives.

Is the rise of a new mode of production a realistic assumption?

It is widely held that the current crisis of Marxism is caused by the awareness
that markets cannot be abolished, that central planning is no viable alternative to capitalism and that the prospect of realising socialism in practice is
unrealistic.[2] Indeed, there is general agreement that following Lenin's death
Marxism experienced a downward spiral throughout the twentieth century and fell to an all-time low after the fall of the Berlin wall. Sève (2004,
pp. 151–55) has appropriately argued that the true cause of this eclipse was
the use of Marxism as a justification for the pro-USSR policies of communist
parties. This – he claimed – is why it collapsed simultaneously with the centrally planned systems established in Eastern European countries.[3]

The question if worker control of firms, the beacon of hope that Oskar
Lange (1957, p. 159) erxpected to rekindle the activism of the working class,
can become the 'new polar star' for the Left[4] is a major focus point of some
of my earlier writings (e.g. Jossa 2012a–c) in which I claimed that what is
known as socialism boils down to democratic democratic firm managemen[5]
and that the topicality of the intuition behind the very first theorisation of
workers' councils[6] has remained intact to this day (just as Anweiler argued
back in 1958 – see Anweiler 1958, p. 472).[7]

Today, worker control of firms is a realistic alternative option to centralised
planning.

To account for this, it is worth starting out from the two basic contradictions affecting capitalism: (a) the mismatch between socialised production
and private appropriation and (b) the opposition between capital and labour.
And while scholars prioritising the importance of the former will emphasise the potential of centralised planning to act as an antidote to the evils
of markets, theorists who give prominence to the latter will provide focus
on the prospects offered by a new mode of production which reverses the
present-day capital-labour relationship.[8]

In the opinion of Bidet, Marx tended to look upon trade relationships as
a phenomenic element – contrasted with class relationships – which is con-
stitutive of the essence, and this is why he described the capitalistic mode of
production as a socio-political notion with special focus on class relations
(Bidet 1990, p. 155).

Besides explaining why worker control of firms is a mode of production,
this suggests the conclusion that just as the system we term capitalism is one
where firms are managed by capitalists, so socialism is a system in which firms
are run by workers.[9]

The plan to introduce democracy into the firm system is associated with
the so-called 'challenge of Condorcet' (see Bascetta 2004), i.e. the need to

prioritise 'collective ownership' over 'State-ownership' that Condorcet magnificently theorised as early as 1791. In his *Mémoires sur l'instruction publique*, this great Enlightenment thinker rejected Rousseau's notion of the 'general will' as the confluence of the individual wishes of the citizens into a common destiny which hangs over them and manipulates them. No individual, he argued, should be deprived of the natural right to make decisions freely and the citizens who submit themselves to an established authority are to retain the right to scrutiny the decisions of this authority day after day and the right to disempower it whenever they should disapprove of its choices. 'Politics' has its roots in the public sphere, in its judgments and in exchanges of opinions which become ever more vigorous at the same pace that knowledge is ever more widely circulated. Community life should neither be governed by particular interests nor by the State: it should always be guided by reason and this is what justifies the special status of scholars, i.e. those by whom knowledge is circulated. According to Condorcet, the power of chance and, especially, probabilities of error are magnified by ignorance.

> Provided it is true that the more an individual knows, the more he will be able to predict the future – he argued – then the effort to work towards dismantling the barriers of ignorance by spreading education has been (and remains) the overriding political and social project for reducing the effects of chance in the lives of individuals and of the community as a whole.
>
> (Bodei 2013, p. 184)

In other words, Condorcet looked upon knowledge as the social good par excellence, as the rational language of the public sphere.

> This public sphere, which is neither the State nor the market and can neither be identified with particular interests nor with the 'general will' – Bascetta argues (2004, p. 104) – is the domain where the 'general intellect' or 'collective intelligence' of a community acts itself out.

In my opinion, the 'challenge of Condorcet', i.e. the hoped-for predominance of the 'socially owned' over the 'state-owned', necessitates introducing democracy into the firm system because it is this that can prevent the State from continuing to bow to the pressure of lobbying groups working in the interests of privately owned monopolistic concerns. Quoting Kouvelakis (2005, p. 203):

> The 'abolition' of 'class property' and the 'management according to a common plan of national production' by 'all cooperative associations' are the only means to keep cooperative production from reaching a dead end or falling into a trap; these are the two pillars of what is clearly characterized as 'communism'.

Be that as it may, since no one has ever been able to make clear how a command planning model can be reconciled with the working of markets, a plan can only draw the broad outlines of a possible product mix.

At this point, it is worth stating my personal opinion concerning the correct role of the State in the economy. Although I firmly believe that the State must play a role in economic affairs, the starting idea of this chapter is that the severest mistake of the Left today is to have ceased believing in socialism as full-fledged democracy and in the ability of worker control to help achieve it. As things stand, the Left clings to the erroneous view that the left-wing, or socialist, character of a political system is directly proportional to the amount of state intervention that is put in place in an attempt to knock markets out of the game. This is the rationale behind my critique of statism as a system and my explitic endorsement of the theory of public choice.

All the same – let this repeated – there can be little doubt that the State must act upon the economy even in a system of democratic firms. As mentioned above, within a democratic economic system even public economic policies will be fully democratic: the typical split between politics and economics of liberalist capitalistic systems is bridged, as is the divide between what is public and what is private.[10]

Producer cooperatives as a new production mode

A great many market socialism models have been theorised over the past years (see, *inter alia*, Stauber 1987; Roemer 1993, 1994a; Schweickart 1993, 2002; Wolff 2012).[11] Among them, the system formed of worker-run enterprises which is the subject of this book is both the simplest to prefigure and the most widely discussed.[12]

The question that the foregoing reflections have failed to answer satisfactorily is whether such a system is actually a new production mode.

It is widely held that the transfer of firm management powers from capitalists to workers would not amount to a revolution proper. According to Sweezy, for instance, to assume that a free market system with state-owned production means and with firms run by non-capitalists gives rise to socialism is to mistake legal relations for production relations because a system where firms are run by workers who strive to maximise profits by manufacturing goods and placing them on the market is a very near proxy for capitalistic production relations (see Sweezy 1968).

Sweezy's argument recalls those of Althusser and Mészàros. Specifically, Althusser maintained that producer cooperatives are part of the capitalistic production mode and may prefigure a socialist production mode "only in the minds of utopians or opportunists", while Mészàros argued that

> capital is a metabolic system, a socio-economic metabolic system of control. You can overthrow the capitalist, but the factory system remains, the division of labour remains, nothing has changed in the metabolic

function of society. The only way to evade the control of capital is to do away with it. [13]

(Mészàros 1995, p. 981)

Both these comments miss the point. Let me specify that within Marx's dialectical or relational approach, capital ceases to exist as soon as hired labour is suppressed, or, put differently, the moment when the relation between capital and labour is reversed (Ollman 2003, p. 26): and since capital necessarily entails the existence of the capitalist, the abolition of hired labour will bring capitalism to an end as a matter of course.

As mentioned in Finelli 2007 (p. 128), Marx looked upon capitalism as a reversed world where

> alienation from labour and the impoverishment of the proletariat will necessarily reach a level at which the contradiction between the earning potential of the class and the misery of its current circumstances will become unbearable and set off a movement capable of putting the world back into kilter.[14]

Clues for a better understanding of this point may come from the distinction between two different types of cooperative firms, the labour-managed firm (LMF) and the worker-managed firm (WMF) (see Vanek 1971a, 1971b). In modern producer cooperative theory (which defines capital consistently with the approach in this paper, i.e. as the bulk of production means), it is the so-called LMF cooperatives (those funding their investments with loan capital) that reverse the existing capital-labour relation. Indeed, whereas in capitalistic systems it is the owners of capital that hire workers (either directly or through managers in their service) pay them a fixed income and appropriate the surplus, in LMF-type cooperatives it is the workers running their own firms that borrow capital pay it a fixed income (interest) and appropriate the surplus themselves.

In other words, there are but two antithetical options: capital goods are either owned or not owned by capitalists. In the former case, the system concerned is capitalism; in the latter case, when firms are owned by workers (and are the LMF-type), the system is non-capitalistic by definition and re-reverses the present-day capsised capital-labour relation. And the change in the production mode entailed in this process triggers a revolution real and proper.

In support of this view, it is worth adding that the information on the nature of a firm we draw from its corporate object reveals a basic difference between capitalistic and worker-controlled firms: whereas the former tend to maximise profit, the latter (as taught by economic theory) tend to maximise the satisfaction of the majority of the workers involved in their decision-making processes.[15]

In Marx's estimation, the capital-labour relation in capitalistic systems clashes with our very notion of freedom. After an analysis of this argument,

Marx writes (1857–1858, p. 210): "Yet it is obvious that this process of inversion is merely an historical necessity, merely a necessity for the development of the productive forces from a definite historical point of departure." And this means he did not rate it as an absolute need inherent in the production process.

> The propertylessness of the worker – he argued – and the property of objectified labour in living labour, or the appropriation of alien labour by capital – both merely expressing the same relation at two opposite poles – are basic conditions of the bourgeois mode of production, by no means indifferent accidental features.

Hence, argued Lukàcs,

> only when man seizes full control of work, or, put differently, when work turns from a 'tool for life' into the 'primary life need', only when man is relieved from the constriction stemming from his self-reproduction, then, and only then, will the social path towards human activity as an end to itself be opened up.
>
> (Lukàcs 1923, p. 40)

A well-known saying by Marx runs that those controlling production are also in control of men's lives because they own tools which allow them to pursue whatsoever aim they may have in mind (see, *inter alia*, Pellicani 1976, p. 62; Bahro 1977, p. 23); and this argument goes to reinforce the idea that revolution is to be understood as the handover of production means from capitalists to workers and the concomitant disempowerment of capital.

The potential of a system of producer cooperatives for triggering a socialist revolution is also called into question by theorists, including Pannekoek and Lukàcs, who distinguish between revolutionaries and revisionists based on whether they advocate the overthrow of the State or look upon it as a neutral institution. From my perspective, instead, the idea that revolution comes down to changing the existing production mode necessitates the conclusion that the establishment of a system of producer cooperatives which reverses the capital-labour relation is a revolution real and proper even if the State is not overthrown.[16]

In support of these reflections, it is possible to argue, with Capitini (1968, p. 48), that when things become common property, they must change of necessity.

The scientific core of socialism

It is a well-known fact that Marx rated existing forms of socialism as 'utopian' and contrasted them with his own 'scientific' approach to socialism.

But what did he mean by 'scientific socialism'?

As mentioned before, in Marx 'scientific socialism' is the theorisation of a new mode of production which will necessarily become a reality at some point in time because it arises and develops right within the capitalistic mode of production.

This begs the question whether a worker-controlled firm system can be said to arise and develop within a capitalistic system.[17]

By general agreement (see, for instance, Ben-Ner 1987, 1988, pp. 295–96), the living standard of the working class is a major determinant of both the advantages granted to LMFs and the difficulties they come up with. There is evidence that workers become less risk-averse and develop greater entrepreneurial skills according as their income levels increase.

This is why I share Zamagni's belief that "as human and social capital acquire a greater strategic role than physical and financial capital, the overriding importance of democratic governance modes becomes more and more evident also on a strictly economic plane" (Zamagni 2006, p. 60). Indeed, the greater a worker's educational levels and qualifications, the less he will be prepared to work at the orders of an employer and the more he will tend to acquire the abilities necessary to run a firm first-hand.[18] Authors emphasising the wish of higher-income workers to run a firm of their own include Bowles and Gintis (1996, p. 82). Very often, they argue, workers in self-managed firms have the feeling that their incomes may be at risk and that they may prove unable to finance a decent standard of living for their families, but this feeling recedes in proportion to increases in income.

In the words of Rosselli (1930, p. 453), "the call for worker control… reflects the emergence of a new kind of average workman, whose dignity requires not only material improvements, but the assertion of an autonomous personality both within and outside the factory".

> Bourgeois individualism necessarily breeds a tendency towards proletarian collectivism – Gramsci wrote (1918, p. 189). "The individual capitalist is matched by the individual association, the shopkeeper by the cooperative.

Hayek (1960) described coercion as a social evil which turns a useful thinking individual into a lifeless tool for the achievement of another's ends. That is why the abolition of hired labour in an employee-managed economy would set off the rise of a fully democratic system where workers, freed from coercion from employers, would no longer be alienated. "Marx, much like German philosophers and chiefly Hegel, conceived of world history as a unitary process and the highroad towards liberation".[19]

In short, it is reasonable to assume that labour management is bound to make headway in history according as manual labour loses importance and workers acquire greater educational and professional qualifications (see, for example, Mandel 1973, p. 349).[20]

From the perspective of Proudhon, revolution is inevitable because the division of labour, while, admittedly, adding to the qualifications of workers, simultaneously worsens their condition by parcelling out jobs (see Ansart 1967, pp. 39–40).[21]

In the words of Harman (1977),

> Gramsci often uses the struggle for power between the bourgeoisie and the feudal class as a metaphor for the struggle for power between workers and capitalists. On closer analysis, this comparison is misleading. As capitalistic production relations are closely associated with commodity production, which may arise within feudal society, the bourgeoisie can use its growing economic dominance to build up its ideological position within the framework of feudalism before seizing power. In contrast, the only way for the working class to become economically dominant is by taking collective control of means of production – an aim which requires rallying to arms in order to seize political power.

On this point, however, it is Gramsci, not his critic, that is right.[22]

Conversely, Sylos Labini (1987, p. 244) maintained that the scientific status of Marxism descended from the attempt to gain an understanding of the tendencies under way in society and further them in manners apt to expedite a transition which would come about spontaneously at some point in time (as mentioned above).

Remote bankruptcy risks in democratic firms

At this point, it is worth examining a specific peculiarity that marks out employee-managed firms from capitalistic companies.

In a system of cooperative firms, business enterprises seldom face insolvency risks. As is well known, a business goes bankrupt when its costs exceed revenues. For this reason, the absence of the largest cost item – wages and salaries – from a democratic firm system would greatly help confine insolvency risks.

In other words, the downward trend in insolvencies is the result of a major difference between capitalistic and employee-managed firms: in the former, workers take precedence over capital providers since they cash their wages and salaries on a monthly basis and are usually not dependent on profit distributions; in the latter, the partners participate in the 'residual' and their incomes, though often paid out in monthly instalments, are determined after the whole of the firm's costs, including capital charges, have been settled.[23]

An additional argument is relevant in this connection: if pay levels in a democratic firm fall below the average for the system, the partners will tend to leave the firm, but due to the aversion to the entry of newcomers postulated by the theoretical producer cooperative model they are likely to have difficulty getting better-paying jobs elsewhere. As a result, workers earning pays below their system's average level will have to put up with meagre incomes. And as the members of worker-controlled firms tend to stay with the firm even in times of financial distress (mobility rates are comparatively lower in cooperatives than in capitalistic businesses), this is an additional factor that helps reduce insolvency risks.[24]

Remote bankruptcy risks are also inter-related with lower risks of dismissal, an additional positive characteristic of cooperatives. Layoffs are the exception because of lesser insolvency risks and because a cooperative may respond to drops in demand by reducing working hours instead of laying off part of the workforce. In other words, employee-managed firms offer the advantage of making jobs both safer and more lasting.

As for competition, which in capitalist systems is often very tough, it is cooled off as a result of reduced insolvency risks. A firm which is aware that it will not go bankrupt is free to resolve not to engage in competition at all. For instance, provided the partners are prepared to accept lower incomes, the firm may decide to grant them more free time by reducing daily working hours or the working week. In such a situation, i.e. when bankruptcy risks are not looming, competition will not be an evil since individual firms will have the option of engaging in the competitive race or, conversely, reducing incomes.[25]

Remoter insolvency risks tend to reduce the impact of oppressive market mechanisms and the resulting obstacles to the free choices of workers. As mentioned above, the workers will be free to reduce their individual work inputs and choose organisation modes likely to avert bankruptcy risks. And this goes to reduce both the paramountcy of markets and alienation, viz. the dominance of inanimate things – means of production – over man.

From this, it follows that historical materialism, i.e. the prioritisation of the economic factor in individual and social choices, would be less pervasive in a democratic firm system than it is in our present world order.

Notes

1 My line of reasoning is at odds with the view (that Bauman thinks to be prevailing in his day) that "progress entails the threat of inexorable and ineluctable changes which preannounce, not prospects of peace and comfort, but crises and enduring anxiety" (see Bauman 2014, p. 127).
2 For the claim that Marxism began to decline after the collapse of the centrally planned Soviet system (see, *inter alia*, Sartori 1969, pp. 316–17; Fukuyama 1989; Marga 1995, p. 85; Longxi 1995, p. 70). For different views (see Kellner 1995; Stone 1998; Livorsi 2009; principally, Cohen (1978 and 2000). From the latter's perspective (p. 389), the failure of the Soviet system should actually be rated as a triumph of Marxism.
3 Ragionieri (1965, pp. 129 ff.) makes it clear that the socialism=centralised planning equation goes back not only to Lenin, but also to the powerful influence of Engels and his *Antidühring* on the Second International. Aron, too (1965, p. 2), looks on Engels's *Antidühring* as the main source of classical Marxism, though he emphasises that Marx did read and praise this book, but was barely aware of the problems associated with centralised planning (see op. cit., p. 3).

The main reasons for the association of Marxism with planning are obviously the success of the 1917 Bolshevik revolution and the adoption of centralised planning in the USSR for over sixty years running. In this connection, Bertrand Russel (1935, p. 263) remarked that, far from catching on promptly in political practice, socialism remained the creed of a minority with no noticeable bearing on reality until 1917. Considering that centralised planning has so far been adopted by all countries under socialism, it hardly comes as a surprise that Marxism, the offshoot of scientific socialism, has always been associated with planning.

4   Gunn (2011) has remarked that in-between worker participation in decision-making and full worker management there are a great many intermediate steps. In this book, I am concerned with situations in which workers are granted full decision powers.

5   An equally relevant quote from Trower (1973, p. 138) runs: "if freedom is our goal, industry will only become democratic when it is governed by those working in it."

6   Garaudy (undated, p. 187) described workers' councils as a crucial component of the struggle between opposed classes.

7   In 1973, Trower argued that the pendulum of democracy was finally swinging back from the opposite extreme in the direction of economic democracy (op. cit., p. 138).

8   In the words of Negri, "communism appears as the concept of the overthrow of work, of its subtraction from command" (see Negri 1998, p. 216).

9   During the proceedings of the Constituent Assembly of the Italian Republic, the Christian Democrat Dominedò spoke of cooperatives as firms that could supplant capitalistic firms, while the Communist Bibolotti remarked that the establishment of a system of cooperatives was the only realistic step towards the implementation of socialism conceivable within a capitalistic society (see Cattabrini 2010).

10   Countries with strong cooperative traditions include Spain, Italy, Canada, the UK, France, Japan, Hungary, India, Chile, Argentina and Indonesia.

11   In this connection, Buchanan (1982, p. 24) has aptly argued that communism in Marx "is not an ideal among competing ideals; it *is* the social form which *will* replace capitalism."

12   For Marx's ideas on firms run by workers (see Jossa 2005a).

13   For comparable approaches, see, *inter alia*, Turati (1897), Mondolfo (1923, p. 93), Labriola (1970, pp. 271–72), Quarter (1992), Westra (2002), McMurtry (2004), Gunn (2006, p. 345). Similarly, Sylos Labini stands firm on the claim that democratic firm management models have little in common with Marxism (see Sylos Labini 2006).

14   Evidence that democratic firm management is as yet in the process of becoming a reality is provided by the experience of ESOPs in the United States, where a number of legislative provisions have granted considerable tax cuts to companies establishing 'employee stock ownership plans' (ESOPs) and to firms handing over to the workforce part of the ownership interests in their capital resources.

15   It is likely that worker-controlled firms will retain hierarchies, but that their managers and officials will be appointed in line with democratic procedures. Accordingly, it should not come as a surprise that Marglin, faced with Engels's argument that "wanting to abolish authority in large-scale industry is tantamount to abolish industry itself" (Engels 1894a, p. 483), described it as "a momentary aberration" (see Marglin 1974, p. 60).

16   Our emphasis on equating the transition from capitalism to a system of producer cooperatives with a real and proper revolution is justified by the awareness that Marxists have always refused to concoct "recipes for a hypothetical future", i.e. to offer a clear outline of the social order they think will take the place of

capitalism. Although Kautsky and many later Marxist theorists were strongly critical of the system that had emerged from the Russian revolution, they did not make it clear how those inimical to the central planning model adopted by the Soviet Union were to picture to themselves a socialist order (for the silence of Kautsky on this point, see Geary 1974, pp. 93–94).

17 Gonnard dismissed socialism as the theoretical model foreshadowing a hypothetical future social order which, as such, cannot be truly scientific (Gonnard 1930, p. 445).

18 The gap between the two principal classes of society tends to be narrowed in proportion to increases in the educational and incombe levels of workers and this induces the latter to call into question the power of their masters.

19 In this connection, Engels wrote that "history moves often in leaps and bounds and in a zigzag line" and never in a linear step-by step fashion (see Nordhal 1982, p. 515).

The idea that history progresses towards the full emancipation of humankind has been called into question by many commentators including Colletti, who has strongly criticised the finalist and teleological component of Marxism (see the 1979 interview reported in Colletti 1979). In Marx's approach, Carandini, for instance (2005, chap. I) perceives a teleological component.

20 The subsumed classes mentioned by Resnick & Wolff (1982) include merchants, money dealers and money lenders (bankers), landlords and mine owners, supervisory managers and shareholders in joint stock companies, as well as state administrators (see pp. 4 and 5). If we accepted this approach to classes, hordes of people would be involved, and this is the reason why we assume that the establishment of socialism is feasible today. For our part – let us clarify – we fully agree with Simone Weil that only when there are material prospects of success should the oppressed be encouraged to revolt.

21 Anyone believing that the transition to socialism is heralded by declining frictions between opposed classes should give their best attention to the younger Marx's saying (see Rapone 2011, pp. 169–70) that the precondition for class conflict to become an element of progress is that the two opposed actors develop an awareness of their respective roles, as well as the determination to follow them through – and this happens during the phase termed industrial capitalism and not in the decadent phase termed financial capitalism.

22 As argued by Bronfenbrenner (1970, p. 135), predictions concerning the transition to socialism invariably fail to specify when or where this event is expected to come about. As a result, they cannot be refuted but are ultimately irrelevant. For my part, I do share the view that there is no way for predicting when and where the transition to socialism will be implemented, but – let this be repeated – there are reasons for assuming that the time horizon will be shortened at the same pace that worker income and education levels are seen to increase.

23 Starting out from the tendency of existing cooperatives to lay aside provisions for future investments instead of distributing the entire residual to the members, Sapelli (2006, p. 51) has argued that the higher survival rates of cooperatives are to be traced, not so much to the lower frequence of bankruptcy cases, as to the primary concern of their members with keeping their firm going rather than maximising bottomline results.

24 Let me add that my arguments in support of low bankruptcy frequency are only relevant to the theoretical cooperative model in which workers earn variable incomes. In actual fact, it is well known that existing cooperatives mostly pay their partners fixed wages and salaries.

The argument that bankruptcies are exceptional in employee-managed firms (though for reasons other than those highlighted in this chapter) is supported by empirical evidence (see Ben-Ner 1988; Stauber 1989; Dow 2003, pp. 226–28).

25 According to Stiglitz (1994, p. 276), cut-throat competition is not always a sure sign that the market economy concerned is more efficient than an economy where competition is softer, and Etzioni (1990, p. 402) remarks, much in the same vein, that while competition is a powerful driving force of a properly regulated economy, it turns into a destructive force whenever it is left without effective government.

The benefits of competition have been forcefully called into question by several authors, including Hirsch (1976) and Hirschman (1982).The most radical critic was certainly Proudhon, who described competition as "the greatest of all evils, a formo f perversion [...] in which the advantage of each depended on, even consisted in, his ability to outwit, defeat or exterminate the others" (Berlin 1963, p. 101).

5   Reform versus revolution

Struve's critique of Marx

Introduction

Two forms of socialist revolution can be postulated in the light of the two main contradictions that Marx used to ascribe to capitalism. Specifically, those theorists who prioritise the capital-labour opposition will argue that a socialist system arises when the capital-labour relation is reversed upon the establishment of a system of labour-managed firm (LMF)-type co-operatives;[1] those who attach more importance to the antithesis between planned production and anarchical distribution are sure to contend that socialism boils down to a centrally planned economic system (see Jossa 2010a, pp. 262–63, 2011).

From my perspective, the first of the two possible forms of socialism should take precedence for a reason which was excellently cast into words by Italian Marxist scholar Raniero Panzieri in the following excerpt (1975, p. 107):

> As the worker as a citizen battling for his political ideas is not distinguishable from the worker seeing to his duties in the factory, it is simply inconceivable that workers should change once they have left the workshop in which they were used up, oppressed and crushed by their masters. The political battle of the workers' movement is fought both in the workshop and on every other social terrain, but the main battlefield is and remains the factory, the true founding stone of capitalistic power.

Marx's earnest concern with producer cooperatives is proved by a wealth of writings on the subject of cooperation, but some theorists object that despite their unquestionable illustrative worth these writings do not tell us much about the real potential that Marx ascribed to cooperation (see Lowit 1962, p. 79; see, also, Jossa 2005a).

The issue to be explored in this chapter is whether a socialist system should be established by way of gradual reform or revolutionary change.

Peter Struve, a Russian Marxist who grew into a Social-Democrat and is now almost forgotten, was one of Marx's acutest critics. As a theorist of social evolution, he developed into a much acuter and more original revisionist than his better-known contemporary Bernstein, with whom he had in common the straightforward rejection of the *very idea* of revolution.[2]

In actual fact, before Struve's idea of social evolution can be endorsed – as I am tempted to do – it is necessary to raise a set of key queries, namely:

a   are evolution and revolution irreconcilable?
b   is the Marxian notion of the 'relations of production' an exclusively legal or solely economic phenomenon or is it a combination of both?
c   what is the true import of the assumed passage from quantitative to qualitative changes?
d   are capitalism and socialism antithetical systems?

An in-depth analysis of these issues will lead to the conclusion that Struve's theory of social evolution, though acceptable in broad terms, is objectionable at its very core since it takes no count of the notions of production mode and, consequently, revolution.

As evolution and revolution are different concepts (as are socialism and capitalism), the precondition for an evolutionary process to initiate a revolution is forging the reformist process in manners that will result in the rise of a different production mode.

As will be shown further on, Struve's overall approach is marred by two additional major faults: on the one hand, he categorises production relations as a strictly legal phenomenon and equates revolution with piecemeal adjustments to the production relations via parliamentary reform and innovative laws; on the other, he does not specify that some reforms – for instance the stepwise attainment of universal suffrage within the capitalistic mode of production – can pave the way for the transition to socialism (but not, in itself, bring it to completion), while others, for instance the takeover of management powers by the workers in an increasing number of enterprises, do expedite the transition to socialism by their very nature.

The transition to socialism

The next question to be raised is will the piecemeal substitution of worker control for the capitalistic management mode actually give rise to a socialist system?

And as this is exactly the point I wish to make in this chapter, it is necessary to glean Marx's work for passages that may contradict this thesis.

Marx once wrote:

> Restricted... to the dwarfish forms into which individual wage slaves can elaborate it by their private efforts, the co-operative system will never transform capitalist society. To convert social production into one large and harmonious system of free and co-operative labour, *general social changes are wanted, changes of the general conditions of society*, never to be

realised save by the transfer of the organised forces of society, viz., state power, from capitalists and landlords to the producers themselves.[3]

Down to our days, these and similar statements by Marx have been read as suggesting that worker management cannot, in itself, bring about socialism since it does not replace one power class with another (see, for instance, Sweezy 1968, p. 3, 1969).[4] "The call for changes of the general conditions of society" can be read in a variety of different ways, even as implying the straightforward abolition of markets (as Sweezy suggests), but Marx made it absolutely clear that markets would have to be retained for a considerable period of time after the end of capitalism. The *Manifesto* includes a string of passages which give us to understand that the transition from the older order to the new one requires disempowering capital as a necessary preliminary step: "The proletariat – Marx and Engels wrote – will use its political supremacy to wrest, by degrees, all capital from the bourgeoisie" (Marx-Engels 1848, p. 505), and the action plan they suggested for the immediate post-takeover period is clear evidence that this process was to be implemented by degrees, specifically by enacting the following provisions (pp. 505–6):

–   the abolition of property in land;
–   a heavy progressive income tax;
–   the confiscation of the property owned by rebels and emigrants;
–   the concentration of credit and transport in the hands of the State and
–   a well-orchestrated nationalisation programme.

The steps of this action plan are clear evidence that Marx and Engels did not think of the transition as a process to be implemented by nationalising all production means at one stroke and instantly establishing a centrally planned system. In polemical attacks on Blanqui first (whose revolutionary model he had previously endorsed) and on Bakunin later, Marx argued that revolution was not to be understood as a sudden uprising, but as the culmination of a stepwise process (see Galli 2010, p. 44).[5]

As it is clear that Marx thought of the handover of political and economic power to the working class as the true precondition for the rise of socialism, it follows that socialism will only become a reality if worker control of firms is established simultaneously with the transfer of political power from capitalists to the working class.[6]

An additional preliminary question worth raising here is how theorists equating socialism with employee management picture to themselves the transition from capitalism to socialism.

Some producer cooperative theorist has fleshed out three possible scenarios for the transition from capitalism to self-management socialism.

The categorisation of cooperatives as 'merit goods' is the core idea behind the first and, in my opinion, principal transition scenario and is usually suggested by theorists who credit an all-cooperatives system with a distinct potential to function at high levels of efficiency. The social benefits flowing from the substitution of cooperatives for capital-owned firms include, first and foremost, the powerful impulse to full-fledged political democracy that is sure to stem from such concomitant developments as the attainment of economic democracy, the disempowerment of capitalists and the abolition of plutocracy (see Jossa 2004, 2009, 2010b, 2011). Insofar as cooperatives are actually 'merit goods' and deserve protection for adding to the workers' well-being, the best way to expedite the advent of this new mode of production is to enforce tax and credit incentive policies enabling them to vie with their capital-owned competitors. In this connection, it is worth mentioning that these provisions should preferably be structured as income tax abatements, since the benefits of tax cuts which reduce production costs are usually outweighed by the adverse effects of the destaffing policies that worker-managed firms tend to put in place under such circumstances. On this point, see Ward 1958 and, *inter alia*, Lepage 1978, pp. 68–69.

Since the precondition for the material implementation of this transition scenario is, quite obviously, a majority of working-class representatives in Parliament, I do not feel I can agree with the democratic firm management theorist Panzieri, who does not deny that socialism can be established via the creation of a workers' democracy but rules out a role of parliaments in this process (see Panzieri 1957; Dalmasso 1995, p. 2).

Struve's idea of social evolution

Struve's revisionism (which is mainly developed in Struve 1899) can be analysed by reference to a case study that sheds light on his line of reasoning.

At the earliest stage of a capitalistic system restaurants are run by capital-owners who make all the decisions concerning menus and the categories of target customers to be catered for. The cooks employed in these restaurants are likely to be poorly educated workers wanting in initiative and thus acting at the orders of their masters. With the passing of time, at the same pace that the cooks and other members of a restaurant's staff manage to secure higher incomes, they are likely to acquire higher educational qualifications and, hence, to see to their tasks ever more autonomously. By degrees, they may be given a say in the owners' decision-making processes and start making suggestions concerning the kind of provisions to be purchased, the composition of the restaurants' menus and the way the dishes are to be cooked and served, etc. In due time these cooks will inevitably conceive the wish to shed their status as salaried workers, switch to own-account work and run restaurants of their own.[7]

Besides illustrating the evolutionary transition from the capitalistic to the socialist organisation of the catering sector, this case study illustrates the overall rule governing social evolution: the transition from capitalism to socialism develops by degrees, in successive steps, as a process resembling evolution in the world of nature.

Inasmuch as this sample case offers a correct outline of the overall rule governing social evolution (as Struve contends), the new firm management mode will assert itself by degrees since wage and salary earners who manage to add to their education and organise themselves effectively will simultaneously develop the ability to shape and force through parliament a set of reforms designed to end their subjugation and help them take over corporate management powers. It goes without saying that a necessary precondition for this to happen is a parliamentary majority of representatives of the working class.[8]

Although Struve does not conceive of socialism as worker management of firms, I am firmly convinced that his evolutionary theory will be better understood and more readily accepted if it is discussed against the background of the theory of socialism as the transfer of sovereign corporate powers from capital-owners to workers (and, accordingly, the progress to a system where title to cash business surpluses is handed over from masters to workers).

Let me emphasise once again that this process can be implemented in piecemeal fashion. The first step would be schemes to entitle workers to ever greater portions of the profits earned by their firms and the crowning step of the process would be the 'expropriation of the expropriators' within the resulting self-managed firm system.

Struve rules out revolution altogether because in his evolutionary approach social relations are seen to be gradually adjusted to the productive forces,[9] capitalistic production relations (viz. master-worker relations) are assumed to be a strictly legal phenomenon[10] and the productive forces, which are the economic factor *per excellence*, are held to develop in unison with changes in production, viz., employer-employee relations.

In Marx's revolutionary conception and orthodox Marxism overall, he detects one gross misconception: as Marx looked on production forces as the economic factor and the true basis of all social relations and on production relations as a merely legal phenomenon, he thought of revolution as the inevitable outcome of the frictions between the economy and the legal sphere (base and superstructure) caused by the fact that the production relations were unaffected by ongoing changes in the productive forces and by the ever more marked socialisation of production activities determined by rises in the average size of firms. Denying the existence of "two qualitatively antithetical forms of social evolution" and the assumption that one of these was developing in full sync with the status quo, while the other was spurring on its transformation and ultimate overthrow, he argued that social evolution was solely of one kind: "piecemeal adjustment of the legal system in force to the socio-economic phenomena under way" (see Struve 1899, p. 126).

In Struve's approach, the stepwise adjustments in production relations are not caused by the fact that the economic factor is the cause and legal relations are the effect, but by the fact that the former is linked to the latter by a relationship of content and form and are simply inconceivable in the absence of the latter.[11]

The reason why he holds class conflicts to be gradually solved thanks spontaneous changes and social reforms is his belief that every step forward the proletariat manages to take will expedite the advent of socialism.[12] On occasion – he wrote – social progress is attained by explaining away reasons for resistance, rather than by a revolutionary upsurge intended to sweep away exacerbated antagonisms at one stroke" (op. cit. p. 128).

Moreover, Struve thinks of socialism as inextricably intertwined with capitalism and bound to come about in due time as a matter of course., as a historical necessity and the culmination of the ongoing evolution of economic phenomena and their legal regulation within capitalistic society. If socialism, a real power, should fail to arise within the existing capitalistic order – he argued – we would have to conclude that it simply cannot exist in any form. In point of fact, an overview of the history of socialism reveals that the world has been steadily progressing towards its advent and, hence, leads us to deny any conceptual antithesis between capitalism and socialism (op. cit., p. 139).

Let me repeat that Struve thought of the transition to socialism as the direct and inevitable effect of the growing power of the proletariat. In his opinion, every genuine revolutionary upsurge has a place in social evolution and that socialist reformism is, by its very nature, a revolutionary process: the term social revolution is nothing but a different name for social evolution.[13] The claim that a social revolution should take the form of a sudden outburst of violence – he concluded – is unwarranted.

While Marx's revolutionary approach stands or falls by its ability to prove the validity of the pauperisation theory (i.e. to offer conclusive evidence that the working class draws no benefits from economic growth and is therefore doomed to impoverishment), Struve and other theorists held that the pauperisation theory had been proved wrong by history and that its validation would necessitate the conclusion that socialism was just *myth*.

The roots of Marx's revolutionary vision

On closer analysis, the train of reasoning adopted by Struve to invalidate the Marxian concept of revolution is far from cogent.

The origins of Marx's radically revolutionary worldview were explored by Tucker in a 1961 book which showed that Marx had chosen revolution and communism even before commencing work on his materialistic conception of history.

Until then, it had been widely assumed that Marx's notion of revolution had its true underpinning in his material conception of history, specifically the passage from the *Preface* to the *Contribution to the Critique of Political Economy* reported below:

> In the real production of their existence men inevitably enter into definite relations, which are independent of their will, namely relations of

production appropriate to a given stage in the development of their material forces of production. The totality of these relations of production
constitutes the economic structure of society, the real foundation on
which arises a legal and political superstructure, and to which correspond
definite forms of social consciousness. At a certain stage of development,
the material productive forces of society come into conflict with the existing relations of production or − this merely expresses the same thing
in legal terms − with the property relations within the framework in
which they have operated hitherto. From forms of development of the
productive forces these relations turn into their fetters. Then begins an
era of social revolution.

(Marx 1859, p. 5)

In contrast with this assumption, Tucker suggested that Marx had become
a communist and revolutionist around 1843, due to the influence of Moses
Hess and, specifically, on gaining an awareness that alienation was mainly
caused by the material processes of economic life in civil society.

As argued by Tucker, Feuerbach's demonstration that 'productive activity'
was a distinctive feature and attribute of the human species had been countered by the reflection of the Feuerbachian theorist Moses Hess that due to
the impact of egotistic drives preventing people from operating cooperatively
the modern world was actually in a state of 'perversion'. From Proudhon, the
father of 'philosophical communism' understood as a combination of Hegel's
philosophy of history with the communistic ideal, Moses Hess had taken
over the notion of property as theft, which became the founding stone of his
Feuerbachian theory of alienation.

These findings induced Tucker to suggest that Marx grew into a communist when he embraced the philosophical communism of Hess and its Hegelian core idea of alienation, but that he wove into his view of communism
the idea of the proletariat as the instigator of a new social order − i.e. a notion
which was unknown to Hess.

As far as the links between Hegel and Marx are concerned, Tucker argued
that Marx had distanced himself from Hegel when he fleshed out his idea of
class struggle as the interpretative key of history, and Sabine (1937, p. 588)
specified that Marx had taken over from Hegel the idea of nations as the true
agents in history (a notion but loosely connected to Hegel's overall system),
had replaced the struggle between antagonistic nations with the notion of
the struggle between opposed social classes. The end result of this process −
Tucker concluded − was the transformation of Hegelianism into a powerful
form of social radicalism through the erasure of its political overtones.

According to Tucker, the idea of the proletariat as the 'midwife' of a new
social order came to Marx from a very influential book written by Lorenz
von Stein. With a sudden turnaround, he argued, in the *Contribution to the
Critique of Hegel's Philosophy of Right*, written at the end of 1843, Marx replaced the image of alienated humanity with that of the proletariat as "the

suffering expression of alienated man in revolt against his condition" within the existing economic system. Just as philosophy finds its *material* weapon in the proletariat, so the proletariat finds its *spiritual* weapon in philosophy, Marx wrote, and Tucker traced this "singular philosophical conception of the proletariat" to the influence of von Stein's book.

In point of fact, von Stein was a conservative thinker whose prime aim was to refute the socialist and communist ideas circulating in his day, but his book helped disseminate the idea that a new class had made its appearance on the world scene and that this propertyless, though intrinsically revolutionary class had engaged in a struggle against capital.

In the *Philosophy of Right*, Hegel denounced the risks inherent in the excessive concentration of wealth in just a few hands but concluded that "poverty in itself does not make people into a rabble". To create a rabble, he wrote, it takes, "joined to poverty, a disposition of mind, an inner indignation against the rich", and according to Tucker the effective description of the proletariat as a rabble in the Hegelian sense was taken from von Stein's book, with which Marx's writings of the middle forties "show a minute textual familiarity" (Tucker 1961, p. 115).

On closer analysis, Marx's response to von Stein's description of communism as the class ideology of the proletariat was altogether antithetical to that of Moses Hess. Whereas Hess objected to von Stein's reading of communism as the response of a single class to its material deprivation, Marx looked upon the proletariat as the class called upon to free humanity from the evils of capitalistic alienation.

These reflections show that the initial step in Marx's progress towards communism was a Hegelian form of 'philosophical communism' [14] which had as its main, and probably permanent underpinning the idea of alienation.

It is worth adding that Marx completed his development into a revolutionary when he formulated his materialist approach to history and the associated idea of modes of production, but that in later years he reconsidered his one-time beliefs and began to speak out for a peaceful transition to socialism.

With reference to the description of universal suffrage as one of the main goals the proletariat was to strive for, a commentator has argued that even in such an early work as the *Manifesto of the Communist Party* Marx described the takeover of the proletariat as a victory in the battle for democracy (see Avineri 1968) and that *Capital* includes passages in which Marx praises universal suffrage, some Factory Acts and other pro-worker legislation passed by a number of British Parliaments (see Sidoti 1987, p. 280).

Marx definitively embraced the idea of a peaceful transition to socialism about 1867, when the Second Reform Bill gave the vote to wage and salary earners in the upper income brackets.

In this connection, Lichtheim (1965, pp. 120–21) reports passages from *The Civil War in France*, written in 1871, which show Marx upholding ultra-democratic views that call to mind his one-time enemy Proudhon.[15]

This said, it is fair to admit that due to the persisting influence of the early educational background that had turned him into a communist, Marx never completely discarded the idea that the new order might have to be established by violent means.

The basic contradiction of capitalism and the Hegelian matrix of Marxism

In an often-quoted passage from *Anti-Dühring*, Engels argues (1878, pp. 303–4) that the proletarian revolution will enable the proletariat to seize power, strip production means from the bourgeoisie and turn them into state property. As a result of this act, Engels contends, means of production are cleansed of their capitalistic connotations and their social nature can act itself out to the full.

On page 289 in the same text, Engels spells out that "the contradiction between socialised production and capitalistic appropriation now presents itself as an antagonism between the proletariat and the bourgeoisie".

With reference to these passages, Sève argued (2004, p. 145) that since the logic behind the contradictions of capitalism of is not the same, Engels could barely be assumed to have classed them as identical in purely abstract terms.

In point of fact, Engels is wrong. The reversal of the capsized capital-labour relation which is triggered by the establishment of a democratic firm system does not solve the conflict of interests which opposes workers to capitalists (one aspect of the capital-labour antithesis), but it does sweep away the mismatch between socialised production and private distribution (since production and distribution instantly become socialised when they are determined by decisions jointly made by the workers).

The need to draw a clear-cut distinction between these contradictions is implied in Struve's argument that the former, unlike the latter, arises from a conflict between economics and law (see Struve 1899).

Still another severe contradiction that Marx perceived in capitalism is reflected in his claim that the world does not 'stand upright', as would be the natural order of things, but is 'upside down'.[16] This metaphor was originally fleshed out in the *Introduction* to such an early work as the *Contribution to the Critique of Hegel's Philosophy of Right*, where Marx wrote:

> This state and this society produce religion, which is an inverted consciousness of the world, because they are an inverted world. Religion is the general theory of this world ... the sigh of the oppressed creature, the heart of a heartless world, and the soul of a soulless condition.
>
> (Marx 1843, pp. 57–58)

Concluding, he argued that "the criticism of religion ends with the teaching that man is the highest essence for man – hence, with the categoric imperative to overthrow all relations in which man is a debased, enslaved, abandoned, despicable being" (Marx 1843, p. 65).

According to Fineschi, the idea of an inverse relation between capital and labour in capitalism is closely linked to Marx's theory of alienation (see Fineschi 2005b, p. 111) and Colletti has brought into focus a number of interconnections between Marx's description of capitalism as a reversed world and his alienation and fetishism theories. Both these processes – the latter argues (see Colletti 1979, p. 70) – "are structured in the same way as is the subject-predicate inversion", and the reversal "affects the realities of the capitalistic world" which is turned upside down (see, also, op. cit., pp. 82–92). From my perspective, this conclusion is to be unconditionally endorsed.

The reason why the mature Marx described capitalism as a 'reversed world' is that (as mentioned before) in modern markets control is not exercised by people over inanimate things (workers over production means), but by things over people (i.e. by capital, which dictates the laws that workers are expected to obey). In Volume III of *Capital*, Marx wrote (p. 311):

> In competition, therefore, everything appears upside down. The finished configuration of economic relations, as these are visible on the surface, in their actual existence, and therefore also in the notions with which the bearers and agents of these relations seek to gain an understanding of them, is very different from the configuration of their inner core, which is essential but concealed, and the concept corresponding to it. It is in fact the very reverse and antithesis of this.

The quotes and reflections reported above seem to prompt the obvious conclusions that the correct capital-labour relation typical of a worker-controlled firms system would put the world back into kilter, that the capital-labour opposition and the antithesis between the currently reversed world and the hoped-for upright world are closely interconnected, and that the capital-labour opposition is associated with the contrast between appearance and reality discussed in Marx's theory of commodities exchange.

A comment on Struve's approach

Coming to the question if Struve's analysis is fully convincing, it certainly deserves praise for describing the transition to socialism as an evolutionary process and taking a first stand against the view (advanced by Plekhanov in stark opposition to Bernstein and Kautsky) that endorsing evolutionism was tantamount to invalidating Marx's theoretical edifice at its roots (see Geary 1974, p. 83). Put differently, it goes to refute the widely held view of orthodox Marxists that reform and revolution are antithetical notions and that the call for reform entails rejecting the very idea of revolution. This orthodox belief was spelt out both by Lenin in a polemical attack on Struve (see Howard & King 1989, p. 186) and by Rosa Luxemburg with the following words:

Legislative reform and revolution are not different methods of historic development that can be picked out at the pleasure from the counter of history, just as one chooses hot or cold sausages. Legislative reform and revolution are different factors in the development of class society. They condition and complement each other, and are at the same time reciprocally exclusive, as are the north and south poles, the bourgeoisie and proletariat" (Luxemburg 1899, p. 192). "That is why people who pronounce themselves in favour of the method of legislative reform in place and in contradistinction to the conquest of political power and social revolution, do not really choose a more tranquil, calmer and slower road to the same goal, but a different goal."

(*idem*, pp. 192–93)

Much in the same vein, Agnes Heller argued that a central idea in Marx's theoretical approach was his belief that people have radical needs which transcend – or contain the possibility of transcending – capitalism. Among these are the need to work, life's prime want, the wish to entertain interpersonal relations and the wish to develop our potential to the full, which are needs that capitalism fails to satisfy.

The crucial role of the concept of revolution is in Marx's approach necessitates deciding if these opinions and Struve's overall line of reasoning are acceptable.

On closer analysis, anyone believing (as I myself do) that reformism and revolution are not necessarily antithetical cannot but reject both Luxemburg's and Struve's arguments.

To refute Luxemburg's claim that the radical needs listed above are incompatible with capitalism, suffice it to argue that where the piecemeal conversion of capital-owned enterprises into LMFs is actually furthered, it is necessary to assume that during the transitional process there will be an intermediate stage at which capitalistic enterprises will, admittedly, still outnumber democratic firms, but some of the above-mentioned primary needs will be met by the existing worker-run firms.

Concerning the true relevance of Struve's theoretical approach, it is a fact that Struve does not distinguish between reforms launched to pave the way for the suppression of the capitalistic production mode and reforms that leave class relations unaltered. By way of example, productivity-indexed pay increases add to the workers' well-being without interfering with the dominion of capitalists over production; if they are commensurate with actual rises in labour productivity, they do not affect a firm's rate of return and will leave the growth potential of capitalism intact. The opposite would be true if such pay increases were fixed at rates above labour productivity rises and, above all, if the reform process were designed to grant workers a say in corporate decisions. In the latter case, if the process were protracted in time until the workers take over corporate management powers, the resulting worker-controlled firm system would set off the transition to socialism, i.e. a socialist revolution. In short, some reforms are unrelated to revolution and do not pave the way for the advent of socialism, while others help further the revolutionary process. And as Struve provides focus exclusively on the latter, he fails to see that some reforms do not undermine the potential of capitalism for unlimited growth.

When Rosa Luxemburg wrote that objective processes under way in capitalistic society are changing the trade union struggle into 'a labour of Sisyphus' of sorts (Luxemburg 1899, p. 73), she basically intended to cast this truth into non-embellished words, but actually suggested the opposite view: the thesis that reforms are unsuited to trigger appreciable change, if not altogether ineffectual.

In point of fact, it is evident that even reforms that do not pave the way for a new social order may nevertheless work to the advantage of workers.

With reference to reforms that expedite the advent of socialism – the only ones with which Struve concerns himself – a preliminary query is whether the transition to socialism is actually a historical necessity – as Struve thinks it is.

This claim is concordantly denied by theorists emphasising the relevance of the concept of 'social formation' (which is not a different designation of the notion of production mode). The term 'social formation' denotes an existing social structure thought to be concomitantly shaped by the prevailing production mode, by remnants of the earlier one and by elements of the one which is just emerging. Some define it as a combination of several production modes which arose at different, not easily determined points in time, which is characterised by the absence of one principal power class, but whose class structure is torn by conflicts of interests between a plurality of power classes.

Further on, I will try to refute Burns's claim that this notion "averts the risk of determinism" (see Burns 2010), but here this argument can help explain why Marxism can neither be categorised as fully deterministic nor as clearly non-deterministic.

According to Burns, the need to rule out determinism arises from the fact that the transition from one production mode to the next one may be a long-drawn-out, even centuries-long process during which the power bloc of a social formation may stave off the advent of the superior production mode. In my estimation, Marx is right when he posits a set of different production modes and describes the most recent production mode as superior to the previous one by definition. Although each social formation is characterised by the simultaneous presence of a plurality of production modes, one of these, specifically the one which is taking the place of the earlier and inferior one, is prevailing from time to time and will in due time be replaced by a superior one which is in the process of gaining the upper hand and whose features are probably already in place at least in part.

Having regard to Marx's view of history as a unilinear process hurried on by the incessant growth of the productive forces, it seems to me that the advent of a chain of different production modes is a historical necessity.

Marx's view of history does have a deterministic colouring, deriving from his belief that the historical course works in the direction of the supersession of the capital-labour opposition and the consequential liberation of workers from their subaltern condition. The same conclusion is reached if we consider that Kant assumed the French Revolution to have "revealed an aptitude and faculty for progress in human nature of a kind that no politician's subtle efforts could have extracted from the course of past events" (see Foucault 2008, p. 28) and that the 'aptitude and faculty for progress' ascribed by Marx to human nature are ultimately at the root of his unilinear conception of history as a process which, albeit with twists and turns, will eventually lead to the attainment of ever fuller freedom.[17]

Concerning the driving force behind the hoped-for movement for the abolition of capitalism, i.e. the class that could be assumed to take the lead in emancipating society, Marx wrote:

> No class of civil society can play this role without arousing a moment of enthusiasm in itself and in the masses, a moment in which it fraternizes and merges with society in general, becomes confused with it and is perceived and acknowledged as its general representative, a moment in which its claims and rights are truly the claims and rights of society itself.... Only in the name of the general rights of society can a particular class vindicate for itself general domination.
>
> (Marx 1843, pp. 67–68)

The class that will wrest society free from the chains of capitalism must be one 'with radical chains', he added, and concluded that it was the proletariat.

In fact, as Marx's claim that the proletarian portion of society would increase much more rapidly than other classes has been proved wrong by history, this is still another point that Struve failed to review critically, but despite this additional weak point of his analysis it remains that his description of society as ceaselessly heading towards socialism deserves credit even today.

Marxists trying to define the true revolutionary agent have been alternatively adopting the viewpoints of such different, but complementary ideologies as workerism versus proletarianism. Accordingly, they either restricted the revolution-oriented part of the population to the proletarians real and proper or, conversely, extended it in such a way as to include additional social groups (as proletarianists do – see Petruccioli 1972, p. 51). From my perspective, the basic distinction is between those who welcome change and those who mistrust it, i.e. between hired and own-account workers.[18] And as available statistics indicate that wage and salary earners (especially blue- and lower rank white-collars) have actually increased in number,[19] they go to validate both Petruccioli's finding that the most noticeable changes in the composition of the Italian population had been a drop in self-employment and a rising trend in hired labour (see Petruccioli 1972, pp. 47–48) and, indirectly, Struve's argument that the transition to socialism would be welcomed by a majority of the population.[20]

The notion of modes of production in Marx

At this point it is time to examine an additional major flaw of Struve's approach.

The most original parts of Marx's theoretical work are widely held to be his analysis of the laws of motion in capitalism and the formulation of a set of interconnected notions such as production modes, class struggle and alienation. In this section, I will be principally discussing the production mode.

The relevance of the concept of production modes is emphasised by all those theorists who rate the 'history-as-totality' notion as the true underpinning of Marx's theory of society.[21]

Althusser dwelt at length on the way we find our way to "an understanding of the determination of the *visible* as visible and, conjointly, of the invisible as invisible, and of the organic link binding the invisible to the visible". "Any object or problem situated on the terrain and within the horizon, i.e., in the definite structured field of the theoretical problematic of a given theoretical discipline, is visible" he wrote (Althusser & Balibar 1965, p. 26).

Consequently, the sheer relevance of this notion determines that those who have no cognizance of it will never be able to apprehend reality to the full. Fleischer 1969 (p. 33) tells us that Althusser described the notion of production modes as a ground-breaking theoretical revolution resulting in the substitution of new concepts such as 'forces of production' and 'relations of production' for the older 'individuals/human essence' couple specific to Feuerbach's conception of history.

The idea that society is shaped by its production methods is often looked upon as Marx's most pregnant finding (see Bloom 1943, p. 58); and Stedman Jones, for his part, described the mode of production as "the core notion around which the materialistic conception of history was to crystallize between 1845 and 1847" (Stedman Jones 1978, p. 34).

These quotes are clear evidence that there is general agreement on this point.

The notion of production modes is both inextricably intertwined with the materialistic conception of history and one of its principal constituents and corollaries. In extremely broad terms, the true underpinning of the materialistic conception is the idea that the economic structure of society, which arises independently of the wills and consciences of people, affects and shapes the political and ideological relations engaging their consciences. The notion of production mode is closely intertwined with the materialistic conception of history because it makes clear that the way production activities are carried on and the existing relations of production are strictly determined by the stage of development of the productive forces; as a result, it turns the spotlight on the fact that parallel trends are under way in a plurality of countries and provides evidence that economic systems develop in accordance with laws comparable to those of material life.

Coming back to the main fault of Struve's analysis (his failure to discuss modes of production), since the relations of production evolve in sync with productive forces and are gradually brought into line with them, Struve is right in arguing that the productive forces are so closely intertwined with the production relations in terms of content and form that we cannot think of the former independently of the latter, but he fails to make clear that (a) the capitalistic essence of the production relations remains intact if capitalists continue to keep production surpluses for themselves and (b) that the precondition for the advent of a new mode of production is therefore the transfer of this right from one class to the other.

Concluding, let me re-emphasise that the greatest fault of Struve's approach is his failure to analyse and discuss production modes.

Further reflections on the notion of production modes

A few additional notes on modes of production will help shed further light on my train of reasoning. In Luporini 1974 (pp. 297–98), the Marxian phrase 'relations of production' is said to describe "the mutual relations which arise between individuals as they appropriate and change nature thanks to the strength of their intelligence, through goal-oriented work inputs and technological processes". As Marx rated them as a distinctively human characteristic, the essence of interpersonal relations and the factor which distinguishes human from animal life. Luporini concludes that they constitute the *materialist* core of the Marxist conception of man and human history. Considering that Luporini's view is shared by most Marxists, the phrase 'production relations' can be looked upon as an umbrella term of sorts with inextricably combined legal and economic implications.[22]

An additional fault of Struve's approach is his attack on Marxists for looking upon production relations as a fixed factor that only revolution can subvert. In actual fact, the one factor that Marxists assume to remain fixed in-between one revolution and the next is the mode of production, and it is this that explains their belief that no new production mode can arise unless management powers and the right to cash production surpluses are stripped from capital-owners.

As illustrated by the sample case examined in Section 3 above, during the evolutionary process towards socialism management powers will not be transferred from capitalists to workers at one stroke, and this means that the establishment of a socialist system, the last step of the process, will not occur until all management powers are firmly in the hands of the working class.

Accordingly, the principal fault of Struve's approach is not his contention that production relations undergo continual change and adjustment to the productive forces, but his failure to appraise the relevance of production modes and, hence, to claim that a reformist process is tantamount to a revolution and comes about in piecemeal fashion, according as production relations evolve.

Concluding, let me argue that Struve's description of a piecemeal reformist process as the highroad to socialism made a much more valuable contribution to reformism than the theoretical approach of his contemporary Bernstein, but that he erroneously equated reform with revolution. In fact, reforms may take the form of a preparatory process for a revolutionary change, but a revolution proper requires the instant transfer of the right to cash surpluses from capitalists to workers.

One of the transition processes discussed at the beginning of this book, specifically the stepwise transfer of firm management powers from capitalists to workers, would seem to recall Struve's approach because it is unrelated to the distinction between reform and revolution. It is this that induced me to use Struve's work as a reference background for my book, which is ultimately intended to advance the thesis that while the transition to socialism can certainly take the form of a piecemeal reformist approach, dialectical thinking has taught that in-between the phase at which firms are still run by capital-owners – the capitalistic phase – and the socialist phase when management powers are firmly in the hands of workers there will be an intermediate step at which quantitative changes turn into qualitative changes and trigger a revolution: the turn from capitalism to socialism.

I do hope my line of reasoning will not be lightly dismissed as mere wordplay or an attempt to endorse a 'Struvean-type' reformist transition to socialism without actually having to admit it. In my estimation – let this be repeated once again – Struve's approach remains objectionable because of his failure to provide focus on the notion of production modes. In other words, on the one hand his revisionism commands respect for painting a reasonable and realistic picture of the reformist transition to socialism; on the other, it is invalidated by a disregard for the issue of production modes. To liken a gradual transition process to a revolution it is necessary to offer conclusive evidence that this process can reach a stage at which corporate management rights will be handed over from capitalists to workers and capitalism will be swept away through the substitution of socialist for capitalistic production relations. While it is true that a reformist process can lead to a revolution, reformism and revolution are and remain two different notions and should therefore be kept strictly apart.

As mentioned before, since Struve contrasts reality with science, i.e. a 'dialectically' contradictory process with an approach founded on the non-contradiction principle, he does conceive of capitalism and socialism as antithetical systems, but holds them to be inextricably intertwined in the real world. On closer analysis, it is this conclusion that invalidates his entire approach. As argued by Marx, since thought reflects reality, conceptually antithetical systems such as capitalism and socialism must be no less antithetical in real terms, that is to say in the real world, where they constitute two antithetical modes of production. The fact that the transition from one to the other mode is usually a piecemeal process does not imply the need to erase such conceptual differences, as Struve does when he describes capitalism and socialism as an inextricably conjoined in the real world.

Criticisms of reformism

The true reasons why Marxists rule out the hypothesis that a reformist process should give rise to a revolution are both the awareness that it will be opposed by capitalists (who are just the class on which capital ownership bestows major power) and principally the persuasion that the State will put in place actions in defence of the status quo.[23]

Whereas in the *Critique of Hegel's Philosophy of Right* and *The Eighteenth Brumaire of Louis Bonaparte*, i.e. in 1843 and again in 1851, Marx argued that a state bureaucracy could seize hold of the authority to make decisions and exercise it independently of the class in power, in later years, with a thorough change of focus, he bluntly proclaimed that the capitalistic state apparatus was firmly in the hands of a single class. This means he had embraced a thesis which was forcefully advanced by Lenin in *State and Revolution* and *The Proletarian Revolution and the Renegade Kautsky* and subsequently revived by Offe in a well-known study dating from 1977. In fact, this view is refuted by quite a lot of authors and Offe himself resolved to back-pedal on this point in later years.[24]

In *The Proletarian Revolution and the Renegade Kautsky*, Lenin wrote that

> the toiling masses are barred from participation in bourgeois parliaments [...] by thousands of obstacles, and the workers know and feel, see and realize perfectly well that bourgeois parliaments are institutions alien to them, instruments for the oppression of the proletarians by the bourgeoisie.
>
> (Lenin 1918, p. 156)

Concluding, he stated that "the exploiters inevitably transform the state (and we are speaking of democracy, i.e., one of the forms of the state) into an instrument of the rule of their class" (Lenin 1918, p. 160).[25]

In Offe's approach, a state becomes a class-based power structure when institutional mechanisms are used to enable its apparatus to orchestrate a selectivity function designed to further given events to the detriment of others. The underlying assumption, here, is that the bourgeoisie uses the State apparatus to further interests which it would otherwise be unable to pursue. Consequently, the primary criterion against which the class character of a State is to be measured is the extent to which the goal selection process of its apparatus is designed to identify and further the 'overall interests of capital' even *in defiance* of individual aggregations of capitalists or lobbying groups. An additional selectivity function is needed to shield capital from the attacks of anti-capitalists.

In short, selectivity may come in two forms: it is positive when the State sets its agenda in ways that will help capital avoid wrong moves; it is negative and repressive when it produces 'non-events' designed to protect capital from its enemies.

Offe defines four institutionally enforced selectivity functions: structure, ideology, process and repression. Structural selectivity, which is exemplified by the protection of private property, is exercised *de facto* in full accordance with the rule of law and is the process which governs the gleaning of goals eligible for inclusion in the government's policy agenda. The process described as ideological selectivity is used to restrict the range of feasible State policies in accordance with the dominant cultural and ideological sentiment. An additional selection mechanism is put in place to pinpoint and implement policy goals that play into the hands of certain lobbies to the detriment of other groups. Lastly, repression is the task of the State's police, military and criminal justice systems. The combined action of these selection mechanisms accounts for the fact that capitalistic systems are unsuited to satisfy a vast array of needs (see Offe 1972, chap. V).[26]

Anyone sharing these views will argue that the core sentiment behind reformism is "the idealistic myth of the primacy of politics" (Ferrajoli 1978, p. 50). As long as economic power remains firmly in the hands of capitalists, the State tends to further the interests of the class in power by putting off its agenda any policies that may run counter to the goals of capital (op. cit., p. 52).

From my perspective, Offe's line of reasoning is questionable since it leaves out of count cases in which power is seized by the representatives of the working class (as may occasionally happen). In such a case, the implementation of a pro-worker action agenda would doubtless be slowed down by the legal system in place, by the prevailing climate of opinions and the resistance the business world is sure to put up in defence of the interests of capitalists, but it is reasonable to assume that working class representatives would nonetheless be able to secure a measure of elbow room, manage to enforce piecemeal adjustments to the legal system in force and exert some influence on the prevailing cultural sentiment.

In other words, in capitalistic systems it is not the State, but the economic agenda of action that is class-oriented, and there can be little doubt that economic-financial requirements may set the agenda for the government even when the representatives of the working class are in power.

When a State is ruled by the representatives of the working class, it ceases to be agent of the bourgeoisie, but its action will continue to be conditioned and constrained by the power of capital. Put differently, although State action will necessarily be constrained by the strong resistance that the bourgeois will put up thanks to their control of the economy, working class interests might nevertheless remain high on the government's agenda and power might at long last be vested in wage and salary earners.

Engels's well-known saying that "periods occur in which the warring classes balance each other so nearly that the State power, as ostensible mediator, acquires, for the moment, a certain degree of independence of both" resounds in the following argument from Tronti 1977, p. 53: "Over the span of history no single class has always had the overhand and no single class has always been in subjection".[27]

As is well known, Wright Mills and other conflict theorists have extensively studied the issue of power elites, i.e. power blocs which are in a position to defy the authority of democratic institutions and prevent rival groups from seizing power. In this connection, Offe contended that the position of ruling bloc is invariably attained by those who are able to bring home the message that they are better able to solve the problems affecting society at large (see Offe 1977, pp. 36–37). In so doing, he argued, they create the illusion that power is not the privilege of a group, but (just as money) a functionally necessary and freely multipliable product of the global systems which generate it and use it to perpetuate their own conditions of equilibrium (see Offe 1972, pp. 36–37).

The 'rival' anti-capitalistic groups Offe had in mind were certainly those advocating the creation of a Soviet-type centrally planned system.

Conversely, if we think of groups speaking out for parliamentary democracy, for instance the establishment of democratic firm management, it is difficult to believe that power elites would actually prevent them from achieving their goals.

Democratic firm management would solve major social problems and correct inadequacies of the democratic system because a social system claiming to be truly democratic can hardly be assumed to withhold power permanently from a movement working towards full-fledged democracy. This is why I do not believe that every political force acquiring autonomy in present-day society is exclusively driven on by the will to further the class interests of the bourgeoisie (see Galli 2010, p. 43).

Let me specify that the aim of this paper is not to refute the core assumption behind the so-called 'theories of influence', i.e. approaches that postulate a more or less far-reaching influence of individual capitalists on government action while denying the influence of capitalists as a class. Although I do endorse Offe's analysis of a dual type of government selectiveness shaped by class influences exercised on the State apparatus and of selection mechanisms framed to further the interests of the economic power bloc, I do not think that he has offered incontestable evidence that the capitalistic State is always class-oriented'.[28] According to Offe (op. cit., p. 145), "the class character of the State becomes evident analytically only in an *ex-post* perspective, namely when the limitation of its functions becomes apparent in class conflict". From my perspective, considering that working class representatives, once in power, will find it hard, but not impossible, to abolish capitalism, it would be more appropriate to speak of 'resistances' rather than 'limitations'.

The Austromarxists Karl Renner, Otto Bauer, Max Adler and Rudolf Hilferding were the first Marxists to challenge the view of the State as consistently concerned with promoting the interests of the bourgeoisie. Renner went so far as to suggest that the State's pro-worker policies were digging a widening gulf between the State apparatus and the business community; Bauer objected that social classes did share in the exercise of State power, Adler maintained that the 'dictatorship of the proletariat' could be exercised as part of political democracy and Hilferding emphasised the need to re-think Marxist political theories, specifically to proceed from anarchism to statism by dropping the base-superstructure distinction and acknowledging the far-reaching influence of the organised forces of the proletariat on the superstructure. As for Kelsen, he argued the case for treading in the steps of Lassalle, rather than Marx, and acknowledging that nothing would prevent the State from framing a democratic agenda designed to further the interests of the proletariat (see Marramao 1980).[29]

Conclusion

In sum, to accept Struve's theory of social evolution we have to integrate it with the notion of modes of production (which Struve surprisingly failed to consider) and spell out in bold letters that evolution and revolution are different notions, just as capitalism and socialism are different modes of production. Against this background it is necessary to make clear that the preconditions for socialism to be attained by reformist means is setting the reform agenda in manners that will bring about a new mode of production.

An additional conclusion implied in the foregoing is that the advent of socialism is no historical necessity (as Struve assumed it to be). A majority of working-class representatives may pass legislative provisions capable of bettering the living standards of the working class, but no truly socialist system will ever be established unless this specific goal is placed at the top of the political agenda and consistently pursued through provisions designed to do away with capitalism for good. An indispensable move is the adoption of a legislative measure enforcing the transfer of management powers to wage and salary earners – a move which has so far been the exception.

"Why take part in the class struggle?" – Tucker asks himself (1961, p. 227). In varying formulations this question has been addressed to Marx and Marxists over and over again by philosophical criticism and some have raised the question why a thinker who regards the victory of the proletariat as historically preordained should actively promote it.

Assuming that wage and salary earners and their allies should succeed in securing a majority in parliament, before they can even think of promoting the establishment of a socialist system, they would have to expedite the transfer of corporate management powers from capitalists to workers.

There is no such thing as a spontaneous advent of socialism, as Struve assumes there is.

Notes

1 LMF-type cooperatives are those that finance their investments solely with loan capital and therefore strictly segregate labour incomes from capital gains (see Vanek 1971a, 1971b). The loan capital used by these firms may in part be self-financed since portions of the surplus can be distributed to the partners in the form of bonds (see Jossa 1998, pp. 88–91).

2 The work to which reference will be made in this paper was written by Struve in 1899, the year when Bernstein published the book which is usually rated as the first effective attempt to offer a theoretical justification of reformist tactics (see, *inter alia*, Geary 1974, p. 82). Lenin is said to have written *Marxism and Empirio-criticism* in opposition to Struve (see Boss 1990, p. 132).

   Let me mention that Struve developed his evolutionist approach on the assumption that he was moving well within the Marxist tradition, while Bernstein's declared goal was to come up with a straightforward anti-revolutionary, non-Marxist approach (see Gustafsson 1974, pp. 109 ff.).

3 As mentioned in Vranicki 1971 (vol. I, p. 165I), this passage is taken from the *Instructions for the Delegates of the Provisional General Council*, a speech delivered by Marx at the first Congress of the First International held in Geneva from 3 to 8 September 1866).

4 Sylos Labini is one of many theorists who do not think of the creation of a system of producer cooperatives as a real and proper revolution. Accordingly, he sees no direct link between self-management theory and Marxism.

5 This is why I reject Berlin's argument that "Marx always looked upon gradualism as camouflage for the attempt of the class in power to misdirect the energies of its enemies to harmless and ineffectual targets" (see Berlin 1963, p. 96).

6 In this connection, Luxemburg wrote (1967, p. 356):

   There are not two different forms of class struggle, economic versus political. The working class is engaged in *a single* form of class struggle whose aim is, at the same time, to combat exploitation within bourgeois society and to do away with exploitation and bourgeois society at one stroke.

7 Soon after the October Revolution, when Lenin opposed the plan to allow workers to manage enterprises by themselves, he never as much as suggested that this was because the times were not ripe for such a move or because workers lacked the entrepreneurial skills needed to run firms on their own. Neither do Marxists or Marxist historians today. The Althusserian theorist Karsz has aptly argued (1974, p. 188) that no technical requirements dictate the need that the users of production means should be non-propertied individuals without power to make decisions regarding the uses of labour power. The separation of ownership from control is observed in most, though not all, production modes and is doubtless specific to the organisation of the productive forces within the capitalistic production mode. In capitalistic systems, the subjection of workers to technicians and engineers is the direct result of the typically capitalistic tendency to over-determine the technical requirements of the productive forces.

8 As argued by Karsz (1974, p. 196), "within modes of production where class relations are relevant 'the political dimension' is the very basis of all existence, not simply the phenomenal expression of the status quo or a veil drawn to justify it."

9 Unlike Struve, Proudhon dismissed partial changes as altogether ineffectual because of interconnected contradictions which only a truly radical process of change could cancel (see Ansart 1967, p. 14).

10 At the other end of the spectrum are Marxists, who think of production relations as an economic phenomenon; see, *inter alia*, Karsz (1974, pp. 184–89).

11   In this connection, Cohen wrote (Cohen 1978 and 2000, p. 98):

> We are arguing that the familiar distinction between forces and relations of production is, in Marx, one of a set of contrasts between nature and society. Commentators have failed to remark how often he use 'material' as the antonym of 'social', and how what is described as material also counts as the 'content' of some form. The upshot of these oppositions and identifications is that the matter or content of a society is nature, whose form is the social form.

On the subject of historical materialism, see, also, Cohen (1983).

12   In Marcuse (1969, p. 180) we read that "the Marxian concept of revolution implies continuity in change."

13   When Lenin rehabilitated the concept of reformism late in life, he (and Bukharin in his wake) spelt out that evolutionism was to be thought of as "economic revolution, not by one stroke of the revolutionary sword, but by organic evolution" (see Cohen 1973, pp. 138–39). But a review of Lenin's writings shows that in earlier years he had rather endorsed the opposite view (see Lenin 1918, p. 261, 1920, p. 14).

14   As far as the influence of Hegel is concerned, I agree with Tucker and Berlin that Marx's immediate successors tended to understate Marx's Hegelian ascendancy without considering that when Marxian theory is read in line with Marx's own perception of himself as a rigorous scientist investigating truth, but without a concomitant focus on the unifying model that helped mould it, his theoretical edifice appears to be splintered into a myriad loosely linked intuitions.

15   The turn of British Marxists to reformism at the end of the nineteenth century has often been traced to a rapid pace of economic growth – a thesis that Lichtheim rejects as barely convincing. As a result of a downward trend in Britain's overseas trade, Lichtheim goes on to argue, money wages hardly rose in those years and continued to stagnate even during the subsequent upswing of the economy (see Lichtheim 1965, pp. 207–8).

16   Marx described bourgeois society as "a bewitched, distorted and upside-down world" (see Marx 1894, p. 242).

17   Marx's conception of history as continual progress towards the realm of freedom has been criticised as a form of uncritical mysticism (see, among others, Fougeyrollas 1959, pp. 86–87, Gurvitch 1962, pp. 148ff).

18   Quoting Sofri (2008, p. 10),

> it is curious, though, admittedly, inevitable, that the description of society as split into two opposed classes has never been so forcefully denied as it tends to be today, when the polarisation of society into 'haves' and 'have nots', and especially, the gap between the two extremes represented by the super-rich and the destitute are escalating at an unprecedented pace.

Quite naturally, on a balance of probability the chances for revolution increase in direct proportion to widening income equalities.

19   For follow-up studies of the composition of Italian society the reader is referred to the revised edition of Sylos Labini's book (Sylos Labini 1984) and to Carboni (1986), Bagnasco (2008) and Pugliese (2008).

20   Catephores is one of numerous authors reporting that the proportion of the population prepared to welcome the demise of capitalism is seen to rise instantly if the phrase 'wage and salary earners' is substituted for the term 'working class' (see Catephores 1989, p. 221).

21   Althusser went so far as to argue that "the bourgeoisie, in its own ideology, keeps silent about the relations of production and the class struggle" (see Althusser 1973, p. 86).

22   Struve, holds that the contradictions in capitalism are caused by a mismatch between the legal system in place and the way economic relations evolve. In a

polemical attack on Struve, Plekhanov (1976, pp. 474ff.) refuted this argument by explaining that Marx did not conceive of these contradictions as the reflection of a contrast between economics and law and that, at any rate, such a contrast was not a key element of Marx's theoretical approach.

23 "The State and I are enemies" – Stirner wrote (1844, p. 195).

24 According to Bobbio, Marx and the workers' movement never worked out a true theory of the State. Unlike Bobbio, Tronti (1977, p. 67) holds that Marx's theoretical approach, to politics, though, admittedly, not a theory of the State proper, was "developed in writings other than *Capital* and the *Grundrisse*, i.e. independently of his critique of political economy".

25 The assumption that exploitation is at the origin of the class character of bourgeois democracy prompts the conclusion that there is "a logical-historical continuity between the labour theory or value and the theory of historically determined forms of political organisation (see Fistetti 1977, p. 7).

26 Much to the same effect, G.D.H. Cole has argued that no government will ever dare to adopt policies that might prove detrimental to the interests of business and industry tycoons.

27 In response to Tronti's analysis of the 'self-standing role of politics', Bobbio objected that 'political power is never autonomous or fully self-sufficient; inasmuch as it 'is needed', i.e. 'functional' to something, it is in a condition of dependence. The political action of a government vesting corporate powers in the workers under the pressure of a revolutionary movement can barely be categorised as fully autonomous because it is probably conditioned by external factors: the economic cycle, the relative weights of the two opposed classes (an additional 'economic factor') and the determined will of workers to take over firm management powers.

28 These reflections recall the objection that Kelsen brought against Bauer in 1943 paper and Bauer's reply to this critique (see Marramao 1977, pp. 69–77).

29 From among authors rejecting the categorisation of the State as the power structure of one class, let me mention Lelio Basso, who emphasised the function of the State as a mediator and 'clearing house of contradictory energies'.

Aconvincing analysis of the reasons why the capitalistic State cannot be said to be a tool in the service of capital and capitalistic relations worldwide, see Bieler, Bruff and Morton's critique of *Open Marxism* (2012). The members of the 'Open Marxism' movement think of capitalistic relations as the sole enablers of human activity and, by extension, of historical growth throughout the world. On closer analysis, though, this movement has been unable to account for the fact that changing State-capital relations have given rise to different, and hence, a-historical, State models. *Open Marxists* think of capital as the founding stone of every State, whatever its model – a stance that must obviously be rejected.

6 Competition in a democratic firm system
Failures and constraints

Introduction

As is well known, in capital-managed businesses employees are paid on a monthly basis, and their wage and salary claims are accorded priority treatment over those of capital providers. At the other end of the spectrum are the partners of a cooperative, who are only entitled to participate in the 're-sidual', the balance which is left when all the firm's costs, including capital charges (but not labour costs) have been settled. This arrangement acts as a shield against bankruptcy. Considering that businesses go bankrupt when their aggregate costs exceed their revenues, it is clear that the cancellation of the largest production cost item-wages and salaries-in an employee-managed firm system is an effective safeguard against bankruptcy.

In addition to this, as the payments accruing to the partners constitute, not wages or salaries proper, but shares in the cooperative's distributions of the surplus, before the partners of firms with revenues below the system's average can leave their firms they have to find more efficient cooperatives prepared to take them on. In point of fact, since closed-membership firms such as cooperatives are mostly averse to the entry of new members, the workers of an all-cooperatives system will seldom be able to do so and will just have the option of putting up with their meagre incomes or setting up a new firm.

The ultimate effect of this combination of circumstances is to make bankruptcy the exception.

Workers risking to see their incomes zeroed must obviously be eligible for effective protection, but as this serious issue is associated with a need for state intervention in the economy, it lies outside the scope of this chapter.

Does this suggest that insolvency is a spectre that may scare democratic firms into accepting the logic of competition just as it does in capitalistic systems? Considering the greater freedom of action deriving to firms from remoter bankruptcy risks, the answer is obviously no. In other words, cut-throat competition is a distinctive characteristic of capitalistic, rather than self-managed firm systems.[1]

This conclusion is in full accord with Petrović's argument that the production mode of as system of producer cooperatives helps overcome both "the division of society into 'quarrelling' spheres" and "the domination of the economy over other spheres" (Petrović 1975, p. 15); in other words, that it puts an end to the war between 'quarrelling spheres' within a class society.

Thanks to this shield against insolvency, producer cooperatives may satisfy the needs of the proletariat at least in part even in a capitalistic system. In short, although socialism can only be fully implemented in a system where employee-managed firms outnumber capitalistic businesses, the relative freedom of action enjoyed by employee-managed firms may create the assumptions for the establishment of 'socialist enclaves' in a capitalistic society.

These reflections suggest that the crisis of European socialism which the theorist of social democracy Georges Sorel traced to a marked turn towards consumerism in his day should rather be blamed on the traditional belief that socialism necessarily entails centralised planning. As is well known, when Bernstein theorised his revisionist approach, he started out from the assumption that the main obstacle to the establishment of a socialist system was not the need to help the proletariat seize power, but the difficulties attending any attempt to rapidly organise production in line with the criteria of a planned economy. No such problems would arise during the transition from capitalism to self-management socialism, which can be implemented in successive steps and without any appreciable organisational requirements.

But is the transition to socialism of worker-managed firms a realistic prospect?

Amartya Sen has argued that pessimism about the ability of society to ensure greater equality is only justified if we hold on to the belief (which Sen himself rejects) that people are exclusively concerned with maximizing their narrow personal interests (see Sen 2015, p. 50). Taking issue with him on this point, I wish to argue that inasmuch as self-employment is more rewarding than hired work and socialism can be established by creating a system of worker-managed or democratic firms, the ultimate advent of socialism is a material prospect even if workers, upon securing higher incomes and a measure of protection against bankruptcy, should exclusively act in their own personal interests.

Solidarity in a system of democratic firms

A well-known passage from the *Preface* to Marx's *Critique of Political Economy* runs as follows:

> In the social production of their existence men inevitably enter into definite relations, which are independent of their will, namely relations of production appropriate to a given stage in the development of their material forces of production. The totality of these relations of production constitutes the economic structure of society, the real foundation on which arises a legal and political superstructure, and to which correspond definite

forms of social consciousness. The mode of production of material life conditions the general process of social, political and intellectual life. It is not the consciousness of men that determines their existence, but their social existence that determines their consciousness. At a certain stage of development, the material productive forces of society come into conflict with the existing relations of production or-this merely expresses the same thing in legal terms-with the property relations within the framework of which they have operated hitherto. From forms of development of the productive forces these relations turn into their fetters. Then begins an era of social revolution.

(Marx 1859, p. 5)

This often-quoted argument has been praised by many authors. In the estimation of Bakunin, for instance (Bakunin 1873, quoted in Plechanov 1895, p. 58), Marx offered the demonstration that economic matters had always taken precedence over legal and political issues throughout the history of societies, peoples and states and this demonstration is one of the primary achievements to his credit.[2]

Defining the materialist approach to history with specific reference to capitalism, Raniero Panzieri wrote (Panzieri 1967, p. 255):

In a capitalistic economy production plays a dual role: on the one hand, it is a specific material process; on the other, it is the general category dominating the process as a whole. If we do not understand this, we will never gain a correct appreciation of the mechanisms governing capitalistic societies.

One major assumption behind the materialistic conception of history is that human character itself is affected by the institutions in place; and the influence of institutions on character suggests that one of the principal evils associated with capitalism is an adverse impact on human nature. In the words of Bataille,

the factory only knows of forces that may serve its purposes, proletarians, middlemen, accountants or technicians, but ignores the individual wherever and whenever this is possible. A firm is driven on by flameless greed, it employs labour without heart and worships its own growth as its only idol.

(Bataille 1976, p. 74)

More recently, the economist F. H. Hahn has called attention to a stark contrast between the innermost driving force behind capitalism and generally recognised ethical values. Since the Jewish-Christian ethic extols virtues such as benevolence and care for our fellow-beings, condemns greed and discourages the accumulation of treasures in this world, he argues, there is nothing to be admired in individuals whose actions are solely guided by the personal profit motive, rather than the duty to take care of their fellow-beings, i.e. in anyone behaving as is expected of people operating in capitalistic systems (Hahn 1993, p. 10).[3]

These reflections indicate that individualism, the true cause of the breakup of interpersonal ties, does not proceed from democracy, but from the age-long development of capitalism, and that the establishment of a system founded on mutual solidarity is an absolute necessity. In capitalism, Gramsci wrote, "all the higher bonds of love and solidarity are dissolved: from the bonds of craftsmen's guilds and social castes to those of religion and the family". That is why the socialist revolution is "the spiritual revolt of humanity against the new and pitiless feudal lords of capitalism. It is the reaction of a society which is striving to remake itself as a harmonious organism, living in solidarity, governed by love and compassion". Thanks to it, "the 'citizen' is displaced by the 'comrade; social atomism by social organization". In a system of workers' councils, "limits are placed on the sway of capital in the workplace" at a stage when capitalism is still in place.

> The worker wins a degree of autonomy for himself, a degree of real, effectual freedom. He is no longer one individual standing against the world: he is a member of collectivities which mesh together into other, ever greater and more powerful collectivities.
>
> (Gramsci 1994, p. 134)

The first author to extol the solidarity-building potential of democratic firm management soon after the establishment of the earliest producer cooperatives was John Stuart Mill. More recently, its ability to counteract egotism and individualism was emphasised by Meade in a book which describes the organisational structure of *Agathotopia* (a society imagined to be based on cooperative principles) and contrasts the sympathetic and cooperative spirit of a typical *Agathotopian* with the tendency of Britons to act in accordance with the 'every man for himself' criterion and grab as much as they can in the shortest time possible (Meade 1989, pp. 8–9).

For my part, I am in full sync with C. Wright Mills when he urges the Left to socialise production means in an attempt to humanise mankind. According to this author, the belief that the new man of a free society will be forged in the factory, rather than the electoral district, explains why left-leaning groups tend to press for the permanent inclusion of worker control in the strategies and bargaining agendas of all trade union organisations (Mills 1948, p. 258).

The thesis advanced in Erich Fromm's *To Have or to Be*, is that the precondition for creating a social order founded on being, rather than having, is the active involvement of all its members in economic life as free citizens. In other words, Fromm explains, to wrest ourselves free from modes of living centred in property we have to be fully and democratically involved in industrial and political life (Fromm 1976, p. 235).

Marshall's idea of cooperation as a character-moulding agent

Alfred Marshall laid special stress on the beneficial effect of cooperation on character.

Specifically, he held that more than by any other influences (unless it be the influence of religious ideals), the character of a man is moulded by his everyday work and by the material resources which he thereby procures, and that consequently the two great forming agencies of the world's history have been the religious and the economic.

In an 1897 paper he wrote:

> Social science or the reasoned history of man, for the two things are the same, is working its way towards a fundamental unity; just as is being done by physical science, or, which is the same thing, by the reasoned history of natural phenomena. Physical science is seeking her hidden unity in the forces that govern molecular movement: social science is seeking her unity in the forces of human character.
>
> (Marshall 1897, p. 228)

In earlier writings, Marshall claimed that human character is not given from the outset, but thoroughly shaped by the environment and its economic structure. In 1873, for example, he wrote "we scarcely realise how subtle, all pervading and powerful may be the effect of the work of man's body in dwarfing the growth of man" (Marshall 1873, pp. 105–6), and in an analysis of the relative weight of religious versus economic factors conducted in the *Principles* he argued that compared to the former, which are more intense, the latter rank higher in terms of pervasiveness since "a man's mind is absorbed by matters associated with his business even when he stops working and, as often is the case, sets out to plan future actions" (Marshall 1890, p. 2).

The belief that work is a powerful agent shaping man's character led Marshall to argue that the main task of a social thinker was to suggest institutional reforms capable of enhancing the best qualities in man, namely the 'high' ethical motives he used to contrast with the 'base motives' behind capitalism, individualism and the profit motive.

All these reflections go to explain why Marshall praised the cooperative movement for its ethical motives and for its main aim: "the production of fine human beings" (Marshall 1889, p. 228).

Overall, Marshall's approach to cooperation was designed to lay stress on the potential of a genuinely democratic system to generate positive externalities and other types of benefits for society at large.

Income distribution in market socialism

An additional point to be explored is the argument of the well-known Italian cooperation specialist Valenti that "cooperative societies are economic institutions designed to redress the greater part of the natural imbalances typifying the distribution of wealth in the present-day free-market system" (Valenti 1901, p. 516).

Insofar as it is true that remoter insolvency risks scale down the impact of markets on income distribution, his argument can be endorsed since the income distribution patterns that would be substituted for the current market-determined ones would be socially determined for the most part and, hence, vouchsafe a juster social order.

Economic theorists (primarily Ward in his 1958 article) have made it clear that the workers of democratic firms should earn pay rates commensurate with pre-fixed percent shares of the firm's surplus ('coefficients'). In particular, the coefficients for entire categories of workers would have to be centrally set for the system as a whole, while those for individual workers might be fixed at firm level (with the important specification that the different production capabilities of each group are likely to induce firms to alter the centrally fixed coefficient pattern in line with firm-specific criteria).

This necessitates raising the question if distribution can be said to be 'socially determined' even under the circumstances outlined above.

In a system of cooperative firms, worker incomes differ both within one and the same firm and between different firms. They are socially determined when they depend on centrally set coefficients, but in this case the different abilities and skills of individual workers of the same category may induce firms to grant some of them higher coefficients than those centrally set. Firm-level coefficients which are fixed by the workers themselves in collective resolutions passed at meetings are socially determined by definition, but as the relevant choices have to be made by reference to the prevailing market conditions, they are so only in part. What really matters is whether, and to what extent, this may help avert insolvency risks and loosen market constraints.

By way of derogation from the neoclassical rule that in every market economy, all prices, including those of the factors of production, are determined by the law of supply and demand, it is possible to argue that socially determined distribution coefficients will tend to reduce inequalities. Factors of production obey different supply and demand mechanisms. Demand for labour is determined by the short-term requirements of businesses, and as firms hire fresh workers according to need, it fluctuates in sync with the conditions prevailing in markets from time to time. Conversely, supply of labour is not solely determined by market factors and tends to fluctuate over considerably longer time-spans. In addition to being far less volatile, it is greatly influenced by the professional qualifications acquired by workers in training programmes, that is to say by social choices and, specifically, by the educational system in place.

The resulting conclusion that the prices of factors of production, unlike those of commodities, are largely unrelated to the law of supply and demand justifies the argument that income distribution is much more strongly influenced by the legal system and the political environment and much less by impersonal market forces than is usually suggested by economic theorists.

Due to the crucial role of the educational system and the practice of re-cruitment by competitive examination, the socially determined nature of income distribution will not be fully neutralised by spontaneous market re-sponses. In essence, the effect of hiring by competitive examinations is to balance out labour supply and demand and there is hardly any need to specify that ancillary services such as career counselling and vocational guidance are integral parts of the mission of any educational system.

On closer analysis, there is scope for arguing that the educational system and recruitment by competitive examination are ultimately designed to at-tain convergent goals. Both of them may help streamline labour supply in manners that will bring the pay rates of different worker categories into line with the desires of society. In other words, if the public hand handles labour supply in such a way as to contrive necessary demand adjustments, the pay rates assigned to the individual factors can be set at levels that social con-science will perceive as fair.

Regarding the issue of manager coefficients in labour-managed firm sys-tems, some authors contend that the assumed rises in worker pays would be matched by cuts on the pay rates of managers. On the assumption that "the hardest work of business management is generally that which makes the least outward show", Marshall argued that those working with their hands tend to underrate the strain involved in the superior work of engineering a business and, consequently, "grudge its being paid for at anything like as high a rate as it could earn elsewhere" (Marshall 1890, p. 292). These reflections, com-bining with a clear analysis of reality in his day, led Marshall to argue that no cooperative firms had so far been able to offer salaries capable of attracting first-rate managers, excepting only cases of excellent men who for the sake of the cooperative faith in them accepted a lower pay than they might have secured by offering their services in the free market.

Unlike him, Korsch suggested that the managers of democratic firms were likely to secure higher remuneration coefficients as soon as the capital owners appropriating corporate profits in our day were successfully ousted from the systems. After all, he argued, this was perfectly in line with the logic of enter-prises which are managed by workers in legal terms but depend on the abil-ities of their managers for their efficient running (Korsch 1922, pp. 33–34).

With reference to the income distribution issue, some authors, including Ben-Ner (1987), have argued that workers expected to take all business risks will hardly be prepared to put up with the volatile income schemes typically associated with the varying fortunes of their firms.

To clear the field of this objection, let me specify that the optimal corpo-rate organisation model of a worker-controlled firm is one in which payroll expenses are kept below the firm's anticipated average bottom-line result and all excess amounts are allocated to a reserve whose proceeds can be used to offset falls in the partners' revenues upon a downturn in business. An alterna-tive option would be pooling corporate tax receipts into a social fund for use by the State in supplementing the meagre distributions likely to be made by firms in temporary financial distress (a solution which, understandably, tends to be met with fierce opposition).

The last, and fairly obvious, remark to be made at this point is that even in situations where income distribution is socially determined the State will be called upon to work towards redressing excessive inequalities, for instance by using tax receipts to award subsidies and putting in place employment-boosting policies (just as happens in capitalistic systems).

Self-management and the 'challenge of Minerva'

The focus point of this section is the claim that the assumed lesser role of the private profit motive in a democratic firm system with markets can be analysed from the perspective of the 'challenge of Minerva' discussed by Serge Latouche in an interesting book (Latouche 1999). Latouche's approach is relevant for a number of reasons. On the one hand, it helps us realise that capitalistic markets differ greatly from the markets of cooperative firm systems; on the other, it suggests that capitalism is not only threatening to destroy the humanistic traditions native to the Mediterranean area, but even to subvert our traditional values by advancing the thesis that despite its closer links with the humanistic tradition the South is more 'backward' than the affluent North.

Minerva is the goddess of reason of the Greeks. As is well known, in Greek myth she is said to have been born directly from Jupiter's head, fully arrayed in arms, and to have two spiritual children: a daughter, Phronesis, the incarnation of prudence, wisdom and, better still, 'reasonableness', and a younger son, Logos, presented as the incarnation of geometrical reason or 'rationality'. In Latouche's approach, Phronesis is a distinctively Mediterranean, feminine entity capable of an acute consciousness of the tragic condition of man, while *Logos*, a protestant masculine entity, appears to be devoid of all passion. In the modern world, he argues, the younger son is about to kill his elder sister – which is tantamount to saying that cold rationality is smothering beauty, our feminine side. Both Freud and Reich characterised capitalism as rational, patricentric and phallocratic.

Max Weber strongly criticised economics as the chronicle of the progress of economic rationalism founded on calculation, which he held to have reached a climax in the modern world. According to Latouche, people used to make a virtue of reasonableness at least until the eighteenth century, when the Western world veered towards rationality in all its problem-solving efforts.

For my part, in this section I wish to advance two closely associated theses, Firstly, as inter-firm competition can help combine rational calculation with reasonableness, there is a chance that a system of producer cooperatives will rise to the challenge of Minerva; secondly, market socialism can protect the values of humanism from the destructive impact of capitalism despite the retention of markets. Paraphrasing Finelli (2007, p. 132), for the first time in the history of mankind in the capitalistic world *reality came to be shaped by an abstract factor*, and *abstraction* itself, trespassing the boundaries of its peculiar domain, logic and cognitive processes, began to build a close-meshed network of economic, practical and, more generally, behavioural, societal and cultural relations in the real world. In a self-managed firm system, this abstraction –viz. capital– is cancelled.

This prompts the interesting conclusion that the materialistic conception of history is not relevant to every historical period and, specifically, is hardly helpful when it comes to analysing a system of producer cooperatives.

In the 1999 book mentioned above, Latouche raises the question if people concerned with maximising utility in an effort to make others happy can be categorised as *reasonable*. As mentioned above, he starts out from the contrast between Minerva's two children, rationality and reasonableness, and sets it against conceptual dichotomies previously posited within Western thought (Pascal's distinction between *exprit de geometrie* and *esprit de finesse*, Kant's and Hegel's reason versus intellect opposition, Pareto's distinction between logical and residual actions, Simon's distinction between bounded and global rationality). His conclusion is that none of these pairs perfectly matches the rationality-reasonableness opposition and that it is definitely surprising that this dichotomy should have been overlooked right to the present day.

Due to the paramount role of economic factors within the overall issue of rational choices, Latouche's specific focus point is, quite obviously, the kind of rationality that is associated with economic calculation. While it is true that rationality is not confined to the domain of economic choices, he argues, given the primacy of the economic factor in today's society it is in economic life that it materialises to the full as its unmistakable paradigm. According to Latouche, the roots of rationality are in the nineteenth century, when mathematical reason was extended to morals. Descartes expressed the hope that someday it would be possible to create a form of truly rational philosophical thinking, a philosophical approach with axioms proved true by mathematical theorems. His project to build a philosophical approach *de more geometrico* was first taken up by Spinoza in an effort to demonstrate that reason could clear the field of all controversy and help flesh out a moral doctrine grounded in rationality, and subsequently by Leibniz in an attempt to work out a mathematical method substituting calculation for discernment. In the estimation of Pareto, all non-economic actions are irrational.

As mentioned before, reason can be made to function in two different and even antithetical manners. One such function is reflected in quantitative appraisals, which have to do with what can be demonstrated and lead to the truth, whereas the other has to do with weighing pros against cons, i.e. judgements on moot cases which are likely to give rise to debatable choices. This means that rationality lays claim to undisputed validity, while reasonableness is associated with debate and conflict.

As argued by Latouche (1999), in a non-capitalistic economy people are said to behave reasonably when they give due consideration to all the constituent elements of the social and human. The 'reasonable reason', he argues, is manifold because it obeys more than one criterion and can consequently lay a claim on embodying, in the words of Rawls, "a full conception of reason that covers the terms 'reasonable' and 'rational' as we often use them" (Rawls 2000, p. 177). And while there are people who do make cost-benefit considerations and test them against the reasonableness criterion, Latouch went on to argue, mainstream economists deny that this holds true for the capitalistic systems of the Western world, where reasonableness was progressively relegated to a back seat at the same pace that rationality, economism and utilitarianism asserted themselves.

Although the belief that reason has little to do with reasonableness is widely shared, it is a fact that the plan to build a society founded on reason and the rejection of tradition and the transcendental can only be implemented by men who are guided by reason.

In line with a well-known Benthamite formula, the aim of society in the present-day world is to achieve the happiness of the greatest possible number of people, that is to say a geometrical form of individualistic society. The hoped-for result is the sum of a number of equivalence relations, for instance the one which posits that happiness = pleasure = standard of living = gross domestic product per capita.

In a capitalistic system, people are solely concerned with needs, utility, interests and whatever can give them pleasure. From the perspective of an economist, love, hatred and passions in general can be looked upon as part of people's utility functions and, as such, enter an individual's cost/benefit calculations much like choices concerning what is to be produced and what is to be consumed. Everything can be bought and sold in the domain of the rational. According to Latouche, economics is the science of all sciences, that is to say the scientific branch which, combined with others, can help solve the vast array of problems we come up against.

It is evident, economists argue, that people draw pleasure from disinterested action and that initiatives designed to make our fellow-beings happy are ultimately taken for the sake of the pleasure we derive from them.

According to Keynes, the interpenetration of the social and economic and the final integration of the economic into society date back to the time when economic science acquired the characteristics of a form of social physics after the Newtonian rational mechanics model, a process which entailed the reduction of happiness to wealth, of wealth to utility and of utility to money.

But why does Latouche deprecate the primacy of rationality over reasonableness?

As this is not the place for an in-depth analysis of his approach, suffice it to mention that the basic assumption behind his line of reasoning (which, surprisingly, is not always perfectly intelligible) is that happiness and pleasure are different things and that the self-respect we draw from ethical behaviour is far more rewarding than pleasure.

And as I feel very much in sympathy with him on this point, let me argue that thanks to its potential for disempowering capital and enabling workers to make free choices (even in areas associated with non-economic benefits), a system of producer cooperatives may prove equal to the task of reconciling rational economic calculation with reasonableness.

Conclusion

In this chapter, I set out from the assumption that the creation of a system of cooperative firms would ensure a marked fall in the number bankruptcies and afford major improvements over capitalism, including beneficial effects on personality and more equitable income distribution patterns. In the middle part, I explored the reasons that may account for the scant attention that cooperation theory has, quite surprisingly, received from mainstream and Marxist economists right to this day. The closing section offers an attempt to refute the assumption that the democratic firm management proposal is a worn-out cliché.

Notes

1 This goes to support Luigi Einaudi's argument that the managers of cooperatives tend to be less pro-active than those of capitalistic businesses.
2 In contrast, in an analysis of the origins of morals Habermas claimed that the great eighteenth century Scots Adam Smith, Adam Ferguson and John Millar had approached this issue in a sociological key, arguing that the power structure, as well as human needs, feelings and behaviour are determined by the *state of society*, which in turn is determined by the configuration society has acquired over the span of its natural evolution (Habermas 1963, pp. 60–61).
3 An additional major point that cannot be examined in depth in this chapter is Marcuse's claim that the inborn inclination to solidarity is stifled in a class society and that the precondition for a climate of mutual solidarity is the abolition of class divisions – the ultimate goal of a worker-controlled firm system.

7 On dialectics and the basic contradiction in capitalism

Introduction

Apparently, a triumph of capitalism, in actual fact globalisation is only its high water mark. By bringing into focus such a crucial Marxist issue as the full power of markets, it poses the need to 'reconcile' Marxism with markets and to draw a clear-cut distinction between socialism and communism.

With regard to this distinction, it is worth specifying right from the start that socialism is a transitional social order which heralds the advent of communism and, above all, that market socialism is a new mode of production that can be expected to take the place of capitalism for long enough to make us cease wondering what will come after it.

Put differently, whereas a Marxist is likely to assume that the transition to socialism lies in the nature of things and is bound to become a reality at some point in time, the advent of the production mode known as communism must be deferred in time since it is strictly dependent on the birth of a new man who has shed part of his egoism and can consequently do without markets.

Today, the prospect of a world without markets is but a utopian dream. As argued by Hodgson (1999, p. 31), no meaningful long-run economic decentralisation process has ever been proposed "without the equivalent decentralisation of the powers to make contracts, set prices, and exchange products and property rights through markets or other forms of property exchange"

Marx did not distinguish between socialism and communism. The idea that socialism and communism are different social organisation models is widely shared, but "for Marx this distinction is non-existent" (see Chattopadhyay 2010, p. 214).

The reason why this distinction necessitates rethinking Marxist theory is that a system categorised as a market economy can only be analysed to the full if it is brought into line with mainstream economic theory. In other words, this determines that a Marxist setting out to analyse socialism will have to do without Hegelian dialectics, an approach which rejects the non-contradiction principle.

One more point that the socialism-versus-communism distinction necessitates redefining is the basic contradiction of capitalism. Indeed, since the contradiction presented as the severest in Marxist theory entails the conclusion that the order to rise from the ashes of capitalism is a centrally planned economy, it is necessary to identify a different contradiction which is compatible with the assumption that the newly emerging production mode, i.e. socialism, will still be a market economy.

This is the working hypothesis of this chapter, which

a   expatiates on dialectics in order to identify a form of dialectic which will not be at odds with mainstream economic thought and
b   subsequently, discusses the basic contradiction of capitalism from a vantage point departing from traditional Marxist approaches.

A group of theorists have recently been treading a different path. Specifically, they argue that "the very ontology of knowledge has grown into an antagonistic contradiction with the commodity form" (Rigi 2013, p. 407), which is tantamount to saying that the ever wider use of computers highlights a different contradiction within capitalism: the contrast between knowledge, which is freely available to anyone by its very nature, and the production of marketable commodities. In their opinion, the production mode of the future, which in fact is already in the making, is peer production, a system which is characterised by the production of socially owned goods made available to the community for free use (see Benkler 2006; Kleiner 2010; Rigi 2013).

A few introductory notes on dialectics

> If ever the time comes when such work is again possible – Marx wrote – I should very much like to write two or three sheets making accessible to the common reader the rational aspect of the method which Hegel not only discovered but also mystified.
>
> (Marx 1858, p. 249)

Regrettably, he never translated this plan into practice, and this may explain why his dialectical method allows of a variety of different interpretations (see Bhaskar 1991).

Although he did not deny the unmistakable Hegelian colouring of all Marx's writings, Schumpeter warned that thinking of Hegelianism as the keystone of Marxism would be tantamount to debasing the scientific standing of Marx's theoretical edifice. In his opinion, Marx had a taste for 'coquetting' with Hegelian phrasing, but did not go any further (see Schumpeter 1954b, p. 9).

Authors convinced that Marx gradually ceased his use of dialectics include Rosenthal 1998 and Bidet 1998 (p. 225), while analytical Marxists look upon dialectical reasoning as altogether misleading and, hence, hardly of any more help than formal logic when it comes to flesh out a social theory (see Meyer 1994, p. 1).[1]

Rodolsky is right in arguing that ever since the publication of the *Grundrisse*, it has no longer been admissible for an academic to write about Marx as an economist without thoroughly analysing his method and its links with Hegel's. Indeed, he contended, whereas in *Capital* Hegelian overtones are just perceived in a few footnotes, the *Rohentwurf* can be described as a string of references to Hegel, specifically his *Logic* (Rosdolsky 1955, p. 8).[2]

Lastly, it is worth noting that the assumed similarities between Marx's and Hegel's dialectical methods have been called into question by a great many authors, with Croce (1899, pp. 4–9), Hyppolite (1969, pp. 300–3) and Garaudy (1969, pp. 312–14) the most prominent among them.[3]

Let me repeat that the main aim of my analysis of dialectics is identifying a contradiction, in capitalism, that Marxists should categorise as the most important of all and that this need is imposed by the fact that the severest contradiction determines what kind of production mode will rise from the ashes of capitalism. The train of reasoning I will be adopting for my analysis is quite an unusual one. Instead of proceeding, as is customary, from the premise to the conclusion, I will take it for granted that the new production mode will be a system of worker-controlled firms and raise the question which of the serious contradictions Marx ascribed to capitalism and which of the dialectical methods he used are best suited to support my view that the new mode of production will be a system of democratically managed firms.

The importance of equating the socialist revolution with the transition from capitalism to a system of worker-controlled firms stems from the fact that Marx, refusing to concoct 'recipes for the cook-shops of the future', failed to provide a clear outline of the social order he expected to take the place of capitalism. Despite the crucial relevance of the post-capitalistic mode of production for a correct perspective on Marxism, neither Kautsky, who described himself as a socialist all his life, nor any other Marxist critical of the way the Russian revolution was evolving ever took the trouble to make it clear how opponents of the Soviet central planning model are to picture to themselves a true socialist order (for Kautsky's silence on this point, see, Geary 1974, pp. 93–94).

As a matter of fact, the categorisation of democratic firm management as a new mode of production is far from widely accepted. Sylos Labini is just one of many academics who reject the assumption that the establishment of a system of producer cooperatives amounts to a revolution, and this is probably the reason why he altogether denies any links between producer cooperative theory and Marxism (see Sylos Labini 2006).

Marx himself did look upon a system of producer cooperatives as a possible new mode of production. In 1864, for instance, he wrote:

> But there was in store a still greater victory of the political economy of labour over the political economy of property. We speak of the co-operative movement, especially of the co-operative factories raised by the unassisted efforts of a few bold 'hands'. The value of these great social

experiments cannot be over-rated. By deed, instead of by argument, they have shown that production on a large scale, and in accord with the behest of modern science, may be carried on without the existence of a class of masters employing a class of hands; that to bear fruit, the means of labour need not be monopolised as a means of dominion over, and of extortion against, the labouring man himself; and that, like slave labour, like serf labour, hired labour is but a transitory and inferior form, destined to disappear before associated labour plying its toil with a willing had, a ready mind, and a joyous heart.[4]

Dialectics as the analysis of a totality with real oppositions

In Marxian theory, production, distribution, exchange and consumption are perceived as links of a single chain. Commenting on this point in a youthful work on historical evolution, Lukàcs wrote that Marx, much like the German philosophers and chiefly Hegel, conceived of world history as a homogeneous revolutionary process consistently geared towards the attainment of freedom. The very core of Marx's conception of history, he argued (Lukàcs 1968b, p. 34), is the supremacy of totality, *i.e.* the pre-eminence of the whole over its artificially detached parts.

In this connection, Rovatti (1973, p. 125) remarks that ever since the publication of Lukàcs's *History and Class Consciousness*, more and more authors have espoused the view that Marx's true aim was to proceed from a fragmented view of the structure of capitalism to an approach capable of highlighting a *totality* moving consistently forward in a single direction. Rusconi (1968, p. 49), for his part, has clarified that Lukàcs rated the 'totality perspective' not only as a speculative aid, but as a real and proper "critical method for the interpretation of society" and "a criterion used to make history intelligible", and Negt (1979, p. 350) has endorsed Lukàcs's view that the totality notion is the key element distinguishing the Marxist from the bourgeois worldview (see, also, Balibar 1993, p. 98).

Lukàcs's suggestion that Marx's totality perspective was closely bound up with Hegel's dialectical method takes us back to one of the aims of this chapter, namely identifying a non-Hegelian dialectical method that even the most orthodox thinkers would probably rate as acceptable. In particular, a form of dialectical thinking that mainstream thinkers are likely to accept is the method of the 'interpenetration of opposites', which is concerned with 'reconciling contradictions' (see Sowell 1985, pp. 28–35) or highlighting a sudden change or reversal of circumstances which until then had been perceived as fixed and given (Luporini 1966, p. 155, 1974, p. IX).[5]

Using the phrase 'unity of differences' to describe mutual relationships, in *Capital*, Marx argued that "the independence of the individuals from each other has as its counterpart and a system of all-round material dependence" (pp. 140–3). Convinced that explaining dialectics was "the only way to begin the theoretical education of the Party", Trotsky (1940a, p. 177) polemically wrote to Burnham: "Your errors are not accidental. You approach each question by isolating it, by splitting it away from its connection with other questions... You lack the dialectic method" (Trotsky 1940a, p. 165). Lenin described dialectics as the most intriguing of all philosophical issues and a tool that reveals the reciprocal interaction of everything with everything else (see Meyer 1957, pp. 19, e 21).

Viewed as the analysis of 'interpenetrating opposites', dialectics helps expand "our notion of anything to include, as aspects of what it is, both the process by which it has become that and the broader interactive context in which it is found" (Ollman 2003, p. 13) and makes us aware that in any dialectical interactions, whether mutual or between unequal poles, the "dominant determination runs from one pole to the other". Without this, Laibman argued (2007, p. 4), "the dialectic characterizes the mutual conditioning of the poles, their relational consistency but does not reveal a dynamic movement in the system that they constitute" (see, also, Sowell 1985, pp. 28–33). In sum, dialectical thinking turns the spotlight on contrasts and contradictions within the dynamics of society (see, *inter alia*, Labriola 1902). In other words, for a contradiction to qualify as dialectical it must express the essence of movement (Lukàcs 1956, p. 92[6]; Colletti 1974, 1980). Indeed, the latter has repeatedly emphasised that the contradictions that are highlighted must be material, not just logical.

The main effect of a totality-focused dialectical approach is to magnify the impact of causality on the context, in terms that its individual components will be perceived as different depending on the specific totality they are part of from time to time. The end result is a compound of effects which impact on the elements constituting the system (Karsz 1974, p. 131).

The importance of a simultaneous focus on the issue concerned and the surrounding totality was also underscored by Althusser. In Althusser's view, this was the only effective way to address and solve an issue dialectically, but he also claimed that this was only applicable to the method used by Marx. Hegel's, he argued, was antithetical to the non-contradiction principle and "completely dependent on the radical presupposition of a simple original unity which develops within itself by virtue of its negativity" and "only ever restores the original simplicity and unity in an ever more 'concrete' totality" throughout its development (Althusser 1965a, p. 175).

From this, it follows that no one sharing Althusser's view of dialectics as totality-focused should use a form of dialectical thinking that can be reinterpreted as economic determinism. In Althusser's approach, therefore, economic determinism descends from the idea of a linear causal chain implying direct cause-effect relations, i.e. relations between a single paramount cause and the effects that passively flow from it. The economic base is the necessary and, in itself, sufficient cause, whereas the superstructure, stripped of its autonomy, becomes ineffectual and production relations are seen to be shaped directly by the prevailing technological standards. Hence, the idea of a predetermined course of things, materialism, gives rise to economic fatalism, i.e. determinism.

On closer analysis, however, this is the conception connoting mechanistic materialism, rather than Marx's approach, and as this conception tends to obliterate the part played by superstructural factors, it is unable to account for the rise of existing forms of society and their different characteristics.

Dialectics as a method and a system of thought

In 1958, Norberto Bobbio drew a distinction between two notions of dialectics.

> Faced with two conflicting entities – he wrote – we may either opt for the 'compenetration-of-opposites' (or mutual-interaction) method or for a method founded on the 'negation of the negation'. When the former is adopted, both entities are kept firm and are assumed to mutually condition each other; when the latter is adopted, it is assumed that the first entity is cancelled by the other at a first stage and the second by the third at a subsequent stage.
>
> (Bobbio 1858a, p. 347)

With reference to these antithetical methods, Badaloni 1962 argued (p. 110) that the former was the method of Marx the mature economist and scientist, while the latter was the method of the younger Marx.

Bobbio's reflects the distinction between Hegel's dialectic (which Sichirollo (1973, p. 149) describes as "the world as it appears in discourse", rather than a method) and the Marxist dialectical method which has already been mentioned above and which I am prepared to endorse since it does not rule out the non-contradiction principle.[7]

For purposes of greater clarity, it is worth emphasising that while Hegel expects us to accept the "union of opposites" as "a result of speculative thinking" without regard for the fact that it may appear "nonsensical to the understanding" (see Hegel 1831, p. 14), Marx's dialectical approach, which I hold to be fully acceptable, is a method which explains the dynamics of reality without calling into question the non-contradiction principle. Both Bobbio 1958 (pp. 343–46) and Dal Pra 1972 (pp. viii–x) are agreed that the latter approach was preferably used by Marx in his maturer years.

An expert on Marx such as Roberto Fineschi 2007 (p. 183) contends that Marx did accept "the self-driven movement of notions, i.e. the laws of dialectics laid down by Hegel", but that he rated them nothing but an effective method for describing things, not for materially creating them.

In fact, there is no denying that Marx used the distinctly Hegelian 'negation of the negation'.

According to Hudis 2000, for instance, a case in point is Marx's proposition that capitalism cannot be superseded by simply suppressing private property.

In Marx's own words, the abolition of private property was just the first negation and, as such, it required a second negation, the negation of capital, as the negation of the negation. A well-known statement by Hegel runs:

> care must be taken to distinguish between the *first* negation as negation in general, and the *second* negation, the negation of the negation; the latter is concrete, *absolute* negativity, just as the former on the contrary is only *abstract* negativity.
>
> (See Hegel 1831, p. 134)

Similarly, in the closing section of his third 1844 *Manuscript*, Marx wrote: "communism is the position as the negation of the negation, and is hence the actual phase necessary for the next stage of historical development in the next stage of historical development in the process of human emancipation and rehabilitation" (Marx 1844b, p. 126). An additional relevant statement from *Capital* runs:

> The capitalist mode of appropriation, which springs from the capitalist mode of production, produces capitalist private property. This is the first negation of individual private property, as founded on the labour of its proprietor. But capitalist production begets, with the inexorability of a natural process, its own negation. This is the negation of the negation.
>
> (Marx 1867a, p. 929)

In the *Postscript* to the second edition of Volume I of *Capital* we also read (Marx 1867a, p. 103): "the mystification which the dialectic suffers in Hegel's hand by no means prevents him from being the first to present its general forms of motion in a comprehensive and conscious manner". In *Antidühring* (which Marx read through and unconditionally endorsed), Engels expatiates on the reasons why he holds that Marx's use of the negation of the negation has nothing in common with Hegel's dialectic (see Engels 1878, pp. 142–43).

These quotes make it impossible to share the widely held view that it was Engels, rather than Marx, who continued to make use of Hegelian dialectics (see, for instance, Cingoli 2005, p. 129).

However, in the light of this line of reasoning and the views of authors suggesting different readings of Marx, I wish to re-emphasise that the thesis I advance in this chapter, namely the compatibility of Marx's dialectical method with formal logic, is not so much backed up by a careful textual analysis of Marx's writings, as by the categorisation of Marxism as a scientific discipline posited by some of these readings (which I endorse).

Defining the basic contradiction of capitalism

At this point, it is time to decide which the contradictions of capitalism is to be classed as the severest of all.

From the vantage point of a Marxist, the severest contradiction of capitalism is the antithesis between capital and labour, i.e. two classes pursuing antithetical interests. This contradiction is held to be unbearable because it originates from the fact that individuals are controlled by capital, that is to say a compound of inanimate things, and not vice versa, as would be in the nature of things. As will be clarified further on, with the passing of time this contradiction tends to be superseded as a result of the laws of motion in capitalism. Although I am aware that the analysis of this well-known contradiction in a Marxist key may appear redundant, from my perspective a few clarifications are necessary.[8]

Let us consider a system of cooperatives of the labour-modified firm (LMF) type defined in Vanek (1971a and 1971b). As is well known, LMFs are worker-run firms which exclusively use loan capital. What would become of the capital–labour opposition – one may ask – in a society which has adopted such a system in place of capitalism?

As is well known, a capitalistic enterprise can be defined one where capital hires labour, runs the operations of the enterprise in its exclusive interests, pays workers fixed incomes (wages and salaries) and appropriates the surplus. In contrast, a Vanek–type LMF is a firm whose workers borrow capital, pay it a fixed income rate (interest), run the firm's business in their own interests and cash the surplus. Hence, the transition from capitalism to a system of Vanek–type firms reverses the existing capital–labour relation by stripping capitalists of their corporate sovereign powers and vesting them in workers along with the right to decide how production shall be managed – as is in the nature of things (see, for instance, Napoleoni 1972, p. 69).

Establishing if, and in what manner, the re-reversal of the present-day capital–labour relation can help supersede this contradiction is no trivial issue. Marx's approach to the contradictions of capitalism is basically dialectical and dialectics, as is well known, is a method which entails the assumption that reality evolves at the same pace that its inherent contradictions are solved and superseded.

Inasmuch as this is true, what it the true import of the claim that a reversed capital–labour relation solves one of the contradictions of capitalism?

Presumably, it would not solve the contrast between capital and labour since this is basically the effect of an income distribution pattern determining that the share of the aggregate national income that is appropriated by one class increases in proportion to the decrease of the share assigned to the other. Although the resulting conflict of interests would be somewhat cooled off by this revolution, it would nevertheless outlast it since capitalists would keep cashing interest on their loans even after the establishment of a worker-controlled firm system. This prompts the conclusion that the capital–labour contradiction and the conflict of interests mentioned above are two different things.[9]

In contrast, the reversed capital–labour relation does solve the capital–labour opposition because the higher incomes and qualifications that workers are sure to acquire with the passing of time will ultimately enable this class to wrest itself free from the capitalistic yoke and take over the management of firms.

Democratic firm management marks a major stride forward in the direction of freedom and Marxism in its truly Marxian version has a unilinear view of history because it assumes that, albeit by the most tortuous of paths, history progresses towards the acquisition of ever greater freedom.

In a world shaped by a correct relation between capital and labour the capital-labour opposition typical of capitalism will be superseded since the laws of motion of capitalism ensure that thanks to the re-reversal of the capitalistic relation between capital and labour the working class will be in a position to appropriate the surplus generated by production. In other words, this re-reversal will create the assumptions for the attainment of the true goal of economic development: enabling humankind to exercise an ever more effective control over the environment.[10]

The basic contradiction of capitalism from the perspective of orthodox Marxists

Neither Engels nor orthodox Marxists think of the capital-labour confrontation as the basic contradiction of capitalism. In orthodox Marxist terms, the basic contradiction originates from a mismatch between the socialised character of production in large-size industrial concerns (where hundreds and even thousands of workers see to their jobs side-by-side) and the private character of appropriation, the very underpinning of privately owned production means (see, for example, Tsuru 1969, pp. 364–65). And according to Engels (and other Marxists), this contradiction is responsible for an additional one, namely the contrast between socialised production and capitalistic appropriation that Engels explained as an antagonism between the organization of production in the individual workshop and the anarchy of production in the society as a whole.

To some degree, Engels's view is supported by the reflection that the transition from capitalistic to democratic firm management will solve both these contradictions at one stroke. As is well known, the aim of socialism is to eradicate the current economic model founded on individualism and private enterprise, replace it with a collaborative socialised model and, hence, solve the contrast between the collective nature of production activity and the private nature of distribution. And as a worker-controlled firm system vests decision powers in matters of production and distribution in collective bodies such as workers' councils, it is possible to conclude that the progress from capitalism to self-management will not only help supersede the capital-labour opposition in the manner explained above, but effectively solve the contrast between socialised production and individualistic distribution as well.

Although these two contradictions are closely interrelated, they are far from identical. The capital-labour confrontation reflects a class conflict, whereas the contrast between socialised production and private appropriation is generated by antithetical aspects of economic activity.

In support of this distinction it is possible to argue that the former, unlike the latter, is grounded in a conflict between economics and law (see Struve 1899, pp. 120–21).

At this point, it is worth discussing an additional serious contradiction that Marx assumed to arise in connection with the fact that the world is 'upside down', *i.e.* with an organisational model which runs counter to the natural order of things determining that the world should be 'standing upright'.

This idea was first discussed in such an early work as the *Contribution to the Critique of Hegel's Philosophy of Right*, whose *Introduction* includes the following statement:

> This state and this society produce religion, which is an inverted consciousness of the world, because they are an inverted world. Religion is the general theory of this world … the sigh of the oppressed creature, the heart of a heartless world, and the soul of a soulless condition.
>
> (Marx 1843, pp. 57–58)

His conclusion is that "the criticism of religion ends with the teaching that *man is the highest essence for man* – hence, with the *categoric imperative to overthrow all relations* in which man is a debased, enslaved, abandoned, despicable being" (Marx 1843, p. 65).

Fineschi 2005b (p. 111) points to close links between Marx's idea of an inverse relation between capital and labour in capitalism and his theory of alienation, while Colletti sees Marx's notion of capitalism as interconnected with his vision of a reversed world and the theories of alienation and fetishism. These processes – he remarks (Colletti 1979, p. 70) – "are structured in the same way as is the subject-predicate inversion", because it is the realty of the capitalistic world that is turned upside down.

The reason why Marx's mature works describe the world as turned upside down is that market mechanisms, while preventing man from exercising control over things (i.e. labour from using means of production), create the assumptions for things to control man and capital to dictate the laws to which labour must conform.

In volume three of *Capital* Marx wrote (p. 311):

> In competition, therefore, everything appears upside down. The finished configuration of economic relations, as these are visible on the surface, in their actual existence, and therefore also in the notions with which the bearers and agents of these relations seek to gain an understanding of them, is very different from the configuration of their inner core, which is essential but concealed, and the concept corresponding to it. It is in fact the very reverse and antithesis of this.

As this suggests that the takeover of firms by workers would reverse the capital-labour relation and put the world back into kilter, it is to be assumed that Marx thought of the capital–labour opposition and the view of the world as upside-down as strictly interconnected issues. In addition to this, my line of reasoning suggests that the capital–labour opposition is also associated with the contrast between appearance and reality which is discussed in the theory of commodities exchange but which the re-reversal of the capital–labour relation would be unable to cancel.

Conclusion

The distinction between socialism and communism must be accepted by any Marxist wishing to come to terms with globalisation. And as this distinction was first made by Lenin, it is to Lenin, rather than Marx or Engels, that he will have to turn for a correct appreciation of the nature of socialism. After his experiments with wartime communism and the Nep, shortly before his death Lenin wrote a seldom-quoted article in which he spelt out that "co-operation is socialism" (Lenin 1923, pp. 1801–2). However, if socialism is a system in which cooperative firms are to operate in the market (though, admittedly, under a measure of State control), any Marxist intending to flesh out a socialist political economy must stop thinking of socialism as a non-market economy and use a method of analysis which is not at odds with mainstream economic science. Specifically, he will have to accept the non-contradiction principle and, consequently, reject Hegelian dialectic thinking.

Inasmuch as it is true that a system of cooperative firms operating in markets is a socialist system, it is impossible to continue holding the traditional Marxist view that the key contradiction of capitalism is the contrast between socialised production activity and private appropriation since such a view will quite naturally lead to the conclusion that socialism is a centrally planned economy. And from this, it clearly follows that the basic contradiction of capitalism must necessarily be the confrontation between capital and labour.

Notes

1 In Settembrini 1975 (p. 9), we read that Trockji likened a non-dialectical Marxist theory to a springless watch."

2 In all probability, the first author to censure Marx for failing to wrest himself free from the influence of Hegel was Conrad Schmidt back in 1865 (see Bernier 1974, p. 167). Major commentators emphasising the close links between Marx and Hegel include the Italian philosopher Giovanni Gentile (1974, pp. 31–33) and, more recently, Rockmore (2005), the author of a masterly analysis concerned with the indissoluble links between Marx and Hegel (see Rockmore 2005).

On the role of dialectics in Marx's approach, see, also, Dal Pra (1972), Bidet (2001), Kincaid (2001), Fine (2001) and Bhaskar (1993).

3 Pellicani (1987, p. 175) argued that Marx had transferred logical contradictions from the domain of thought to the real world of being and objected that such an action, which is based on the identification of being with thought, is justified in Hegelian philosophy, but can hardly make sense in a philosophical approach that Marx himself described as thoroughly materialist in character.

4 The statement, in the *Manifesto*, that the aim of revolution was enabling the proletariat to use its political supremacy to "centralise all the instruments of production in the hands of the State" (see Marx & Engels 1848, p. 312) is of little consequence. Indeed, since Marx did not start fine-tuning his system until 1857, his earlier works can be described as preparatory steps for the full development of his system. Until the time of the Paris Commune, Marx and Engels were persuaded that socialism would be implemented by centralising all powers firmly in the hands of the State. It was the Paris Commune that induced them to reconsider this belief and to conceive of socialism as a system connoted by fully democratic production processes (see Screpanti 2007, pp. 145–46). The publication of the *Inaugural Address* in 1864 marked an end to the period during which they associated communism with the Paris Commune (see Lichtheim 1965, p. 228). However, it was only in the last years of his life, specifically when Marx wrote the *Critique of the Gotha Programme*, that he definitively espoused the idea that socialism was to be a centrally planned system.

5 In this connection, the theorist of world systems, Immanuel Wallerstein, has argued (2006, p. 14) that "the division of knowledge into distinct boxes – disciplines – is an obstacle, not an aid, to understanding the world."

6 In the opinion of Lefebvre (1968, p. 124), unless the purpose is stopping a process, contrasting one term with another is not enough to secure comprehension. Each opposition entails, i.e. dissimulates and reveals, a dialectical movement.

7 Tosel (2007, p. 299) has argued that Hegel's rejection of the non-contradiction principle is to be traced to his wish to have the logical fall in with what is real (see, also, Popper); the reason why Marxists do accept the principle or non-contradiction, he argues, is they do not attach equal importance to this need.

8 It has long been customary to describe political economy as a scientific discipline concerned with demonstrating that capital and labour are not in conflict. A nineteenth-century economist once wrote that thanks to the effective circulation of the teachings of economic science right across the nation British workers had ceased looking on capital as the enemy of labour, has stopped breaking machinery and had come to bear the sufferings associated with the American crisis with exemplary resignation (cited in Favilli 2001, p. 383).

9 Hence, I cannot agree with Settembrini that "in a genuinely socialist regime the antithesis between the working class and the ruling class would be a contradiction in terms" (see Settembrini 1975, p. 35).

10 A Marxist of the calibre of Pierpaolo Pasolini maintained that in mature capitalistic systems the overriding issue is no longer the capital–labour opposition. As he himself put it "In times past, capitalists felt it in their best interests to relegate peasants to the fields, workers to factories and middle-class people to offices and schools, and so forth. The watchword was, what else are class differences for? The situation has been turning round for quite a lot of years now. It would seem that the overriding concern of capitalists is – adopting, as it were, an anthropological rationale – to start off a mounting vampirisation process of sorts intended to scale people up and down to the status of petty bourgeois right across the country, from north to south" (Pasolini 1995, pp. 273–74; see, also, Pasolini 1975, p. 72). And the rationale behind this effort is the awareness that consumerism is the common characteristic of people across classes.

8   Is socialism a utopian
        dream?

Introduction

The idea that a socialist revolution can take form in two different ways, through the establishment of a centrally planned system or a worker-controlled firm system, is rejected by orthodox Marxists who do not accept the equation of socialism with democratic firm control. Yet, this idea is closely associated with the two main contradictions that Marx perceived in capitalism: the capital-labour conflict and the mismatch between planned production and anarchical distribution. Anyone emphasising the latter contradiction will think of socialism as a centrally planned economy, while those prioritising the capital-labour conflict tend to argue that socialism arises when the functions of the 'primary factors of production' are reversed upon the establishment a system of producer cooperatives of the LMF type (see Jossa 2010a, pp. 262–63, 2011).[1]

As a result, it is difficult to accept the view that Marx's theorisation of 'rational planning' is better organised than his approach to worker management of firms and participative democracy (see, *inter alia*, Screpanti 2007b, p. 167).[2]

The terms of the problem can be stated by raising a number of questions:

- which of the above-mentioned forms of revolution fits human nature better?
- which of them is more closely associated with Darwinian evolutionism?
- is it correct to assume that democratic firm management tends to improve human nature?

The first of these questions will be answered in the light of the recent biological theory that 'genes are selfish'; the assumption for answering the second is, quite obviously, an analysis of Social Darwinism; the third will just be touched upon in passing because it is the subject of another chapter.

Accordingly, Section 2 provides a cursory outline of the modern biological theory of selfish genes; Section 3 examines Marx's and Engels's views of human nature; Section 4 analyses human nature from the perspective of the materialistic conception of history; Section 5 is a succinct analysis of Social

Darwinism; Section 6 is intended to establish which of the two models of socialism discussed in this book is in line with the assumption that human nature is shaped by selfish genes; Sections 7 reports my conclusions.

The selfish gene

The biological theory that the actions of living beings are governed by selfish genes is expounded in a book by Dawkins (1989) which raises the following questions:

a   where altruism originates and
b   whether or not human beings are exceptions to the biological rule.

> We are survival machines – Dawkins writes (op. cit., p. vii) – robot vehicles blindly programmed to preserve the selfish molecules known as genes. On being first made explicit in the nineteen-sixties – he argues – this idea appeared revolutionary, but today it has gained wide acceptance within the scientific community. Though originally deriving from Darwinism – he continues – it is expressed in a way which is not Darwin's since rather than focus on the individual organism, it takes a gene's eye view of nature.

Darwin's theory of evolution, which today is nowhere called into question, explains why living beings exist and how they act; but, although great biologists such as Lorenz and Eibl-Eibesfeldt did tread in the wake of Darwin, they had as yet not fully realised how evolution works in actual fact. Only recently, major breakthroughs in biological research have highlighted the unitary nature of all living beings at microscope level (see Di Siena 1972, p. 244). In general terms, it is selfish genes that are responsible for the egoistic behaviour of individuals, but selfishness is a connotation of the gene, rather than the individual. It may come as a surprise that elementary chemical processes and all such within-body interactions as trigger the development and growth of all living beings, including humans, basically involve proteins, but this is what contemporary biology has taught (*ibid.*).

Nonetheless, there are circumstances under which the selfishness of a gene may foster a limited form of altruism in individual animals. Dawkins defines selfishness and altruism in behavioural, rather than subjective terms. An altruistic man, he argues, is one who helps others *at the expense of his own well-being*, but actions perceived as altruistic are often nothing but gestures of dissimulated selfishness. A typical case is the individual who will help others only on condition that he will receive something in return.

In Dawkins's view, both the assumption that the instinct for survival connotes the species and the theory of 'group selection' that biologists long assumed to be true are actually misconceptions. It is not species, but genes, that engage in the Darwinian struggle for existence, and it is not true that the individual must be sacrificed for the sake of the superior interest of the species. Evolution is blind to the future: if only the genes had the gift of foresight – he adds (p. 10) – they could see that their best interests lie in restraining their selfish greed in order to prevent the extinction of their species.

Not always, however – Dawkins clarifies – are we obliged to obey our selfish genes; but where we should observe genuinely altruistic human behaviour, we would be "faced with something puzzling, something that needs explaining" (p. 6): "among animals, man is uniquely dominated by culture, by influences learned and handed down, and to understand altruism we have to understand the relation between nature and culture".[3]

Evolution is not only biological but also cultural. The gene is not the only basis of our ideas on evolution. What is unusual about man – Dawkins argues – can be summed up in a single word: 'culture' (p. 198). Although cultural transmission is not unique to man, it does carry far greater importance for the human species. In short, the role that altruism plays in human behaviour is closely intertwined with culture – in the broadest possible meaning of this word.[4]

In line with the above reflections, Dawkins concludes with the following statement: "if you wish to build a society in which individuals cooperate towards a common good, you can expect little help from biological nature. Let us try to *teach* generosity and altruism, because we are born selfish" (p. 5).[5]

Marx and Engels on human nature

A few words on Marx's view of human nature can help make a final judgment on Dawkin's line of reasoning.

As is well known, Marx's sixth *Thesis on Feuerbach* (which dates from 1845) states that the essence of man is not given, but changes in accordance with the social relations that are in place.[6] The English version of Marx's sixth thesis on Feuerbach runs as follows:

> Feuerbach resolves the religious essence into the human essence. But the human essence is no abstraction inherent in each individual. In its reality it is the ensemble of the social relations.[7]
>
> (See Marx 1845, p. 7)

The anthropological conception of man is also criticised in a later work, *The German Ideology*, where Marx and Engels find fault with the tendency of philosophers to conceive of individuals no longer as subject to the division of labour, but as an ideal under the name of 'Man', "so that at every historical stage 'Man' was substituted for the individuals and shown as the driving force of history" (Marx & Engels 1845–1846, p. 65). And in the much praised 'Preface' to *A Contribution to the Critique of Political Economy*, dated 1859, Marx spelt out in bold letters: "The mode of production of material life conditions the general process of social, political and intellectual life. It is not the consciousness of men that determines their existence, but their social existence that determines their consciousness."[8]

In Marxist terms, therefore, as people living in a capitalistic society tend to develop values and modes of being which depart from those prevailing in non-capitalistic contexts, to understand the real nature of human beings we have to focus on social relations of production.

In Marx's words, "society is the complete unity of man with nature... the consistent naturalism of man and the consistent humanism of nature", and "just as society itself produces man so is society produced by him" (Marx 1844a, p. 113). Analysing Marx's approach to this issue in a fine book dating from 1948, Cornu claimed that the common thread running through modern philosophical thought is the grand issue of man's integration into nature and society.

According to Marx, man's basic unity with nature entails that nature undergoes continual changes as a result of human productive activity, that human beings realise themselves as they act upon nature and that the ambit affected by human action includes both the natural environment and the production system in which people operate. As pointed out by Cornu (1955, p. 455), Feuerbach, too, held that the essence of man is realised in his relations with the environment, but unlike Marx he was thinking of the natural, rather than social environment.

Although Marx rated the influence of the production system as more pervading than that of the natural environment, he, too, spelt out that the actions of human beings were influenced by nature. This is why he wrote (Marx 1844, p. 122) that "history itself is a real part of natural history – of nature developing into man", and then clarified (*idem*, pp. 122–23):

> sense-perception (see Feuerbach) must be the basis of all science. Only when it proceeds from sense-perception – in the two-fold form of sensuous consciousness and sensuous need – is it true science. History itself is a real part of natural history – of nature developing into man.... The social reality of nature, and human natural science, or the natural science of man, are identical terms.
>
> (*idem*, p. 137)

This begs the question if modern science – specifically the gene selfishness theory – is at odds with the belief (held both by Marx and Aristotle) that men and women are social beings because they are shaped by the prevailing production relations, by the environment in which they live and by the interrelations they establish during their lives. From the perspective of Dawkins, inasmuch as this contrast is a reality, it is easily solved because the awareness that selfishness is a connotation of genes, not individuals, makes it possible to assume that human nature, though influenced by gene selfishness, is likely to be principally shaped by the prevailing mode of production and by the environment – two influences that make for sociability and concern with one's fellow-beings.

A materialistic analysis of human nature in different economic systems

In Marx's approach, a mode of production is a form of society in which one prevailing production model, conceived of as a compound of productive forces and production relations, confers significance on the system as a whole (see Luporini 1966, p. 170).

This is how Engels underscores the importance of this notion in his review of *A Contribution to the Critique of Political Economy*:

> The proposition that 'the process of social, political and intellectual life is altogether necessitated by the mode of production of material life'... was a revolutionary discovery not only for economics but also for all historical sciences – and all branches of science which are not natural sciences are historical sciences.[9]
>
> (Marx 1859, p. 203)

Similarly, Althusser remarked that Marx's theorisation of modes of production and the way they arise, grow and die away is a formidable contribution to scientific knowledge. By virtue of this discovery, he added, Marx laid the foundations of a theory which is the true underpinning of all the sciences relevant to the 'continent of history', not only of history, sociology, human geography, economics, demographics, but also of psychology, 'social psychology', the disciplines generally known as 'social sciences' and, still more generally, all the 'human sciences' (see Althusser 1969 and 1995, p. 23; see, also, Althusser 1972, pp. 50–51). According to Althusser, therefore, the notion of modes of production becomes central to historical materialism and, consequently, of Marxism as a whole (see Therborn 1971, p. 104).[10]

In other words, in Marx's view it is only by monitoring the product relations in which human beings act out their respective roles that we can have a correct appreciation of their essence. And the reason is, men only exist thanks to these relations (see Karsz 1974, p. 187).

While Marx's stance is probably too radical to be shared, one need not be a Marxist or an advocate of the materialistic conception of history to accept the idea that character and psyche are strongly influenced by the relations of production. In the opinion of Fromm (1962, p. 38), the assumption that something as a human nature or the essence of man should actually exist has long been a discredited theory and Karsz, for his part (1974, p. 176), has argued that any attempt at grasping what is termed the 'universal human spirit' entails postulating the most idealistic of categories: human nature. Rawls, too, holds that economic and political institutions determine in part both the sort of persons we want to be and the sort of persons we actually are (Rawls 1971, p. 229).[11]

The influence of institutions on character would seem to justify the argument that one of the main defects of capitalism is its adverse impact on human nature.

With reference to historical materialism, the finding that in capitalistic systems selfishness and greed are specific to a higher social standing is confirmed by numerous psychological surveys. More often than not, the members of the upper classes are seen to be less generous, less altruistic and also less cooperative than lower-class people (see Piff et al. 2012); they are more likely to engage in unethical behaviour, tend to donate a smaller portion of their income to charity and are more likely to cheat. In other words, what is known as 'the bourgeois mentality' is typical of the upper middle class, rather than other classes of society.

The importance that upper-class individuals attach to their position in society indicates that social class reshuffling may lead to changes in attitudes and that more collaborative attitudes are likely to develop in a cooperative system (see Ratner 2013).

As argued by Bataille,

> the factory only knows of forces that may serve its purposes, proletarians, middlemen, accountants or technicians, but ignores the individual whenever possible. Those caught up in the wheels of this system know nothing of meaningful interpersonal communication: a firm is driven on by flameless greed, it employs labour without heart and worships its own growth as the only divinity.
>
> (Bataille 1996, p. 64)

More recently, the economist F. H. Hahn has drawn attention to a stark contrast between the innermost driving force of capitalism and generally recognised ethical values. The Jewish-Christian ethic, he argues, extols virtues such as benevolence and care for our fellow-beings, condemns greed and discourages the accumulation of treasures within this world. In line with this moral code, there is nothing to be admired in individuals who pursue their personal profit rather than sticking to their duties or taking care of their fellow-beings – i.e. in individuals who adopt exactly that kind of behaviour that is expected of people operating in a capitalistic system.[12]

This is the rationale behind my claim that in worker-controlled systems – compared to capitalism – greed would lose clout and benevolence and concern for others would become prominent.[13] Self-management socialism is a system in which firms are run by workers who compete in markets, and today there is general agreement that the primary behavioural principle shaping economic activity in these firms is the aim to maximise the average incomes of their workers.

Although the per-capita income maximisation criterion was rigorously enunciated by Ward no earlier than 1958, it was probably not unknown to cooperative theorists even before. On closer analysis, however, far from being a newly discovered third behavioural principle governing the actions of humans (the other two being selfish individualism and ethical motivation), it is nothing but the application of the utility principle to cooperation economics.

In Keynes's definition (see Keynes 1979, p. 66), self-management is an economic system in which the factors of production are remunerated by dividing the actual product of their joint input into prefixed pro-rata shares. Inasmuch as this is true, workers who *strive to maximise individual utility* in self-managed firms act rationally if they work towards maximising the aggregate income of the firm because this will enable them to maximise both their own and the other members' shares in the residual of the firm.

In other words, the per-capita income maximisation principle teaches that people tend to pursue their personal profit (and denies the thesis that people are by nature altruistic), but within a system of cooperative firms it is turned into a solidarity principle since the specific organisational criteria of such a system determine that the partners striving to increase their own income will, at the same time, add to the incomes of their fellow-partners as well.

Concluding, there is sufficient evidence to suggest that a cooperative firm system tends to breed feelings of solidarity that may counteract selfish drives in man.

The revolt of elites against the backdrop of self-management theory

In a very interesting book, Christopher Lasch theorises the 'revolt of elites' and backs up his thesis with arguments intended to demonstrate that democratic firm management may scale down the tendency to excessive individualism he complains of in the present-day world.

The revolt of the elites is an epoch-making change away from an older, more markedly communitarian world that Lasch claims to have observed in recent years. Ortega y Gasset, he argues (see Lasch 1995, p. 34), used to teach that the traditions of Western culture were jeopardised by the risk of uprisings of the masses; today, the threat seems to come mainly from those at the top of the social hierarchy.

The distinctive trait of contemporary elites is not so much a given ideology, as a style of life. They are a mix of bankers, scientists, publishers, TV producers and directors, university professors and representatives of various business sectors who do not share a common political orientation, but operate within an international context to which they are loyal. Lasch estimates them at about 20% of the world population and holds them to stretch across national borders. Their main concern is securing the smooth working of the system as a whole, rather than is individual parts. As they attend the best universities the world round, they feel at home in a cosmopolitan climate and achieve their very best in team work. Unlike traditional intellectuals, they tend to settle in specialised geographical locations such as Cambridge, Silicon Valley or Hollywood. "The privileged classes in Los Angeles feel much more akin to their Japanese, Korean and Singapore counterparts than their own countrymen" (*idem*, p. 52).

The members of this new class think of themselves as a *self-made élite* owing their privileges exclusively to their own efforts, but "meritocracy is a parody of democracy" (Lasch 1995, p. 47). At first sight, the talented members of the aristocracy might appear rich in attractions, but actually "the talented retain many of the vices of aristocracy without its virtues" (*idem*, p. 50). Due to the ties linking them to the world at large, they are indifferent to what goes on in their own nations. The denationalisation process under way in large-size concerns tends to generate a cosmopolitan class whose members do not feel responsible for the fates of their own home countries.

As for wage and salary earners, in capitalist systems there is a tendency to paint an idealised picture of the working class and to emphasise their chances of becoming well-off thanks to saving. In actual fact, considering that unlike capitalists, slave owners were, if nothing else, responsible for clothing and feeding their slaves, their status can be said to be below a slave's. The faith in upward social mobility or economic growth as the core of the theory of free work is no justification for wage labour.

The role that elites play today is evidence that 'debate began to decline from the beginning of the nineteenth century'. Indeed, the precondition for democracy to survive is vigorous public debate, i.e. putting our ideas on the world to the test of public controversy in an effort to gain a deeper understanding of what we already know. Unfortunately, in the present-day world this aim is unattainable because debate has become 'a lost art'. All such knowledge as every community needs – be it a team of scientific researchers or a political organisation – argues Lasch – can only be generated by dialogue and mutual exchanges of information (op cit., p. 179).

The reflections just reported induced Lasch to argue (1995, pp. 115–16) that any philosophical approach concerned with defining the interests of mankind in the twenty-first century would have to prioritise community interests over the right of individuals to make their private decisions, i.e. that emphasis would have to be laid on responsibilities, rather than rights. The challenge facing us, Lasch wrote, is shaping a community structure capable of outperforming the welfare state and restrict the scope of markets and the power of corporations without replacing them with a centralised State bureaucracy.

According to Lasch, evils such as withering democracy and mounting individualism would be swept away if workers were allowed to run their enterprises on their own. Democratic firm management would once again set off debate and discourage individualism in favour of a communitarian view of life.

In full accord with some eighteen century economists I hold that markets, far from being an evil straightaway, are actually beneficial mechanisms because competition ensures the generation of benefits for the community just as individuals pursue their personal interests. However, for a market to operate as beneficial mechanism it has to be organised in accordance with fully democratic principles. In this connection, it is worth noting that even in a system of democratic firms of the type suggested in this book man-made decisions will be given priority over market-imposed choices, i.e. that the benefits made possible by a democratic market are strictly dependent on the prioritisation of collective human will over the individualistic choices made in markets.

A summary analysis of Social Darwinism

At the beginning I raised the question if Marx's approach was consistent with Darwinism. Before this question is answered, it is necessary to establish if this applies to the Darwinian idea of evolution in nature or to Social Darwinism.

Although the claim that Darwin's evolutionary theory can be extended to economics is now shared by a wealth of evolutionary theorists, including Veblen (see, *inter alia*, Hamilton 1999, pp. 25–28; Hodgson 2003), I feel that the idea of a cumulative causation process assumed to be constantly at work in social life (the specific methodological point of Darwinism that Veblen tends to emphasise) should not be accepted without prior in-depth scrutiny.

Modern-day science, Veblen wrote (1964, p. 21), theorises a process where causes and effects, far from being observed separately in their own right, are, as it were, the links of a chain formed of a continuous sequence of cumulative changes. In all branches of science – he specified (1964, p. 40) – research is invariably conducted as a process or active sequence, in terms that each finding becomes the starting point for the next step, in a cumulative sequence. In this connection, several institutionalists have been found to use cumulative processes in their analyses (among authors holding this view, see Hodgson 2003, pp. 87–90; Miller 2003, pp. 54–55;).

In point of fact, in economic theory a less rigorous cumulative causation process than Myrdal's or Kaldor's is envisaged as a possibility, but not as a general rule.

The core idea behind economic theory is that economic processes tend to move towards stability – the exact opposite of the notion underlying cumulative causation;[14] and while it is true that the importance of circular causation processes should not be underrated, I hold that the equilibrium, rather than cumulative causation view is the correct interpretative approach to economic phenomena.[15]

As mentioned by Hodgson, critics of the idea that economic phenomena unroll like a natural selection process include J. R. Commons, who claims that such evolutionary processes as are observed in the economy are not natural, but artificially induced (see Commons 1924, pp. 376).

A great many authors have emphasised that Darwin did not rule out a measure of intentionality in the selection process, but spelt out in bold letters that any intentions, where assumed, had to be explained (see Copeland 1931, 1936, pp. 343–44; Hodgson 2003, p. 91). Hence, Commons's criticism of Social Darwinism is certainly cogent enough.

The underlying rationale is the belief that socio-economic evolution and biological evolution are governed by altogether different mechanisms (Nisbet

1977, pp. 159–61; Gallino 1987, pp. 215ff; Hodgson 2003, p. 86).[16] Whereas evolution determines the success of the strongest in either case (and in economic selection processes the strongest are usually those who are found to be most efficient), economic events are generally conditioned by the power issue and organised forces can halt the progress of any firm, however efficient.[17]

In this wording, the objection is not aimed at the distinctively Darwinian principle of the survival of the fittest, but at a particular version of Social Darwinism in which economic power is equated with efficiency and the most efficient economic organisations are assumed to prevail in the long run.

At any rate, there are solid reasons for arguing that economic selection mechanisms differ greatly from those that govern natural selection.[18] In economic matters, to say that the strongest tend to prevail is just a tautology and, as such, will hardly add much to our understanding. Things would stand differently if it were possible to say, as social Darwinists mistakenly do, that the best economic performers are also the best organisations.

What, then, is the real bearing of Social Darwinism on a notion such as socialism?

The claim that workers are sure to acquire the right to self-manage their firms at some point in time is doubtless in line with the rationale behind Social Darwinism. Both Marx and Croce were firmly persuaded that the long-term direction of history was one leading to ever greater freedom, while Social Darwinists, though holding that evolution proceeds in a given direction, reject any teleological approaches. Hence there is good ground for assuming that in due time – borrowing the words of Giuseppe Mazzini – workers will "get rid of the wage-yoke" and succeed in managing their firms on their own.

The direction in which evolution is heading has as its starting point the sway of nature over man, the sway of capital over labour as an intermediate step and the liberation of man from the oppressive power of capital as its point of arrival. Inasmuch as it is true that history progresses in a precise direction, there can be little doubt that the economy will be heading towards self-management, a system in which alienation would be significantly lower compared to its level under capitalism (see Jossa 2012b).

As mentioned in Finelli 2007 (p. 128), Marx looked upon capitalism as a reversed world where alienation from labour and the impoverishment of the proletariat cannot exceed a certain level, at which the contradiction between the earning potential of the members of this class and the misery of their current circumstances will become so unbearable as to trigger the re-reversal of the currently inverse capital-labour relation.

The same cannot be said of centralised planning. Planning is hardly reconcilable with markets. The prerequisite for any attempt at reconciliation would be leaving with markets the most important choices – and this would be in stark contradiction with the very nature of planning. Accordingly, inasmuch as the rationale behind planning is substituting centrally made choices for the choices made by individuals, there is no way of justifying it from the perspective of Social Darwinism. After all, it is difficult to see why individuals destined to attain ever more freedom should hand over their freedom of choice to a planning board which disregards the decisions made by the members of society.

Additional notes on the relevance of the selfish gene theory to socialism

The distinction between profit and efficiency will be clearly recognized if we bear in mind that – assuming equal pay rates – profit is determined both by the output per labour unit generated in one hour of work and by the amount of work performed in one hour. And while it is true that the productivity level of the work performed is a good measure of efficiency, they conclude, the amount of work accomplished in a single hour is mainly an indicator of the employer's ability to put in place effective control procedures. Accordingly, if the workers of a cooperative should outperform their capitalist competitors by streamlining production processes more effectively, they would attain higher efficiency levels even though they should resolve to work at a slower pace and put up with lesser profits.

Individuals are often said to be moved on by self-love and love for others, both of which are instincts that further the survival of the species, and capitalism is said to differ from socialism because the former is the outgrowth of self-love and the latter is mainly based on harmonious relationships with our fellow-beings. This view is shared by the known Italian journalist and intellectual Eugenio Scalfari (1995, pp. 836–47), who holds that morals are but a reflection of the instinct for survival of the human species.[19]

However, since advocates of the above-mentioned gene selfishness assumption tend to reject this distinction, it is convenient to follow the line of reasoning of a number of modern biologists who contend that genes are selfish, that the behaviour of all living beings is principally governed by their genes and that the survival instinct is not inherent in the species. These assumptions may justify the contention that, while capitalism is the product of gene selfishness, socialism is typified by a special attention for culture, in addition to instinct, which leads it to prioritise all such organisational forms as may result in a favourable terrain for feelings of solidarity (Rifkin 2009).

The reader is likely to wonder what bearing these reflections have on the claim that socialism can be established by creating a self-managed firm system. The answer seems to be that modern producer cooperative theory (to which the socialism-worker control equation is linked – see, for example, Jossa 2012a, 2014) – is realistic since it does reckon with the selfishness of individuals, whereas a centrally planned system cannot function efficiently because it fails to leverage both the profit motive and cultural interests.

This point needs to be analysed in greater depth.

The claim that selfishness is a connotation of genes, rather than individuals, suggests stating the terms of the problem as follows: inasmuch as the gene selfishness theory is correct and Dawkins and Marx are right in claiming that unselfishness is a child of culture (specifically of interrelations established in the workplace), a system expected to outperform competing ones must simultaneously leverage selfishness and create solidarity relationships between individual producers.

Now then, considering that a system of producer cooperatives apportions corporate surpluses among all the partners of its constituent firms, it meets both these requirements in that it simultaneously leverages the private profit motive and generates feelings of mutual solidarity between the partners. At the other end of the spectrum is a centrally planned system, which disregards the selfish drives of individuals and where individual producers, far from being bound to each other by solidarity, felt hatred for the planning board that monitors their work inputs. On all accounts, to suggest that the awareness that work is being undertaken for the benefit of the community as a whole may breed sufficient worker inputs and inter-worker solidarity is hardly realistic.

In other words, if culture is equated with the social environment and intellectual climate generated by a production mode, the argument that the culture of a centrally planned system with nationalised means of production breeds solidarity and commitment to production activities will barely hold. In Engels's words, "in communist society, where the interests of individuals are not opposed to one another, but, on the contrary, are united, competition is eliminated... Private gain, the aim of the individual to enrich himself on his own, disappears".

If we ask ourselves if Engels's is a realistic scenario, the answer must be that a Soviet-type planning model may play a role in stifling the selfish drives that reign supreme in a capitalist society, but that the selfish gene theory necessitates asking ourselves what breeding ground would be available for nourishing germs capable of fostering solidarity feelings in the population and what feelings might induce individuals to engage in production despite their selfish genes.

Bearing in mind that revolutionary enthusiasm tends to be short-lived, it is difficult to argue that culture, i.e. the desire for interpersonal relationships that culture tends to breed, should justify centralised planning. It is worker control, not planning, that generates solidarity by its very nature and that satisfies the need to entertain harmonious interpersonal relationships.

As is well known, in worker-run firms all the members are equally interested in the efficient management of their firm and decisions are made jointly, often following in-depth discussion and exchanges of opinions. And it is hard to think of anything capable of generating more solidarity than the joint discussion of the means that will best help achieve shared goals.

The idea that association is a means of emancipating workers was shared by John Stuart Mill. If workers are joined into cooperatives (where they become 'their own masters') – he wrote – the productiveness of labour tends to increase thanks to "the vast stimulus given to productive energies" by the awareness of the members that their increased work inputs will boost their incomes, but this material benefit – he added – "is as nothing compared with the moral revolution in society that would accompany it" thanks to the potential of cooperation for furthering "the transformation of human life, from a conflict of classes struggling for opposite interests, to a friendly rivalry in the pursuit of a good common to all, the elevation of the dignity of labour, a new sense of security and independence in the labouring class; and the conversion of each human being's daily occupation into a school of the social sympathies and the practical intelligence". Elsewhere in the same book, Mill described cooperatives as "a course of education in those moral and active qualities by which alone success can be either deserved or attained".

Marshall, too, was persuaded that cooperation "does rest in a great measure on ethical motives" and "has a special charm for those in whose tempers the social element is stronger" (see Marshall 1890, p. 292). The true co-operator, he wrote, "combines a keen business intellect with a spirit full of an earnest faith" and the cooperative movement "makes it its task to develop the spontaneous energies of individuals by educating them to collective action and teaching them to use collective resources for the attainment of shared goals". Although he did not deny affinities between cooperation and other movements, he emphasised that no other movement was as directly aimed to improve the quality of man himself (see Marshall 1889, p. 227); and he put "the production of fine human beings" at the top of the list of the primary goals of this movement (see Marshall 1889, p. 228).[20]

My line of reasoning so far may explain why I strongly disagree with all those Marxists who declare an interest in cooperation, but cling to the view that centralised planning (though not of the Soviet type) is a necessary constituent of socialism. Marx and Engels thought of socialism as a planned system because they were averse to markets and this aversion can quite naturally be traced to their Aristotelian view of man as a social animal. In two fine books, Cornu, who is one of the acutest commentators of Marx, tells us that Feuerbach and Hess thought of economic and social contradictions as generated by an ethical conflict between egoism and altruism (see Cornu 1948, 1955). When Marx dealt with this conflict in the *Introduction* to the *Critique of Hegel's Philosophy of Right* (which dates from 1843) – Cornu argues – he translated it into a social conflict proper and by so doing he turned Communism into a doctrine of action, transferred the social problem to the ethical plain (as Feuerbach had done).

Marx's view of human nature has already been discussed above. Here, it is interesting to note that both his firm choice of communism and his aversion to markets, which account for his advocacy of centralised planning, date back to 1943, his twenty-fifth year of age, and it is a well-known fact that youthful decisions, especially if prompted by strong emotions, tend to remain pervasive influences throughout a man's life.

The same misconception is apparent in Gramsci, a supporter of the Bolshevik Revolution who went to far as to argue that in a socialist society "the average proletarian psychology will quickly lose all the mythological, utopian, religious, petit-bourgeois ideologies: the communist psychology will quickly and permanently be consolidated, constantly roused by revolutionary enthusiasm" (Gramsci 1919–1920, p. 30). In addition to this, he wrote that "it is possible to imagine the coercive element of the State withering away by degrees, as ever more conspicuous elements of regulated society (ethical State or civil society) make their appearance" (Gramsci 1975, vol. II, p. 764).[21] On closer analysis, however, these reflections are not only unrelated to gene selfishness and where they should be brought to bear on issues associated with centralised planning they would have to be supported by evidence (which Gramsci did not provide) that a planned system would actually generate solidarity feelings. Not for nothing his claim was proved utterly wrong by the course of events in the countries organised in keeping with the system known as 'state socialism'.

Conclusion

The main thesis advanced in this chapter is that democratic firm management, one of the two ways to establish socialism, is more consistent with the nature of man as shaped by selfish genes. My second thesis is that democratic firm management is more easily implemented than centralised planning since the retention of markets allows the selfish drives of human beings to act themselves out to the full.

The third is that democratic firm management is a form of socialist revolution that may appear to be in keeping with Darwinian evolutionism.

Notes

1 Although many of Marx's writings bear witness to his concern with producer cooperatives, several commentators have argued that the relevant works are just descriptive in nature and do not reveal Marx's overall evaluation of the real potential of cooperation (see Lowit 1962, p. 79; see, also, Jossa 2005).

2 The distinction between two forms of socialist revolution is in conflict with the following well-known saying by Bernstein (1901, p. 234): "I am singularly uninterested in understanding what people commonly mean by 'the final goal of socialism'. This goal, whatever it may be, means nothing to me; it is the movement itself which is everything".

3 Mazzini rated altruism as a cultural attitude because he looked upon fraternity as the essence of being in an organic community poised to achieve shared aims (Sabattini 2014, p. 51).

4 Rawls (2000, p. 158) has pointed out that Kant, unlike Hume, held that any attempt at identifying this principle "does not proceed as part of a lager science of human nature, but begins analytically by elucidating the underlying principle(s) implicit in our commonsense judgments of moral worth".

5 Marcuse, instead, postulated the existence of an "inborn inclination to solidarity" (see Marcuse 1969, p. 22); and Rifkin (2014, p. 226) wrote:

> Considering the long-espoused idea that a basic trait of humans is selfishness, most economists are likely to rate this as a bewildering thesis. The thought that people may resolve to pursue collective interests of their own accord will

strike most economists as quite unconceivable, and the point they are sure to reject is that solidarity is not a cultural attitude, but inherent in human nature.

6 Concerning Marx's conception of man and, specifically, his reflections on man in the *Theses on Feuerbach*, see Mondolfo 1909; Fromm 1961; Mondolfo 1962, pp. 312 ff.; Markus 1966 and a collection of papers by Schaff and Sève (see Schaff & Sève 1975).

7 Schaff (1971) warns that this version of Marx's text is wrong although it features in quite a lot of French, Italian, Polish, Russian and other translations. The correct translation, he argues, which does appear in a few French and Italian versions (see Marx 1845, pp. 77 ff.), is not "the essence of man (*das menschliche Wesen*) is, in its reality, the ensemble of social relationships", but "*the individual (i.e. the non-abstract 'man')* is, in *his* reality, the ensemble of the social relationships. And while it is true that this version somewhat bends the letter of Marx's text, it is fully consistent with Marx's thought. As argued by Althusser (1965a, pp. 218–19), "if we take this phrase literally ... it means nothing at all" because there is no such thing as a 'human essence', an abstract human being, and in order to trace a real, non-abstract man we have to turn to society."

For a more exhaustive analysis of Marx's view of the essence of man, see Althusser (1965a, pp. 202–6), the *Preface* to Althusser (1965b) and Sève (2004, pp. 111–36).

8 See Marx (1859, p. 5). Nonetheless, it is worth considering that Marx also wrote:

The materialist doctrine concerning the changing of circumstances and up-bringing forgets that circumstances are changed by men and that it is essential to educate the educator himself. This doctrine must, therefore, divide society into two parts, one of which is superior to society.

(See Marx 1845, p. 3)

9 From Orfeo 1970 (p. 271) we learn that Antonio Labriola described the materialistic conception of history as "an effective means of splitting the huge and extremely complex working mechanism of society into its simplest constituent parts."

10 Bloom (1943, p. 5) holds that the notion of society as shaped by its production methods is the climax of Marx's doctrine and Althusser, for his part, emphasised that Marx's theorisation of modes of production marked an epistemological break with the traditional approach to the philosophy of history (see Althusser 1965a, p. 217). For the evolution of the concept of Marxism, see Haupt (1978, pp. 115–45).

11 Authors endorsing this view include Donnaruma and Partyka (2012, p. 50), who stress the significant part that economic structures play in shaping the lives and conditions of people in society (Donnaruma & Partyka 2012, p. 50).

12 An additional major point that will not be entered upon in this paper is Herbert Marcuse's claim that solidarity, though grounded in instinct, is stifled in a society which is based on classes and that the precondition for a climate of solidarity is consequently the suppression of class divisions – a goal that would be attained in a worker-controlled firm system (see Marcuse 1969, p. 22).

13 Gustafsson also has recently emphasised that one of the salient characteristics of capitalism is to prioritise corrective motives and actions, rather than an impulse to cooperation (see Gustafsson 1993, p. XVI).

14 In a well-known 1953 book by Hamilton, cumulative causation and equilibrium are presented as antithetical principles (see Dugger 2003, pp. 65–66).

15 In fact, most institutionalists reject the neo-classical approach to equilibrium as unacceptable (see, for example, Miller 2002, p. 252, 2003, p. 52, as well as Hamilton 2003, pp. 12–14).

16 Authors critical of Social Darwinism include Bowles and Gintis. According to them, this argument misses the point since it fails to distinguish between economic-financial performance and efficiency. In competitive markets – they write (1986, p. 84) – survival is a function of profit, which should not be mistaken for efficiency.

17 Authors critical of Social Darwinism include Bowles and Gintis. According to them, this argument misses the point since it fails to distinguish between economic-financial performance and efficiency. In competitive markets – they write (1986, p. 84) – survival is a function of profit, which should not be mistaken for efficiency.

18 Marx, who was otherwise a great admirer of Darwin, denied the relevance of the Darwinian logic in areas such as history and politics.

19 In a well-known book Singer (1980) provides an exhaustive analysis of the ethical foundations of Marx's theoretical approach and concludes that all Marx's propositions reflect the wish to get rid of a system in which individuals behave selfishly without the least regard to the needs of their fellow-beings.

20 As argued by Vanek (1971a, p. 107), the fact that every week a man spends no fewer than forty of the most active hours of his life in a working environment where conflict is endemic must necessarily have an adverse impact on his whole life (Cornu 1948, pp. 154–55).

21 An additional interesting passage runs as follows:

> Worker solidarity which in the union developed in the struggle against capitalism, in suffering and sacrifice, in the council is positive, is permanent, is made flesh even in the most negligible of moments of industrial production, is contained in the glorious consciousness of being an organic whole, a homogeneous and compact system which, by working usefully and *disinterestedly* producing social wealth, affirms its sovereignty and its power and freedom to create history.
>
> (Gramsci 1919–1920, pp. 36–37; italics added)

9   Schweickart's approach to economic democracy

Introduction

This chapter is intended to revisit ideas I first advanced and further developed in numerous writings (Jossa 1979, 1980, 1981, 1982, 1985, 1986a, 1986b, 1988, 1989a, 1989b, 1990, 1992, 1993, 1994a, 1997, 2004, 2008b, 2016, 2017). Occasionally, my approach to economic democracy may appear to be interchangeable with those of theorists such as David Schweickart and Richard Wolff, but it is different from either of them and, especially, from the model of market socialism with State-controlled investment that Schweickart first theorised back in 1993, re-proposed in a slightly modified version in 2000 (when he further developed elements of an earlier 1980 study) and then fleshed out in its final version in 2002 (Schweickart 2002).

Accordingly, instead of providing a detailed resume of Schweickart's train of reasoning, in this chapter I will principally focus on the points that mark out Schweickart's model from my own.

A workable form of socialism

As Schweickart's model is one in which means of production are publicly owned, doubtless it fits into socialism.[1] Specifically, it is a model of *market socialism* in which the prices of raw materials and capital and consumer goods are largely determined by supply and demand, firms are free to make decisions based on profit calculations, and the residuals they earn are distributed to their worker-partners. Due to the workers' right to run firms freely and exercise their decision powers in line with the 'one person, one vote' principle, it can be described as a model of economic democracy in which income distribution is democratically devised.

The market socialism model I recommend is mainly characterised by worker-owned production means, full autonomy, and democratically managed firms operating in a free market system and socially devised income distribution patterns. To these three aspects Schweickart adds a fourth, State-controlled investment, which is specific to his model and will be addressed in greater detail further on in this chapter.

As the Marxian aspect of Schweickart's model, State-owned means of production, is likely to arouse suspicion in economic liberalists, it is worth spending a few words on it right from the start.

In a system where firms are autonomous and workers can freely 'dispose' of the means of production they use (in terms of being authorised to buy and sell them at their discretion), the 'publicly-owned-production-means' formula is of very little consequence: the only constraint associated with it in Schweickart's model is the obligation of firms to keep the aggregate capital stock intact, i.e. to maintain a depreciation fund (see Schweickart 2002, p. 48).

In particular, the fact that firm ownership titles are vested in society at large has nothing to do with planning, for Schweickart makes it absolutely clear that "centralized planning, the most commonly advocated socialist alternative to market allocation, is inherently flawed, and that schemes for decentralized, non-market planning are unworkable" (Schweickart 2002, p. 49; see, also, Schweickart 1998, p. 10). Hence, the State's ownership of production means constitutes a fairly negligible aspect of Schweickart's model, neither a major merit nor a defect of some consequence.[2] This subject will be dwelt on in greater depth further on.[3]

An additional point worth making preliminarily is that Schweickart's 'basic model' makes no provision for private saving and that State funding of investment can consequently be described as a public service (see below). In partial contrast with the foregoing, this may rather suggest that the State's ownership title in means of production is a major aspect of Schweickart's model: the State appropriates part of the returns on the publicly owned capital goods and uses them to accumulate public savings and investment funding becomes a public service because it is made through the use of public savings. On closer analysis, though, in Schweickart's model publicly owned means of production are not a necessary prerequisite for public investment funding. For this purpose, the public hand uses the fiscal system and the resources needed to fund investments can be raised by taxing private capital.

Although I feel that Schweickart is barely familiar with the vast body of self-management literature, it must be admitted that his analysis of the pros and cons of democratic firm management is, at several points, of absorbing interest. One fault of his approach is his failure to mention the difficulties that labour-managed firms come up against when it comes to raising investment resources, and considering that Schweickart's model is designed to solve exactly this problem, his silence on this point strikes me is all the more surprising.

On other advantages and disadvantages of labour management Schweickart dwells at length and in part with original arguments.

Well-known advantages of labour management such as an inducement to increase work inputs and socially determined income distribution are given adequate attention, while Schweickart's analysis of unemployment in self-managed firms is less exhaustive and, thus, barely conclusive.

As has been made sufficiently clear in the existing body of self-management literature, under certain circumstances unemployment levels tend to be higher in a system of democratically managed firms than in capitalist systems both because democratic firms deem it expedient to adopt more capital-intensive technologies and, above all, because thriving firms often do not respond to price increases by increasing their workforces (see Vanek 1970, chaps 2 and 3; Dubravcic 1970; Meade 1972, 1979; Estrin 1983).

Relevant employment-related aspects of a system of democratically managed firms include (a) the tendency to generate little Keynesian un-employment thanks to the tendency of the partners not to fire each other light-heartedly (see Domar 1966; Berman 1977; Ireland & Law 1981; Stephen 1984; Jossa & Cuomo 1997, pp. 188–207) and, overall, (b) lower unemployment levels made possible by the absence of conventional payroll costs (and, consequently, of high-wage unemployment). In particular, the 'discipline effect' discussed in efficiency wage theory, i.e. the tendency of firms to keep wages high in order to generate a level of unemployment that will lead workers to regard job loss as a great danger, is non-existent in a system of labour-managed firms (see, *inter alia*, Schweickart 1993, pp. 252–53; Jossa 2001, pp. 123–26).

In a review of these aspects, Schweickart emphasises that his model system would literally root out unemployment for two main reasons; on the one hand, because the banking system would be assigned the mission to work towards boosting employment and, on the other, because the State would be called upon to act as 'employer-of-last-resort' (see Schweickart 1993, pp. 110–11, 2002, pp. 135–38).

As far as I can see, the idea to make banks responsible for framing employment-boosting investment policies should be treated with utmost caution because it conflicts with the market orientation that any market so-cialism model should uphold wherever possible or reasonable. Schweickart's proposal is prompted by the fear that a system of democratically managed firms may generate unemployment, but as will be shown below, his model has other economic policy tools that can be used to combat unemployment.

Whereas the State's role as 'employer-of-last-resort' in a system of labour-managed firms is one of the most interesting aspects of Schweickart's model (and has also been theorised by other authors), its principal weak point is the failure to lay down in detail the procedures that the public hand can adopt in exercising tight control over investment for the purpose of ensuring full employment.

This point will now be entered upon in greater depth.

Public investment funding

State-controlled investment is an integral part of the socialist tradition.

In numerous contributions to the debate on economic calculation in socialism, Maurice Dobb drew on Keynes's teachings in describing corporate investment decisions in a market economy as "acts of faith *par excellence*". In-deed, he explained, as managers are usually unaware of the business strategies that other enterprises are putting in place, the decisions they make "are both arbitrary and short-sighted in that they involve the systematic underrating of future needs and, as a result, a tendency towards underinvestment".[4]

> Within a changing and developing environment – he went on to argue – it is not correct to assume consumer preferences as given, for it is impossible to imagine a process of growth which is not accompanied by radical changes in human needs.

And as consumer preferences are determined by society, the growth strategies framed by political decision-makers will influence the ever-changing spectrum of consumer needs: "if this is right, decisions concerning the kinds of goods to be produced are, at least in part, political actions and politicians must not abdicate their responsibilities in decision-making" (see Dobb 1953, pp. 78ff.; see, also, *inter alia*, Kaldor 1972, p. 1240).

Additional relevant details include Dobb's thesis that investment decisions should pursue the dual aim of meeting meet consumer needs and reconciling individual with collective choices and the argument that since "many choices concerning commodities to be produced are 'expert decisions', it is not surprising if the community will rely on planners to make them" (see Dobb 1953, pp. 69–74, e 84–86).

Dobb's thesis that public investment choices are to be tightly monitored is doubtless dictated by the need to flesh out a model suited to address the income distribution issue. Without due governance – he argued – investment resources tend to be channelled to regions where growth is already in progress, driven by the fact that external economies increase *pari passu* with the growth of the region concerned. This is likely to result in unbalanced growth and, what is more, will tend to produce cumulative effects (see Dobb 1953, pp. 65–67, 1956, p. 1122).[5]

Although Schweickart shares the views of Dobb and other economists that investment decisions should not be left to private initiative, his main aims seem to be (a) abolishing capital gains straightaway and (b) creating the assumptions for greater distributive justice by apportioning investment resources more equitably among regions. This is the rationale behind his argument that

> generating the investment fund by taxing enterprise rather than by 'bribing' individuals to save, not only shuts down a major source of capitalist inequality, namely interest payments to private individuals, but frees an economy from its dependence on the 'animal spirits' of savers and investors.
>
> (Schweickart 1998, p. 17)

The benefits associated with the suppression of capital incomes are apparent and need not be entered upon here. In Schweickart's model, they flow directly from State control over investment, i.e. from the fact that firms are funded with State resources.

The second aim Schweickart sets out to pursue, distributive justice, can be achieved thanks to the social criteria that govern the allocation of investment resources and the types of public investment control he envisages. The core idea behind his approach is that the investment fund must be prorated among regions based on their respective population numbers and is justified as follows:

> We observe that it would not be fair simply to return to each region the investment funds collected (via the capital asset tax) from that region, since that amount merely reflects the quantity of capital assets in that region. The fact that one region has a larger capital base than another is not due to the greater effort expended by the people in that region, or to their greater intelligence or moral worth, but to the region's specific history.
> (Schweickart 2002, p. 52)

Even more specifically, the need to prorate investment fund allocations in accordance with principles of equality (the 'fair share' principle) is justified by:

a   the State's task to counteract imbalances originating from the market allocation mechanism;
b   the need to help people stay in their home regions, i.e. where they were born and grew up and
c   the fact that investment and savings are the result of the 'specific history of the region', not of particular virtuous actions of the individuals concerned (abstinence, productive energy, etc.) that society must necessarily value highly.

Specifically, the population-linked apportionment of investment fund resources among regions is justified by a principle that Schweickart doubtless accepts and even mentions in passing, but on which he lays insufficient emphasis: the right of all citizens to the same amount of public services of the same quality level.

This principle is implicit in the wording of Article 3 of the Italian Constitution which states that 'all citizens have equal social dignity and are equal in the eyes of the law' and vests in the Republic the task of 'removing any economic and social obstacles that may limit the citizens' freedom and equality or thwart an individual's potential for full development'. Nowhere, let me add, does the Italian Constitution state that public services must be made available to citizens in proportion to their income levels or the aggregate income of the region in which they live. And this, no less than the very wording of Article 3, can be rated as an implicit assertion of the principle that each citizen is entitled to receive the same amount of similar quality public services (on this subject, see Pica 2000, pp. 133–35).

Investment control and publicly owned means of production

In today's world, innovations such as economic democracy, the apportionment of profits among workers and the 'fair share' principle in investment allocation are enough, in themselves, to arouse interest in Schweickart's proposal.

In Schweickart's model firms are allowed to make investment decisions in their exclusive interests, i.e. based on profit calculations. This entails an inducement to workers to select optimal investment projects and to see to their tasks with utmost efficiency in the awareness that their efforts will help boost both outputs and earnings.

Coming back to the public or private nature of investment, it is clear that in Schweickart's model propensity for saving ceases to be a specific virtue and merit of the individual because it is made compulsory by the government through taxation. At the other end of the spectrum is investment, which is and remains the result of the entrepreneurial skills of business managers. In other words, the pro rata allocation of investment resources cannot be justified on grounds that capital accumulation is neither a difficult nor a meritorious action (for this would mean confounding savings and investment), but only, as suggested before, by arguing that the suggested business funding method is a public service. In the opinion of Schweickart, "since investment funds are publicly, non-privately, generated, their allocation back into the economy is a public, not a private, matter" (Schweickart 2002, p. 50).

On closer analysis, though, it is possible to argue that investment funding becomes a public service when investment resources are apportioned among regions (and thus among firms) in line with social (in lieu of efficiency) criteria: public funding can be categorised as a 'public service' because it is governed by social criteria – much like school, postal or similar services.

At this point it is worth clarifying how the 'investment fund' accumulated by the central government should be allocated and used.

The two most radical options, central planning and the allocation of the entire investment fund to a network of banks operating in line with capitalist criteria, are ruled out because Schweickart is critical of the idea of substituting planning for the working of markets (see Schweickart 1993, p. 72, 2002, pp. 50–51). Hence, Schweickart opts for a system which lies 'between these extremes' (Schweickart 2002, p. 51), i.e. the above-mentioned fair share' criterion providing that public revenues are to be preferably used to fund non-decentralized public services, the lower levels of government and public capital investment. Allocations to firms constitute the second step and are made after the former process has been completed and in line with a variety of different criteria. At the regional level, part of the resources is used to fund regional public services and the remainder is allocated to smaller communities, for instance municipalities, in accordance with the population-linked distribution criterion and used to fund local public services there. The rest is managed by a system of public banks.

In Schweickart's model, banks are non-profit institutions. Representatives of the bank's in-house staff serve on the bank council along with those of the bank's main credit holders and representatives of the community's development planning agency. Moreover, as banks are public institutions, they are instructed to allocate their funds in accordance with democratically devised criteria. Financial performance is just *one* criterion, for banks are also expected to prioritise financing applications from firms committed to employment-boosting business strategies (Schweickart 1993, pp. 74–77, 2002, pp. 53–56).

An additional point to be clarified is the criterion that should govern the apportionment of aggregate resources among banks. In Schweickart's view, the proportion of the aggregate resources to be allocated to each bank should be fixed by reference to the number and dimensions of its corporate credit holders, to the bank's own efficiency level as reflected in bottomline results and, above all, to its track record in allocating funds to firms capable of creating new jobs.

Is per capita allocation an efficient investment fund management method?

This section is intended to examine the pros and cons of State-controlled investment, the aspect which marks out Schweickart's from other models of economic democracy.

Self-financing is doubtless a 'commendable' business policy. Not only is it a clear sign of initiative on the part of the business enterprise concerned, but it bears witness to the firm's determination to cope with competition, seize the opportunities arising in the market and its ability to attract private savings by projecting a positive image of its business projects. Conversely, when investment is publicly funded in a system where firms freely make their decisions and the investment fund is allocated based on criteria other than profit, acquisitions of capital goods remain private business deals which, as such may prove rewarding (or detrimental) to the firms making the relevant investment decisions but are nonetheless made possible by the provision of a public service – State-funding. And the moment business funding is looked upon as a public service, there can be little doubt that the idea of having the investment fund allocated in line with the population-linked criterion becomes fully acceptable: indeed, it is difficult to imagine that the fairness of the principle of taxing accumulated capital in line with proportional criteria or the idea of providing public services to the citizens of a country on an equal basis should be called into question.

As mentioned before, one of the strong points of Schweickart's model is the abolition of capital incomes, but an additional, far from negligible merit to his credit is the demonstration that the method of apportioning investment funds among regions and communities is both rational and fair.

Coming to the issue if the equitable population-linked allocation of the investment fund may ensure efficiency, there is a material risk that some regions or firms might be allotted resources in excess of those they are able to use and that allocations to other regions may fall short of expectations and oblige some firms to renounce profitable investments. To counter this objection, Schweickart makes it clear that all the funds remaining unused because of insufficient investment opportunities would be returned to the central government and redirected to areas where demand is greater.

The risk of losing part of their allocations, he argues, would induce the communities concerned and the banks themselves to devise fresh investment strategies and set up agencies in charge of this specific task. The result would be the establishment of entrepreneurial divisions with the specific mission of creating new firms and strengthening existing ones (see Schweickart 1993, p. 76, 2002, p. 54). Both Schweickart and other authors hold that the successful track record of the Spanish Mondragon group goes to back up this thesis (see Thomas & Logan 1982, p. 49; Schweickart 1993, p. 110).

The principle ruling that the investment fund is to be allotted in accordance with the laws in force, Schweickart adds, "confronts squarely what may be the single most destructive feature of contemporary capitalism: the hypermobility of capital" (Schweickart 1998, p. 108); firstly, it avoids flights of capital from given regions or communities and favours a less unstable kind of growth; secondly, it prevents those in search of jobs from having to move to regions offering greater investment opportunities and, thirdly, it may induce people to engage in local politics in the effort to devise profitable ways of investing the funds allotted to their region or community.

From Schweickart's perspective, the idea that capital mobility makes for efficient resource allocation is just a commonplace of neo-classical theory and an "act of faith" (see Schweickart 1993, pp. 78–88, 2002, p. 64).

Few, if any, orthodox theoreticians will be prepared to subscribe to this radical argument, which Schweickart traces back to externalities and to imperfect information, i.e. lack of the information that would be needed to allocate investment funds in line with rational criteria.

As Schweickart's State-controlled investment system is certainly designed to minimise distributive imbalances between regions, the following reflections are in place.

It is an obvious fact that an alternative option to capital mobility is labour mobility; and in a system of democratically managed firms it is both reasonable and socially expedient to empower the citizens to freely decide if they prefer to stay in their home regions (where return on capital is assumed to be fairly low) or move to areas with higher returns on investment. From the perspective of neo-classical theory, the population-linked apportionment of the investment fund resources among regions is thought to generate allocative inefficiencies. In Italy, for example, investment opportunities are known to be greater in the more developed northern regions than in the South. Assuming return on investment to stand at 20% in the North versus 10% in the South, neo-classical theory teaches that capital resources should be left free to migrate northward for purposes of efficiency and that a ban on capital transfers to areas with higher returns on investment would result in losses for the nation as a whole.

Though probably relevant to a capitalist economy, this objection is barely applicable to a system of worker-run enterprises, where no revenues are earned on capital by simply detaching coupons. In such a system, it is up to workers in the South (where unemployment is likely to be highest) to decide if they prefer to move and set up firms in the North (where return on investment averages 20%) or stay and be satisfied with cashing a meagre 10%.

The unemployment issue

As his model makes provision for levying the investment fund tax on the aggregate capital of business enterprises instead of profits only (viz. not charging it to the account of thriving firms only), Schweickart raises the question if this tax may soar to levels that may result in underinvestment. From the fact that no dividend of interest payments are envisaged in favour of share- or bondholders, he adds, it follows that this is actually a material risks since the investment tax would be comparable to the interest that firms currently pay on borrowed funds (see Schweickart 1993, pp. 71 and 153–54, 2002, p. 54) and would be stepped up or down in the event the resources earmarked for capital accumulation should fall short of, or exceed, demand.

The fact that publicly funded firms are in a position to solve their traditional investment funding problems, i.e. the main obstacle which has so far prevented them from gaining a firm foothold, is a major strong point of Schweickart's model that has been highlighted by more than one author (see, inter alia, Drèze 1989, 1993; Gintis 1989; Gui 1993; Putterman 1993; Mygind 1997; Dow 1998), whereas an additional advantage seems to have been overlooked by Schweickart himself and other theorists.

Assuming that the aim of balancing aggregate demand and supply of goods and services at full plant capacity utilisation should be pursued through the fiscal system as a whole (not – as Schweickart suggests – by taxing accumulated capital resources only), the aggregate fiscal takings, including accumulation fund tax revenues, might be used to equate savings and investments at full plant capacity utilisation and drive up capital growth to levels that may ensure full employment.

In other words, in a socialist market economy the public hand would be called upon to perform two different, though equally basic functions: (a) balancing out aggregate demand and aggregate supply and (b) adjusting the accumulation rate in manners that will ensure full employment (by reducing structural unemployment).

As Schweickart analyses the (a) function only, he simply suggests fixing the investment accumulation tax at the level at which demand for investment resources will equal aggregate public savings. On closer analysis, though, the (b) function is no less fundamental because a government succeeding to make aggregate demand equate aggregate supply by different means would be in a position to pursue a second aim, i.e. driving up growth to levels at which structural unemployment would be cancelled straightaway.

As Schweickart holds State support to be a precondition for preventing rises in unemployment in an economic democracy (see Schweickart 2002, pp. 135–36), at this point it is worth clarifying in what way public action should be used to combat unemployment.

As is well known, unemployment is traced to three main causes (1) high labour costs (classical unemployment); (2) low aggregate demand (Keynesian unemployment) and (3) insufficient accumulation levels (structural unemployment). In an economic democracy, 'classical' unemployment – i.e. loss of jobs caused by wage hikes – is ruled out by definition, but the government is expected to put in place effective economic policy tools geared towards combating both 'Keynesian' and 'structural' unemployment.

Schweickart suggests using the accumulation fund tax to combat Keynesian unemployment,[6] but he fails to specify that the fiscal system can be effectively used to reduce structural unemployment as well. And this is a major shortcoming of his model.

These reflections will now be used as the starting point for a re-examination of the issue of the State as 'employer–of–last–resort'.

One of Schweickart's main aims is to devise a system where those unable to find jobs in the market can be hired by the State; but this solution is likely to arouse much criticism. Instead of acting as 'employer–of–last–resort', the government should rather fight structural unemployment by managing the investment fund in manners that will drive up the country's actual rate of growth to levels corresponding to the level that Harrod termed 'natural'.

Since unemployment is likely to be a major problem in any worker-managed firm system, it is probably worth repeating that Schweickart's failure to analyse the considerable role that investment fund tax can play in combating structural unemployment is doubtless a major fault of his model.

While few, if any, economists will be prepared to accept a State performing the function of an 'employer–of–last–resort' in charge of guaranteeing full employment,[7] the argument that the government should counteract structural unemployment by such an easy move as stepping up the accumulation fund tax is probably much less objectionable.

Schweickart's 'basic' model can be described as genuinely and radically socialist because it cancels capital incomes altogether. Private savings do exist, but they do not bear any interest and investment is funded with public saving. Besides this basic model, however, Schweickart fleshed out an enlarged one in which "it would not be unreasonable to allow a network of profit-oriented, cooperative savings and loan associations to develop" (Schweickart 2002, p. 81).

This prompts the question if an economic democracy is actually required to do without capital incomes altogether.

Holding that "business investment, as opposed to consumer credit, is too important to the overall health of the economy to be left to the vagaries of the market", Schweickart argues that a socialist society should only authorise interest payments on borrowings fitting within the category of consumer credit (*idem*, p. 82).

This point will be discussed in greater detail in the next section.

More criticisms of Schweickart's model

If the organisational structure of a capitalist society is set against innovations such as economic democracy, the distribution of business profits to workers and the *per capita* apportionment of investment resources among regions, economic democracy can be said to amount to a revolution real and proper, but as Schweickart's model is sure to be forcefully opposed by advocates of capitalism, it probably makes sense to abstain from introducing further complications, for instance rules which are either difficult to observe or likely to cause losses of efficiency.

The second mission – combating unemployment – that Schweickart vests in banks and firms has at least one major downside: the risk that institutions expected to adopt two different criteria may end up by making arbitrary lending decisions. In other words, the principle that a bank should provide its funds preferably to profit-making firms is an efficiency criterion that can easily be complied with and will seldom result in discretion or arbitrariness, but its combination with a second selection criterion, providing funds to employment-boosting firms, would open the way for discretionary and even arbitrary credit authorisation practices.

Coming to Schweickart's aim to ensure that "concerns for justice and efficiency are balanced by using a mix of market and non-market criteria" and to introduce the practice "to allocate the centrally collected funds according to a principle of fairness first, and then to bring in competition to promote efficiency" (*idem*, p. 51), it is fair to admit that Schweickart's failure to specify that both banks and business enterprises should work towards efficiency is clear evidence that his original idea was not developed to its ultimate logical consequences.

An additional weak point of Schweickart's model descends from the status of banks as public agencies providing financings at no cost. As far as I can see, the only way to ensure efficiency in a system of worker-directed firms is to extend the self-management model to banks, i.e. to have banks managed democratically and authorise them to operate for profit and distribute their revenues to their partners. On the one hand, this would not conflict with the population-linked investment distribution criterion because following regional allocations the governments of the recipient regions might be authorised to grant their resources to those banks that are prepared to pay the highest interest rates. On the other hand, under this arrangement the banking system would arguably strive to maximise revenues by giving priority to efficiency-maximising firms over employment-boosting ones. More precisely, my objection is that obliging banks to prioritise financing applications from firms adopting employment-boosting strategies is not only far from expedient, but probably redundant, since Schweickart's model does envisage a different tool that the government can put in place to work towards full employment.

To induce enterprises to make efficiency their top priority, the banking system should be instructed to allocate government funds by exclusive reference to the earning potentials, i.e. the prospective revenues of the corporate applicants for funding.

In sum, my objection is that the apportionment of the investment fund resources should be governed by two main criteria: principles of fairness and the need to induce firms to pursue efficiency by all means. But if this objection is rated as cogent, Schweickart's model will have to be changed by authorising banks to use the interest rate as a means of selecting optimal business projects – with the inevitable effect of automatically re-introducing capital incomes, even though only in the banking sector.

On closer analysis, though, when the interest rate is reintroduced as a criterion for the selection of optimal investment projects, principles of fairness will dictate the need to empower savers also to earn interest on government bonds. From my perspective, interest-bearing savings are out of place in a system where savers are mostly capitalists in control of economic activity, but not (or much less so) in a society where business enterprises are run by workers and capitalists have been deprived of all power. After all, a model of society in which the State is empowered to self-finance itself by issuing bonds and using the private savings of its citizens has its perks, in terms of reducing the need for the public hand to raise resources by taxing business capital at disproportionate rates (i.e. by increasing the strains on business enterprises to be point of discouraging new investment).

The risk that the transformation of banks into self-managed firms concerned with maximising profits for their partners might inhibit the flows of financings needed to create new firms has been emphasised in a vast body of literature,[8] However, as this is not the place to dwell on such a complex issue (that Schweickart himself has not addressed), suffice it to mention that the obstacles to firm creation might be reduced through the introduction of *ad hoc* legislation into the legal system concerned.

The changes suggested in this chapter would help solve an additional weakness of Schweickart's model: 'the obligation of firms to keep the aggregate capital stock intact'. As this is a point that Schweickart has failed to expand upon, it is not clear what institutions would be responsible for monitoring compliance with this obligation or by what means the monitoring function might be effectively enforced.[9]

If the corrections suggested above were actually introduced into Schweickart's model, the distinction between investment credit and consumer credit on which Schweickart dwells at considerable length would become redundant, but his model would automatically come in for an additional criticism.

If the main credit authorisation criterion adopted by banks is the interest rate that applicants are willing to pay, firms in regions with higher investment levels will be charged higher interest rates than those in regions with lesser investment opportunities. To prevent the resulting interregional capital flows from subverting the equitable resource allocation process devised by Schweickart, it would be necessary to closely monitor interregional capital transfers and the necessary controls would probably not be easy to put in place or enforce.

The risk that firms in regions with greater investment opportunities might attract capital from other regions by paying interest *under the counter* (i.e. illegally) is, admittedly, far from remote, but on closer analysis the resulting objection can be refuted by emphasising that the need for close controls would also arise in Schweickart's original model (where firms do not pay any interest on the financings received from banks).

The main weakness of Schweickart's original model (with or without the corrections suggested above) is therefore the risk of illegal capital transfers between regions, but the following reflections may help counter this criticism as well.

As socialism is a controlled economy, critics of state control have no option but to espouse economic liberalism. In particular, Schweickart's model will be rejected both by theorists who object to interregional capital transfers and by advocates of market socialism, who are likely to prioritise the model of Ward and Vanek (which does not require control of capital transfers). In point of fact, control of capital transfers has long been a distinctive feature of the Bretton Woods system and is still endorsed by advocates of the Tobin tax today. From my perspective, the latter (who are currently all but few) are sure to reject Schweickart's model regardless of whether they do or do not share the criticisms set forth in this chapter.

As Schweickart's banks are non-profit organisations, their revenues must be entirely and exclusively used to cover operating costs and payroll expenses. Accordingly, in Schweickart's model they are to be allocated by the State according to a formula which links "income to the bank's success in making profit-enhancing grants and creating employment" (Schweickart 2002, p. 54) but is unlikely to work efficiently.

The above-mentioned conversion of banks into self-managed firms would ensure the additional dual advantage of reducing system malfunctions and sweeping away a mechanism which makes for discretionary choices.

Conclusion

The fact that the population-linked investment fund allocation criterion does not conflict with the principles of economic liberalism has been emphasised in my analysis of the apportionment of public savings as a public service.

As far as State control over investment is concerned, its advantages can be summed up as follows:

a   the provision of adequate allocations to firms thanks to the fact that the aggregate amount of the investment resources is unrelated to private utility calculations;
b   a balanced growth model made possible by the fact that the investment fund resources would be allocated in proportion to the number of inhabitants of each region and
c   a potential to combat unemployment for the reasons highlighted above.

In all probability, free market liberals will reject Schweickart's solution to have investment controlled by the State as excessively radical or tainted by statism, but the corrections suggested in this chapter would considerably reduce this defect.

Concluding, Schweickart's model should be attentively explored for two main reasons: firstly, because it is not at odds with the principles of a market economy and, secondly, because it goes to refute the main objection which is usually raised against Ward and Vanek's model.

Concluding, let me repeat that Schweickart's is an interesting model of market socialism which State control over investment, but that the type of State control devised by Schweickart has at least three main weak points.

One is inherent in the public-service function of the investment fund itself. As mentioned above, Schweickart does suggest allocating investment resources based on a population-linked criterion, but he fails to explain why the investment fund resources should be allocated in this manner.

The second aspect of investment control that Schweickart has failed to account for to the full is the asserted potential of the investment fund to ensure full employment. By its very nature, the tax which is levied for the purpose of creating the investment fund is a tool for counteracting structural unemployment and can consequently be used to ensure that the actual rate of growth is permanently brought into line with Harrod's 'natural rate of growth'.

Thirdly, it is possible to argue that firms and banks which are expected to adopt employment-boosting policies will barely be able to pursue maximum efficiency. The only way to remedy this shortcoming is not to require the banking system to allocate lending at no cost (i.e. to authorise the government to levy taxes on the relevant financings) and to turn banks into self-managed firms empowered to operate for profit by charging interest on their financings.

Notes

1   Quoting Dobb, "a treatment of the essence of a socialist economy as being other than the social ownership of means of production would represent a definitive breach with the tradition of socialist thought as this was inherited from the past century" (see Dobb 1969, p. 141; see, also, Roemer 1992, 1994b). For a different opinion, see Mises (1932, 1951, p. 211).

2 This may counter Kornai's argument that market socialism is altogether inconsistent as a system since it claims to reconcile two mutually exclusive elements: the market and publicly owned means of production (see Kornai 1992, p. 50).

3 One main implication of publicly owned means of production is the fact that these resources cannot be bequeathed to heirs. In our opinion, this is in line with the conclusion reached by Roemer when trying to establish whether the equalisation is a means of attaining distributive justice or the outcome of such distributive justice: "it is not difficult to argue that public ownership of the means of production will result in greater equality of all the above equalizanda than private ownership of such means will entail" (Roemer 1992, p. 288).

4 See Dobb (1939a, pp. 253–24); see, also, Dobb (1939b, pp. 41ff, 1953, pp. 74ff).

5 Concerning the traditional debate on public investment control, see, also, *inter alia*, Dickinson (1933, pp. 237 ff.); Napoleoni (1962a, pp. 200–3, 1962b, pp. 479–80); Nuti (1978, pp. 192–95) and Erlich (1978).

6 In Schweickart's view, in a system of economic democracy Keynesian unemployment would be confined to very low levels, since the workers of a firm can barely be assumed to sack one another (see Schweickart 1993, pp. 109–10, 2002, pp. 128–29).

7 For a different opinion, see Aspromourgos (2000).

8 The firm creation issue is analysed in depth in Vanek (1970, chap. 14).

9 In Schweickart's model, bank financings are granted for an indefinite term without repayment of principal. Conversely, in our modified proposal financings are turned into reimbursable bank loans on which the capital tax rate is levied at a rate proportional to the capital of the firm net of its borrowed funds.

10 Richard Wolff's democracy at work; a cure for capitalism

Introduction

The idea that firms should be run by the workers themselves was suggested by Schweickart and myself in numerous writings and is also the main focus point of a book written by Wolff in 2012.

The background against which Wolff develops his analysis is United States politics, described as tainted by illegal party and campaign financing, corporate lobbying and little worker participation. As for the latter, levels were low even before the 1970s but showed a sharply declining trend, especially during the country's neo-liberalist stage. In the opening section of his book Wolff argues that the iniquity of capitalism and its recurrent crises in the years before he wrote his book had induced him to elaborate upon his long-held conviction that production activities gain in efficiency when they are conducted in accordance with democratic and collective criteria and vest sovereign powers in workers. Accordingly, he suggests creating a system of worker-run enterprises (named WSDEs, i.e. workers' self-directed enterprises) discussed against the backdrop of Marx's 'class analysis' and production, appropriation and distribution theory.

Wolff's proposal is designed to offer an alternative option to the interventionist economic strategy that Franklin D. Roosevelt is known to have adopted in his day and that Wolff does not deem to be effectively applicable in the present-day world.

Wolff's WSDE

The model to be set against capitalism in Wolff's approach is a mix of numerous basic components. First and foremost, this model is expected to put an end to the recurrent crises our system is seen to face; secondly, it is aimed to redress the serious inequalities typifying the present-day world scene; thirdly, it is intended to expedite the rise of a corporate organisation model making for a more equitable power structure in the workplace and the community at large. In sum, this new model should further democracy and break up the capitalist class structure that currently enables one part of the population to exploit the subordinate class by using its services. From Wolff's perspective, these goals are attainable because the conversion of existing firms into WSDEs would erase the distinction between capitalists and workers (just as capitalism itself cancelled the distinction between masters and serfs) and vest in each individual the double status of employer and employee (Wolff 2012, p. 13). Structurally speaking, a system of WSDEs would give workers the right to appropriate and distribute the surpluses earned, and hence create the assumptions for the extinction of the State theorised by a number of Marxists (*ibid.*).

According to Wolff, the alternative option to capitalism and to a Soviet-type centrally planned system offered by a system of WSDEs is badly needed since any critique of capitalism that fails to suggest an alternative model capable of doing away with State control of the economy or Soviet-type socialism would lack the strength needed to fire the enthusiasm of the masses and mobilise them into a social movement.

In the new system, he argues, workers would be assigned to two types of tasks. On the one hand, each of them would have to perform a job fitting within the framework of a conventional labour division scheme; on the other, all of them would be entitled to cast votes in the joint decision-making processes designed to frame the business plans of their firms and their surplus apportionment criteria – with the resulting abolition of the one-time distinction between intellectual and manual work, between controllers and those controlled. The workers would be allowed to make collective decisions concerning the production mixes of their respective firms, the required technological solutions, the locations of their production plants, and so forth. Outsiders, i.e. individuals not directly involved in production, would be barred from sitting on the board of a WSDE.

To demonstrate that existing cooperative firms are not equivalent to WSDEs, Wolff makes it clear that solutions possible in the current system, for instance the case of a of a group of farmers collectively purchasing and owning land, hiring farmhands and other personnel and running their business in line with capitalist criteria, would be no options in a system of WSDEs.

From Wolff's perspective, in the existing system workers are ousted from corporate economic-financial decision-making processes, and this explains why many of them refuse involvement in other collective decision processes and oblige the class in power to incur considerable expenditure in resisting union demands. Conversely, the precondition for furthering the transition to the new system is providing subsidies, incentives and technical support to worker-run enterprises.

The way WSDEs work

WSDEs are free to use professional managers, as is the rule in capital-owned enterprises, or opt for different practices, for instance vesting management powers in individual members in rotation.

Provision accounts formed by putting aside prior year surpluses may prove useful in times of crisis or upon the adoption of destaffing policies made possible by the introduction of innovative technological aids. The relevant funds would be administered by an agency in charge of interviewing redundant workers and train selected candidates for vacancies in other firms. It is evident that such a solution would effectively help combat unemployment.

With regard to crises, Wolff argues that workers prepared to help their firms out of financial difficulties by accepting temporary cuts on their earnings would be entitled to greater portions of the firms' post-crisis revenues (p. 159).

In terms of roles in production and title to surplus distributions, the workers of a WSDE fall into two categories. Surplus-producing workers have title to sit on the board of the WSDE and are in charge of the work that goes to fashion the WSDE's output; the other group, 'enablers' in Wolff's definition, is formed of workers providing the ancillary services required for the surplus-producing workers to perform their tasks, i.e. clerical workers, security officers, cleaning staff, receptionists, architects, members of the legal department, etc. In capitalist systems, Wolff argues, this distinction is obliterated because all the workers are treated as wage and salary earners, proletarians or employees.

For a WSDE to work efficiently, these two categories of workers must operate in perfect harmony since all the decisions in matters of surplus generation, appropriation and distribution are to be jointly made. The same principle, i.e. joint democratic decision-making, applies to matters with respect to which the interests of the two groups are likely to diverge, for instance the portion of the surplus to be re-invested in new technological aids. Although surplus appropriation and distribution decisions are the exclusive prerogative of surplus-producing workers (*idem*, p. 129), thanks to the effective collaboration of surplus producers and enabler workers in all decision-making processes the risk that one group of workers may exploit the other group is indeed remote (*idem*, p. 166).

> SDEs are most easily understood as relatively small enterprises [...] where the members of the board of directors can personally know one another, gather in subgroups and reach reasoned consensus on directorial decisions.
>
> (*idem*, p. 160)

Thanks to institutions and mechanisms called upon to frame pro-worker strategies, in the transitional period the establishment of a system of WDEs would strengthen union action and other forms of anti-capitalist protest. "Instead of anxious workers and unions deciding between caving in or calling the capitalist's possible bluff, their alliance with coops and a movement for WESDEs gives those workers and their union a new weapon in their struggle" (*idem*, p. 174).

Ownership rights, markets and planning

In a system of WSDEs, ownership rights may be structured in different ways. Capital goods can either be publicly owned and made available to WSDEs by the State or directly owned by the workers themselves: "Ownership rights might be vested in part in government agencies at various levels and in part in the workers of the WSDEs" (*idem*, p. 142), i.e. partially centralised and decentralised. Examples in point are Yugoslavia and the Mondragon complex. From Wolff's perspective, for workers to play a part in the democratic governance of society they must first secure the expertise and knowledge needed to exercise governance powers in the workplace. Indeed, what prevents them from taking an active interest in the policy-framing processes of capitalist enterprises is just their subordinate role in the workplace.

If WSDEs are to secure the gains in efficiency that will enable them to vie with capital-owned enterprises and finally fend off their competition the workers will have to increase their workouts as much as they can, cut managerial costs (for instance by serving on the board themselves in rotation) and do without dividend distributions. To rate a system of WSDEs as incapable of trouncing the competition of capitalist enterprises would be tantamount to calling into question its viability as an alternative option to capitalism.

Conclusion

This somewhat detailed analysis of Wolff's work is clear evidence that despite interesting comments, his approach is thoroughly indebted to ideas that were developed by Schweickart and myself in books and a considerable body of writings which he fails to quote although they appeared in authoritative scientific magazines.

An additional point which is worth clarifying and on which both Wolff and I myself have failed to provide sufficient focus is the way worker-run firms can be set up.

Instead of hiring workers, paying them fixed wages and salaries and keeping the surplus for himself, a businessman meaning to set up a new enterprise is likely to enter into an agreement with potential workers, negotiate the percent rates of the prospective firm's net revenue to be respectively paid to them and retained by himself and lay down these details in an agreement to be signed by all the parties involved.

At first sight, this procedure might seem to be at odds with the joint decision-making principle applicable to self-managed firms; in point of fact, this is not the case since the detailed breakdown of the prospective revenue distribution scheme to be submitted by the founding member to his prospective partners, where accepted, constitutes the decision jointly made by the founding member and the other partners.

Difficulties are likely to arise when the newly founded enterprise takes on fresh personnel to support its growth. Will the revenue distribution scheme have to be renegotiated every time a new partner enters the firm? It is clear that this is one more difficulty facing self-managed firms.

11 Critical perspectives on self-management theory

Introduction

In the words of a well-known Italian cooperation theorist, it is dangerous, if not fatal, to cling to illusions; considering that workers carrying on business on their own will come up against obstacles as a matter of course, the creation of a producer cooperative system will turn out to be an all but easy undertaking (see Rabbeno 1889, p. 609).

These obstacles are the main subject of a book published by Dow in 2018.

Ever since the formulation of Ward's theory of price determination in co-operatives back in 1958, the efficiency of worker-run enterprises has been called into question by several other authors as well. One objection was raised by Ward himself and has to do with the 'perverse', i.e. downward slope of the supply curve of a cooperative (see Vanek 1970, chap. 3). Initially, his objection was perceived as destructive, but later on the research work of several other theorists, including Domar (1966), Horvat (1975), Meade (1972, pp. 409–10), Berman (1977), Steinherr and Thisse (1979a and 1979b), Sertel (1982), Brewer and Browning (1982), Miyazaki and Neary (1983), Hansmann (1996, pp. 84–85), Jossa and Cuomo (1997, chap. IX), Dow (1993b) and Jossa (1999, 2002, chap. II, 2005b, chaps IV–VI), helped put the issue in its right perspective.

According to Dow, the perverse slope of the labour-managed firm (LMF) cooperative is not caused by worker control, but by the fact that cooperatives face no opportunity costs in respect of external labour (see Dow 1993, p. 992), but surveys conducted by Miyazaki and Neary and Craig and Pencavel (1995) in later years proved it to be empirically negligible. Specifically, these and other authors claimed that the thesis of the declining trend in the supply curve had to be backed up by the demonstration that its downward slope was steeper than that of the demand curve and that this was a cause of instability – a barely realistic conclusion.[1]

An additional objection worth mentioning right from the start is the assumption that workers are hardly eager to become masters in their firms. Togliatti, for instance, described workers as even more inimical to economic democracy than industrialists themselves. When an Italian businessman accepts the takeover of his company by its employees, he wrote, his true aim is turning its shareholders into creditors of the prospective cooperative firm. As soon as he has achieved this goal, he will wash his hands of the firm's management, production, marketing and other business activities. Satisfied with cashing the fixed interest accruing on his credits, he will not spare a single thought for the fate of the industrial sector as a whole" (Togliatti 1920, p. 183). Tornquist, for his part, went so far as to suggest that industrial democracy would set workers free for the exclusive purpose of obliging them to try their hands at the uncongenial role of businessmen striving to maximise profits (see Tornquist 1973, p. 393).

Downsides of democratic firm management include the problem of lodging the collateral needed to back up loans, the underinvestment issue, lack of portfolio diversification opportunities, as well as the monitoring and control issues. As will be shown below, some of these problems can be solved if cooperatives are organised in accordance with the LMF model.

The first of the problems listed above is extensively addressed in the literature (see, for instance, Furubotn & Pejovich 1970, 1973; Vanek 1971a and 1971b; Furubotn 1976, 1980; Jossa & Casavola 1993; Jossa 2005a, chap. VIII). A recurring objection has it that the majority resolutions required for a cooperative to authorise fresh investments tend to cause underinvestment. Considering that exiting partners forfeit their titles in the labour incomes generated by the cooperative, those about to leave the firm for seniority or other reasons will tend to vote against investment resolutions. In point of fact, the prevailing opinion expressed in the published literature on this subject is that underinvestment is the rule in worker-managed-firms (WMFs), but an exception in LMFs. Specifically, it has been found that the limited time horizon problem postulated by the Furubotn-Pejovich effect can be solved by allowing self-financed LMFs to allot their partners bonds in amounts commensurate with the earnings they would have cashed if the surplus had been distributed. When this is the case, exiting members will retain and can freely dispose of the bonds they were allotted upon the passing of the self-financing resolution. The organisational model of an LMF provides that the partners will be jointly liable for the firm's debts as long as they stay with the firm and vests in them claims in the amounts they made available to the cooperative upon the launch of investment projects. Conversely, exiting partners will be relieved of their obligation to third parties without forfeiting their claims against the firm.

The LFM model just described would simultaneously avert the risk (which was faced by State-owned Yugoslav firms) that the partners should "swallow up their firms", i.e. dismantle them, sell capital goods and apportion the proceeds of the sales among themselves (see, *inter alia*, Vanek 1972, pp. 220–21). If the workers are liable for the firm's debts, such a move would expose them to the risk of defaulting on their obligations.

These reflections explain why a cooperative of the type just described would also help solve the above-mentioned diversification issue at least in part. It is well known that risk diversification difficulties are one of the main downsides of self-management. Whereas investors in capital-owned companies are able to diversify their investment portfolios at will, in a cooperative firm system each worker is tied to the single firm for which he works. The firm model suggested in this chapter would enable bondholding partners to diversify their investment portfolios by selling the bonds of their firm to third parties and underwriting bonds of other cooperatives. As this solution is not applicable to WMFs, which self-finance their investments without allotting any bonds, the partners of these firms are unable to diversify the returns on their investments.

An additional point worth discussing is the fact that self-management socialism, i.e. a system of producer cooperatives, has to be democratically established following a majority vote of the population and that a referendum on this issue will obviously be launched only if and when incomes in the country reach levels at which a majority of the population feel they can afford the risks associated with the direct management of firms.

Incidentally speaking, there is good ground for arguing that the partners of a cooperative run lesser risks than the employees of capitalist companies: in situations of overstaffing, they will seldom lose their jobs because their fellow-partners will be reluctant to fire them and, at any rate, because any such resolutions will have to be made either by drawing lots or by holding democratic voting rounds.[2] Let me specify that the cooperatives of the system discussed in this chapter have the right to hire a limited number of wage or salary earners, which means that risk-averse individuals would be in a position to opt for a conventional contract of employment.

As far as the plant monitoring issue is concerned, in a 1972 article Alchian and Demsetz objected that the exiting partners of a WMF would hardly think it in their interests to fund necessary capital goods maintenance expenses. To counter this objection, it is worth bearing in mind that the exiting partners of LMF cooperatives who are allowed to retain the bonds received upon the adoption of self-investment resolutions will, conversely, deem it in their best interests to keep their firms going even after their exit.

The capital goods maintenance issue is inextricably intertwined with the control issue. Jensen and Meckling wrote (1979, p. 487):

> It seems to us unlikely that outside investors would voluntarily entrust their funds to a labour-managed enterprise in which the workers maintained complete control and the investors were allowed to hope that the worker-managers would behave in such a way as to leave something for them.

At first sight, the fact that the worker partners can prevent non-partner financers from exercising any control over the cooperative is a plus point which might induce us to prioritise WMFs over LMFs, but on closer analysis the fact that the exiting partners of an LMF retaining their bonds will find it in their interests to keep the firm going even after their exit necessitates the conclusion that LMFs are the better option.

With regard to the decision-making problem, Jensen and Meckling (1979, pp. 488–89) complained that no theorist had so far come up with a viable suggestion concerning the solution of this issue in cooperatives.

> No one – they wrote – has specified a well-defined set of procedures for solving the decision-making problem within the firm when the preferences of the workers are not all identical. It is usually simply assumed that the workers will have a common set of preferences and that no conflicts will arise in translating these into operational policies at the firm level.

From my perspective, an organisational scheme allowing cooperatives to appoint managers empowered to run the corporate business in utter freedom would not only clear the field of this objection but might put medium-large size cooperatives in a position to head towards a major performance.

In a much-praised 1996 book, Hansmann suggested that collective decision-making costs were by far the main problem facing cooperative firms, but his detailed analysis of this point was restricted to a sample of cooperatives operating in the Western world in his day which did not include any firms fitting within the model fleshed out by modern cooperation theorists. Provided the criteria recommended by contemporary economic theorists are adopted and managers are given full freedom of action, the issue raised by Hansmann will be ruled out by definition.

Obstacles to the establishment of producer cooperatives

Whereas brisk firm creation is a major need both in capitalist systems and in a system of democratic firms (see, for example, Meade 1972, pp. 420–21, 1979, p. 787; Jensen & Meckling 1979, pp. 478–79), there are grounds for arguing that odds at the formation stage of a cooperative by far exceed those faced by the founders of a capital-owned enterprise.

As is well known, a capitalist enterprise is set up when one or more persons of large means resolve to hire personnel on the assumption that the collateral they are able to lodge will help them raise more capital in case of need. A person with capital resources and organisational talents will hardly deem it convenient to found a cooperative and share corporate powers and revenues with others. Such a person is likely to opt for a capitalist firm, in which he will both hold all power and keep all the firm's profits for himself as long as he remains sole owner (see, for example, Ben-Ner 1987; Dow 2003, p. 17; Gunn 2006, p. 346).

Those theorists who emphasise this point also draw attention to the fact that the proposer of a cooperative investment project is not entitled to appropriate all the resulting revenues for two reasons: (a) because he has to share the net earnings from his project with the other partners and (b) because on leaving he will forfeit his claim on the income the firm is likely to earn in future thanks to his initiative.

According to Ben-Ner, a new firm can opt for the cooperative form provided its founding partners meet the following four requirements: they must be able to (a) define both a business concept and the associated action plan; (b) face the risk of losses; (c) raise capital and (d) cover start-up expenses. And the same author made it clear that the odds are against workers (compared to capitalists) in all these areas (Ben-Ner 1987, pp. 289–90).

As suggested by two well-known cooperation theorists,

> as soon as a capitalist raising capital for a profit-oriented business project starts carefully weighing the comparative advantages of different legal forms, he is likely to set up a limited partnership or company, while the establishment of a cooperative will barely enter his estimate of advantages.[3]
>
> (Riguzzi & Porcari 1925, p. 5)

This prompts the obvious conclusion that only persons without financial means or appreciable entrepreneurial talents may think of founding a cooperative.

In point of fact, while there is no denying that the scant propensity of investors to lend capital to property-less operators is a major drawback to the growth of the cooperative movement, it is a fact that most existing LMFs operate at satisfactory levels of efficiency (see Section 7).

The reflections developed above would seem to suggest that a system exclusively composed of democratic firms is barely the ideal solution and that policies for the enforcement of such a system would prove abortive. Advocates of the cooperative ideal will probably be agreed that a better (or probably necessary) solution would be to leave up the formation of small firms (e.g. those with headcounts below 10 or 20) to individual initiative and restrict government aid to firms above a given dimensional threshold.[4] The experience of the Mondragon cooperatives has shown that work relations tend to deteriorate in firms which employ 1,000 members or more (Thomas & Logan 1982, pp. 178–82).

The most authoritative analysis of the obstacles to the creation of new cooperatives is developed in a 1970 book by Vanek. In a chapter on specific drawbacks to the growth of the cooperative movement, Vanek suggested that governments could make up for formation difficulties by building industrial sheds and making them available to cooperatives. Although Vanek's proposal deserves careful consideration, I rather think that an effective solution is offered by a system where efficient small size cooperative firms would be freely competing with capitalist firms and medium-large cooperatives only (considering their classification as 'merit firms'; see, further on, chap. X) would be eligible for tax benefits and subsidised rate loans. Eligibility for tax benefits should obviously be made conditional on the ability of the cooperative to generate 'external economies', i.e. benefits for the community at large. And it goes without saying that many economists, irrespective of political faith, agreed that the criterion of granting benefits to firms that can be categorised as merit firms obeys a pro-competition rationale, rather than a statist one.

The funding difficulties of producer cooperatives

Economists have long been arguing that the severest obstacle to the self-driven growth of an employee-managed firm system in a capitalist economy is the so-called 'collateral dilemma' (Vanek 1970, p. 318): working-class operators without any property of their own are often unable to lodge the collateral that potential providers of funds require as a form of security to back repayment of their loans.

Although this means that producer cooperatives face considerable funding difficulties, it is necessary to distinguish between the obstacles respectively faced by LMFs and WMFs.

As risk taking is a sure sign of the operator's confidence in the success of an enterprise, outside capital providers tend to grant more loan capital to firms that self-finance large portions of their investments. Very often, the interest rates charged increase in an inverse ratio to the self-financed part of a firm's investments. And in line with the 'increased risk principle' theorised in Kalecki 1937 (see, also, Baumol 1953; Stiglitz 1969), the risks taken by owners of firm increase in direct proportion to the part of the firm's investments that is funded with loan capital. As a result, if the firm is an LMF financing its operations solely with loan capital, the risks taken by its members are likely to be maximised since the firm will only obtain loans at fairly high interest rates.

These are the reflections that led Drèze to emphasise (1989, chap. IV, 1993, pp. 257–262) that the risks associated with fixed-rate loan capital in capital-intensive or high-risk cooperatives may greatly erode, if not altogether nullify, the incomes of workers in the event of a downturn in the firm's business.[5] According to Drèze, capital-intensive firms and firms in high-risk business sectors are often compelled to use risk capital and joint-stock companies arose and made rapid headway in capitalist systems exactly because they offered means of effectively solving problems in these two critical situations.

Economic theorists have drawn attention to an additional major point with a distinct bearing on LMFs: if the cooperative is a limited liability firm, its members may venture into particularly risky investments on the assumption that while the success of a risky investment will step up their earnings, in the event of a failure they can leave the firm without honouring their obligations to external providers of funds (see Drèze 1976; Schlicht & Weizsäcker 1977; Gui 1982, 1985; Eswaran & Kotwal 1989, Putterman, Roemer & Silvestre 1998, pp. 886–97; Pittatore & Turati 2000, p. 27). This fear on the part of financers, it is argued, adds to the difficulties that LMFs whose members do not invest their own resources in the firm are seen to face when it comes to borrowing funds to finance their investments.

The question now is, are these objections really as weighty as they may appear at first sight?

Possible solutions to the funding problems of LMFs

Consistently with my reflections in the previous section and with Vanek's approach, before I can proceed to discuss the financing difficulty issue with special focus on LMFs I have to examine the procedures open to LMFS meaning to gain access to credit.

As mentioned in the introduction, an LMF resolving to self-finance its investments can issue bonds for underwriting by its partners.[6] This self-financing case can be broken down into two sub-cases, depending on whether the firm's bonds issues are allotted to the members entirely or in part (in which case the rest is offered to the general public).

Either decision may give rise to conflicts of interests because it requires a majority resolution by the members. In the former sub-case, a conflict is likely to arise over the rate of interest the securities will have to bear: since any increase in the capital income assigned to these securities will produce a pro-rata decrease in the member's labour incomes, there will obviously be differences of opinion between those wishing to remunerate the bonds with a greater or lesser part of the firm's revenues and over the proportion of the global issuance to be allotted to the members. The partners wishing to increase the firm's investments are likely to prioritise self-financing, while others might be altogether averse to self-financing or wish to minimise the self-financed proportion and maximise the surplus available for distribution.

On closer analysis, however, although these conflicts of interests are material enough, they are far from insurmountable obstacles to the viability of an LMF issuing bonds for member financing.

Providing more effective security to external financers would greatly further the self-financing practice. One method is to establish the rule that interest on the members' bonds is to be paid out only after external loans have been remunerated. As a result of this rule, the bonds issued by democratic firms would fall into two categories: (a) internal bonds, i.e. bonds for distribution to the members issued at the direction of the manager or by a majority resolution of the members and (b) external bonds, i.e. bonds for subscription by third parties in general (external financers and members). And preference rights would only attach to those bonds that are freely offered to the general public (see Cuomo 2003).

In Chapters 6 and 9, I have provided evidence that there are sound reasons for arguing that self-managed firms should be owned by the State as the ultimate obligor for their debts. Indeed, as lenders would derive formidable security from such an arrangement, it is often argued that an all-cooperatives system is only conceivable on condition that the firms concerned are declared to be state property.

Equity financing

An additional point to be discussed preliminarily is whether the members of worker-run firm facing financing difficulties should or should not be authorised to issue voting and/or non-voting equities. In this connection, it is worth specifying right from the start that the precondition for equity issues to prove a reasonable solution is fixing the proportion of the firm's profits to be allotted to them right upon their issuance.

Voting-equity financing is the rule in the mixed worker and capital controlled system of cooperative firms theorised by Meade (1989). However, although this mixed solution was doubtless devised with intent to tackle the funding issue, Meade's is not a system of worker control proper. Moreover, as a cooperative, issuing voting equities tends to be gradually turned into a capitalist firm, the best solution is to restrict the analysis to models of employee-controlled firms that do not adopt this form of member financing.[7]

Turning to the case of a cooperative resolving to issue non-voting equities or variable rate bonds (see, *inter alia*, Nutzinger 1975, p. 181; Drèze 1976, pp. 1133–35; Mc Cain 1977, p. 365; Vanek 1977a, pp. 226–28; Jay 1980; Gui 1982, p. 267; Thomas 1990, pp. 17ff; Thomas & Defournay 1990; Major 1996; Waldmann & Smith 1999), it is worth clarifying that this option is not at odds with the logic behind self-management, albeit in its strictest or narrowest form: just as profit-sharing agreements with workers are occasionally used in capitalist systems, so income-sharing agreements with capitalists should be an option in a system of self-managed firms.

Non-voting equities are fully in line with Drèze's approach to the funding issue, namely his proposal that firms should enter into 'financing agreements' that would transfer all risks from the firm's partners to its financers. In this connection, Drèze (1989, 1993) draws attention to 'implicit contract theory', i.e. the finding that the workers of capital-owned enterprises (who are barely prepared to share risks with capitalists) can be said to enter into tacit contracts entailing acceptance of lower wages in exchange for the employer's commitment not to reduce wage levels in periods of crisis (i.e. in exchange for the fact that it is employers that run the relevant risks). If workers under capitalism deem it in their interests to renounce part of their earnings in order to self-insure themselves against the risk of fluctuations in their incomes – Drèze contends – the same should be applicable to a labour-managed economy, where workers might find it expedient to change their variable incomes into fixed incomes by executing contracts with providers of funds and thus transferring business risks onto capitalists.[8]

However, as this proposal may sound exceedingly radical, it is probably expedient to approach the problem from a different viewpoint and to state that a LMF experiencing funding problems should be authorised to issue non-voting equities.

The issuance of non-voting equities is a case in which incentives for members and incentives for outside capital providers might turn out to be mutually exclusive. The members of a cooperative raising funds by issuing non-voting equities or quasi-shares may resolve to launch investment projects designed to make work more agreeable without generating any appreciable monetary gains. Possible options include in-house crèche and kindergarten facilities, workplace embellishments, new machinery to alleviate work, and so forth (see, *inter alia*, Waldmann & Smith 1999, p. 247; Nuti 2000, pp. 95–96) but also investments aimed to safeguard employment levels within the firm. Secondly, the members might decide to conceal the returns on their investment and use them to finance new investment projects instead of making them available for distribution (see Wolfstetter, Brown & Meran 1984; Waldmann & Smith 1999, p. 267).

To minimise the first of these risks, Major suggests including the value of fringe benefits in the residual used as a basis to calculate the yield of the bonds (see Major 1996, p. 557); to avert problems altogether, others recommend linking the yields of the quasi-shares to the industry-wide index (see Waldmann & Smith 1999). However, in either case it is fair to admit that the solution proposed would neither be easy to implement, nor effectively outweigh this risk.

Opponents of the non-voting-equity financing hypothesis draw attention to the risk of conflicts of interests between simple working members and workers who are also financers. Examples in point are particularly risky high-income projects which might jeopardise the firm's current employment levels or financial performance. Under such circumstances, worker-members financing the firm can be assumed to be voting for the investment in contrast to simple working members, and the result would be investments that one or the other member category does not deem in its best interests.[9]

Addressing the case of variable-income securities entirely and exclusively allotted to the members of the firm, Hansmann pointed to an additional potential risk: the conflicts of interests that are likely to arise between owners of greater or lesser stakes in the firm when it comes to passing the resolution needed to fix the capital income / labour income distribution ratio (see Hansmann 1996, p. 90).

The option of variable-income non-voting-equity financing is often held to be open to the additional objection that LMF securities would have no market if the members were free to resolve not to pay any dividends on them and their outside capital suppliers were prevented from reversing such a resolution. On closer analysis, however, the suggestion that the proportion of the firm's profits to be allotted to such equities should be fixed right upon the issuance of the securities (see above) goes to refute this objection.

One further problem requires proper consideration at this point: once the workers have resolved to assign part of the cooperative's income to equity owners, they will quite naturally tend to take a further step forward in this process, in terms of issuing voting equities to apportion business risks and corporate control functions between themselves and their financers. The problems stemming from such a decision have been highlighted by more than one authors. To confine the firm's risk profile within socially optimal levels, risk capital providers might require some control over the firm's management; and as there can be little doubt that the workers' determination to attract risk capital would induce them to grant financers a certain measure of control, the resulting external control over an LMF would impair the democratic nature of its management and thereby set off a piecemeal return to capitalism (see

Gintis 1989; Bowles & Gintis 1993, p. 35; Drèze 1993, pp. 257–62; Putterman 1993; Putterman, Roemer & Silvestre 1998, pp. 886–87; Dow 2003).

In conclusion, this weighty counterargument seems to suggest that this financing mode is not the ideal solution.[10]

Non-distributable reserves

An issue to be examined in depth at this point is the risk that a cooperative which self-finances itself as mentioned above, i.e. by allotting to its partners bonds in the aggregate value of its undivided profits, would find it more difficult to obtain external financings than one allocating all its profits to the non-distributable reserve.

Inter alia, non-distributable reserves are useful when it comes to providing security to external financers. This is why it is worth raising the question if cooperative which self-finances itself by allotting bonds to its partners and leaving its non-distributable reserves intact would continue to reap the benefits that cooperatives draw from such reserves.

This question might be answered positively if the bonds were declared to be non-transferable. On closer analysis, though, since it would be unreasonable to allot bonds to outsiders, this option will only apply to situations in which the partners are not planning to leave the firm.

Hence, a cooperative has two options: (a) restricting the allotment of its non-transferable bonds to the period the partners continue to stay with the firm or (b) allocating part of its profits to the non-distributable reserve.

Coming to an additional function performed by this kind of reserve, it is widely held that workers today shy from running cooperatives because they do not want to accept variable incomes in place of fixed wages and salaries. Insofar as this is true, to get around this problem a cooperative may use its non-distributable reserves to cover the outlays needed to pay the partners a minimum fixed pay rate and, hence, ensure more stable incomes.

As is obvious, this solution will prove workable so long as the firm continues to operate at a profit, but as downturns in business can barely be ruled out, to avert risks of bankruptcy and, simultaneously, guarantee fixed minimum worker incomes the cooperative will have to keep the aggregate amount of its non-distributable reserves at levels which will allow it to cover its fixed personnel costs even in times of crisis.

This specific situation is governed by section 254ter of the new Italian Civil Code, which rules that "non-distributable reserves may be used to cover losses only after the provisions allocated for capitalisation purposes or allotment to the partners upon the dissolution of the firm have been entirely used."

Risk diversification in democratically managed firms

Today, portfolio diversification is a means of hedging against uncertainties associated with stakes in enterprises carrying on particularly high-risk business activities. Shares are one way to achieve this end. In a capitalist system, investors entitled to residual claims on the profits of a company may diversify their investment portfolios by purchasing equities of companies with different risk profiles. The same is not true of a system of democratic firms, where a worker living on the residual of his firm is bound to that particular firm and cannot diversify his labour investment by working simultaneously for more than one firm.

On closer analysis, though, a very simple institutional measure would enable the partners of democratic firms to participate in the lives and business activities of more than one firm at least indirectly: a number of cooperatives might join to form a 'second-level cooperative', i.e. a firm whose members are not individuals, but cooperative firms themselves.[11]

The member cooperatives would staff the second-level firm with part of their own working members and would receive shares of the second-level cooperative's income in proportion to the number and qualifications of the workers seconded to it by each of them. Moreover, to spread risks the second-level cooperative's revenues would have to be distributed to the affiliates.

The funding methods of the second-level cooperative would be the same as those of its first-level affiliates, but the resulting pyramid of firms would reduce funding difficulties since the affiliates would finance the second-level cooperative either with direct capital contributions or with loans backed up by collateral lodged by it. A second-level cooperative negotiating a financing agreement would act in the name and for the account of the whole group and the resulting business differentiation within the group would reduce both the aggregate risks of the group and those taken by the financers of the second-level cooperative's individual investment projects.

Thanks to these second-level cooperatives, ordinary LMF-type firms resolving to venture into high-risk business activities or launching large-scale manufacturing projects which would otherwise be outside their reach would automatically have access to a risk-spreading mechanism comparable to the portfolio diversification strategies available to investors in capitalist countries.

An additional question worth examining is why existing cooperatives are mostly the WMF-type. One explanation is that financing difficulties are highest at the start-up stage, i.e. when the newly-founded firm has as yet not acquired any fixed assets or accumulated resources that can be lodged as collateral to raise outside loan capital. The only way out of such a situation is opting for the establishment of a WMF, a firm which uses the greater part of its earnings for self-financing purposes and which is all but easily turned into an LMF at a later stage.

Further reflections on the financing difficulties of LMFs

As the voting equity hypothesis has been ruled out in Section 5 above, it remains to decide if an LMF which opts for bond financing will necessarily have to face shortage of funds.

Vis-à-vis financers of limited companies, providers of funds to democratic firms face the considerable disadvantage of being unable to choose between shares of bonds. However, provided democratic firms are shown to be less risk-prone than capital-owned enterprises this disadvantage would be offset by a lower risk profile.

An additional major advantage is associated with the fact that (theoretical model) cooperatives remunerate loan capital prior to labour. From this, it follows that financers of LMFs face lesser risks than providers of funds to limited companies in which labour is to be remunerated prior to capital. In capital-owned enterprises, workers receive their wages and/or salaries month after month, as production activities progress, whereas loan capital is remunerated at longer intervals of time and risk capital only appropriates the residual. At the other end of the spectrum are cooperatives, in which the cooperative's partners rank last in terms of remuneration.[12] As a result, loans granted to cooperative firms are, in this respect, safer than loans to public limited companies;[13] and this goes to refute the assumption that cooperatives face particularly serious difficulties when it comes to raising investment funds.[14]

A comparative analysis of limited liability companies with large-size cooperatives will show that this conclusion is not at odds with my initial argument that cooperatives do face funding difficulties when the greater part of their partners does not own property that can be offered as collateral to potential providers of funds. Considering that the former companies are liable to creditors only for the value of their investments, this more than counterweighs the alleged disadvantage associated with the fact that most of the partners of cooperative firms are usually property-less.

Let me emphasise that the reflections developed so far tend to endorse the view that cooperatives do not face particularly serious funding difficulties. Further on, this preliminary conclusion will be backed up by analyses of competition, insolvency risks and ownership structure, as well as by notes on risk diversification options and Schweickart's interesting proposal to apportion available savings among LMFs. The first three of these points will be dealt with in the next chapters, while the last two are addressed below in this chapter.

Notes

1 Craig and Pencavel's survey of cooperatives in the US plywood industry – probably the best analysis of the behaviour of the supply curves in cooperative firms – provides evidence that these curves are, admittedly, less sensitive to price variations in cooperatives than they tend to be in capitalist enterprises, but hardly ever show the 'perverse' slope attributed to them by Dow.

2 In point of fact, this conclusion has been called into question by quite a lot of theror ists. According to Cole, for instance, a worker-run enterprise "will have leaders, discipline and authority in a fuller and more real sense than these can exist under the industrial autocracy of capitalism" (1920, p. 51).

3 The assumption that start-up capital raising problems are by far the main barrier to firm creation is confirmed by the history of the cooperative movement and endorsed by numerous economic theorists (*inter alia*, Cole 1953, vol. I, chaps XIV and XXIV, vol. II, chap V and IX; as well as Putterman 1982, pp. 150–51; Zangheri et al. 1987; Gunn 2006, p. 35).

4 This idea is shared by Schweickart (2005), who suggested that a sector of small-size capitalist firms is a necessary prerequisite for the proper working of a socialist system both at the initial stage and, probably, throughout its lifespan.

5 Quoting Drèze (1993, p. 254), the funding issue is "central to understanding why labor management does not spread in capitalist economies".

6 Come scrive Pérotin (2006, p. 298), "not having access to capital market or to cheap bank finance, cooperative founders may need each other for funding and collateral, as suggested by Walras (1865)".

7 Meade's proposal is analysed in depth in Cuomo 2010, chap. VII.

8 Dréze himself used the words "paradoxical" and "surprising" to describe his conclusion that the workers of an LMF can indifferently opt for either a financial agreement or a labour agreement. In the former case they would fix the dividends owed to financers in given circumstances; in the latter, they would define their own workloads and wage rates in the same situations (see Drèze 1989, pp. 92–93, 1993, p. 260). In a perfect-competition environment both these agreements would ensure the same results. In a situation of uncertainty and imperfect markets, the actuals-versus-budget balance would be charged to financers in one case and to workers in the other.

9 Unlike other conflicts of interests, "this is not a conflict between principal and agent, but one opposing principal to principal" (Nuti 1997, p. 135).

10 Major obstacles stand in the way of equity financing in Eastern European countries: firstly, banks seldom provide loans to investors wishing to buy securities without having the necessary cash on hand; secondly, given the scarce bottom-line results of firms and their resulting inability to distribute dividends, it would take years before any returns on such investments can be expected to accrue (see Kalmi 2000, pp. 6–7). All the same, workers in those countries have traditionally practised equity investing.

11 This idea is based on the experience of the Spanish 'Mondragon' group and was suggested to me by Gaetano Cuomo (see, also, Smith & Ye 1987; Gunn 2011, p. 325).

12 A different case is that of Italian cooperatives, whose members are hired workers. Based on Law no. 142/2001, the workers' wage claims are classed as priority claims and are consequently to be settled prior to any others (on this point, see Reito 2008).

13 "The residually remunerated resource suppliers can be thought of as 'insuring' the suppliers of resources for some of their risks" (Zafiris 1986, p. 37).

14 In addition to or instead of lodging collateral, the firm might allow outside capital providers to inspect its operations and accounting records (see Bonin & Putterman 1987, pp. 63–64).

12 Marxist criticisms of democratic firm management

Introduction

The idea that 'those who work in the mills should own them' – that is to say that firms should be run by the workers on their own – was suggested, among others, by the greatest social thinker of the twentieth century, John Dewey, but was shared by Marxists such as Anton Pannekoek, Karl Korsch, Angelo Tasca, Antonio Gramsci, Richard Wolff and Ernesto Screpanti, as well as by socialists including Pierre Proudhon, John Stuart Mill, Karl Polanyi and G.D.H. Cole – to mention just a few.

Ever since John Stuart Mill described a cooperative firm system as "the nearest approach to social justice and the most beneficial ordering of industrial affairs for the universal good which it is possible at present to foresee" (Mill 1871, p. 792), economic theorists have concerned themselves closely with worker control of firms and have offered convincing evidence that such a system would not only work efficiently but would even ensure appreciable improvements over capitalism.

Hence, it is possible to endorse both Sartre's claim that such obviously democratic institutions as workers' committees may act as "the founding stones of the future socialist society" (see Sartre 1960, p. 29) and Landauer's description of a cooperative firm system as "the first true step towards a strong stand against capitalism" (quoted in Candela 2014, p. 210).

The Italian patriot Giuseppe Mazzini put the matter in this way: Acquiring title in the fruits of our labour is the goal that lies ahead, and as the combination of capital and productive work in the same hands will result in immense advantages not only for workers, but for society at large, it is our duty to work towards its attainment (Mazzini 1862, p. 233). R. Tawney, for his part, maintained that the preconditions for attaining full freedom are absence of repression and, most importantly, opportunities for self-advancement through the extension of representative institutions to industry (see Tawney 1918, p. 103). In sync with both of them, Marcovic emphasised that no theoretical approach could be rated as truly radical or revolutionary unless it was designed to create conditions under which producers in association would be able to freely dispose of the output of their work (Marcovic 1969, p. 143).[1]

In the January 1970 issue of the *Manifesto mensile* Lucio Magri wrote that workers' councils, though certainly an integral component of Marxist revolutionary theory, had never been materially established since the times were never thought to be ripe for such a move, but that a fresh impetus in this direction was the prerequisite for dismantling the obstacles standing in the way of the emergence of a revolutionary bloc (see Magri 1970, p. 72).

The proposal to have workers run business enterprises on their own is closely associated with the dramatic crisis of capitalism today, with the collapse of the Soviet-type centralised planning model and, even more generally, with the crisis of statism and the evident decline of kingship.

In this connection, Bobbio argued that

> the leading actors in political affairs are invariably groups, i.e. organisations such as associations, unions of various trades and professions, as well as political parties propounding a gamut of different ideologies». Consequently – he concluded – «it is groups, rather than individuals, that loom large in the political agenda of a democratic society without a king.
> (for this argument of Bobbio's, see Bolaffi 2002, p. 156)

The belief that a system of producer cooperatives gives rise to a new mode of production goes hand in hand with the assumption that a well-organised system of this kind ensures effective control of production without interfering with free market mechanisms and is true to the traditional socialist and Marxist vision notwithstanding its market orientation.

A preliminary question to be raised at this point is why market-oriented cooperatives should be analysed against the background of Marxian theory – an approach which I rate as essential and therefore adopted in previous studies as well (see Jossa 2012a, 2014, 2015).[2]

From the perspective of those who think that Marx's revolution in social science is comparable to Copernicus' revolution in astronomy (Plechanov 1911, p. 2), that Marxist thought «will never die» (Gramsci 1917, p. 43) or that it takes a revolution to change the current mode of production, cross-references to Marxian thought are not only necessary but constitute the sole mode of scholarly reflection that any social scientist is expected to adopt.

In this connection, Wright Mills went so far as to contend that no one could think of himself as a modern social thinker if he failed to come to terms with Marx's theoretical approach (see Wright Mills 1962, p. 7), and Bloom remarked that "each great cultural era of the globe seems to be fated to live through an absorbing and usually bitter controversy over the merits and relevance of the doctrines of Karl Marx" (1943, p. 53).[3]

The question arising at this point is: what is socialism?

Before I attempt to answer this question, let me specify that ever since the close of the nineteenth century the ongoing debate over the comparative merits of capitalism versus socialism has always revolved around a form of socialism typified by centralised planning. It is common knowledge that Marx and Engels strongly argued against Bakuninism on account of its failure to acknowledge the State and abstentionism in politics. The call for the suppression of the State – Engels wrote to Cafiero in 1871 – is an old slogan we used to spout as young men, but it would be stupid to include it in our programme for the International (see Engels 1871).

Pareto is one of many academics who emphasised the statist strain running beneath the socialist ideas circulating in Europe. The extent to which this is true is confirmed by his own and Hayek's later argument that any scientific approach to socialism requires a comparative analysis of two antithetical systems, namely free competition versus state-controlled production.

It is well known that Marx always consistently refused to concern himself with what he termed 'the cook-shops of the future'. In Wright Mills 1962 (p. 90), for instance, we read that Marx thought it beyond our power to predict with certainty what the post-capitalist society would be like and that he dismissed detailed scenarios of this future as nothing but the mental constructs of utopians and dreamers. Just as Marx hated indulging in daydreams, Wright Mills concluded, so he shrank from going into details about the future.

Although this goes to rule out any conflicts between Marx's approach and the claim that socialism is democratic firm control, rather than statism or social democracy, Marxists tend to be cynical about the prospects of creating a system of worker-controlled firms – the main focus point of this chapter.

Early Marxist criticisms of democratic firm management

The Marxist Tronti thought of self-management as part of the ideology of extreme left-wing socialists and old-style communists (see Tronti 1978, p. 292); Fraenkel dismissed it as a form of reactionary romanticism (see Fraenkel 1972, p. 80),[4] Bettelheim remarked that passages from Marx which acknowledge the major potential of cooperation had been consigned to oblivion, and Adler described workers' councils as the 'forsaken children' of the working class (see Adler 1974, p. 246).[5] Some authors flatly deny that the transfer of corporate management powers from capitalists to workers would amount to a revolution proper. According to Sweezy, for instance, to assume that a free market system with state-owned production means and firms run by non-capitalists constitutes a socialist order is to mistake legal relations for production relations, because a system where firms are run by groups of workers set on maximising profits by manufacturing goods and placing them on the market is a near proxy for capitalistic production relations (see Sweezy 1968).

In my estimation, it is principally the market and private profit orientation of cooperative firms that accounts for the non-supportive attitude of Marxists towards such a system.[6] On this point, Sen has argued that right to this day most Marxists and socialists have refused to accept the idea that being generically against markets is "as odd as being generically against conversation" (Sen 1999, p. 12).[7] In fact, this attitude is also in stark conflict with

Lenin's call for a socialist system capable of making the most of "personal incentive, personal interest and business principles" (Lenin 1921, p. 44) and his idea that socialism cannot do without actions designed to promote competition "between practical organisers from among workers and peasants" (Lenin 1919, p. 393).

Hence, the querelle between Marxists and theorists equating socialism with a system of democratic firms operating in a market environment calls to mind the criticisms that Marxists used to level against Kautsky's and Bernstein's tendency to approach Marxism from the narrow perspective of their democratic-liberal views in politics and evolutionary worldviews (see Matthias 1957, p. 58).

In part, the tepid attitude of Marxists towards cooperation can also be explained as follows.

It is well known that the natural relation between work implements and workers is capsized in capitalism: it is the human body that has to adapt to such implements and not vice versa, as would be natural. On closer analysis, however, it is worth noting that the re-reversal of the capsized capital-labour relationship that democratic firm management is expected to trigger would actually oblige society to retrace, as it were, its steps and to re-adopt the organisational model of pre-capitalistic times. Moreover, having regard to Marx's denial of a «human nature in general» (he believed that human nature changes incessantly over time), in strictly scientific terms it is impossible to contend that the re-reversed capital-labour relationship would be consistent with human nature. In the words of Fineschi:

> If something as the essence of man did exist and if it were appropriate to read the 'natural' work process from such a perspective, the only way to eradicate estrangement would be restoring this process to its proper status, that is to say re-reversing the capsized subject-object relation typical of the capitalistic working mode and, in essence, reverting to individual work, the 'natural' process. But this is not what Marx had in mind.
>
> (Fineschi 2006, p. 101)

To refute this objection, let me stress – in contrast with Marx's more mature approach – that a human nature in general does exist, though it tends to change over time. A quote from Marx's *Economic-Philosophical Manuscripts of 1844* is clear evidence that the younger Marx did not deny the existence of a human nature in general:

> Industry – he wrote – is the actual, historical relationship of nature, and therefore of natural science, to man. If, therefore, industry is conceived as the exoteric revelation of man's essential powers, we also gain an understanding of the human essence of nature, or the *natural essence of man*.
>
> (Marx 1844a, p. 121; italics added)

Similarly, in the *Grundrisse* (vol. II, p. 123) we read that man originally appears "as a *species-being* (*Gattungswesen*), *clan-being, herd animal*", and even in Marx's more mature works, from which the idea of a general human nature has disappeared, we still perceive a persistent element of naturalism: man is no ape.

Leaving aside the issue of Marx's actual thought for the moment, there is no denying that a modern Marxist may well claim that a general human nature does exist, though it changes in accordance with the prevailing production mode. Today – let this be repeated – a man is a man and, as such, different from his ape ancestor.

Specifically, anyone denying the existence of a general human nature may nonetheless believe that within a democratic firm system such typical evils of capitalism as estrangement and alienation would at the very least be alleviated. And there can be little doubt that abating alienation is the precondition for realizing human nature to the full. Although Marx formulated his alienation theory in the *Economic-Philosophical Manuscripts of 1844*, that is to say when he did believe in the existence of a general human nature, nowhere in that work did he claim that the precondition for eradicating alienation was restoring the appropriate work process by re-reversing the capsized capital-labour relationship typical of capitalism. As Marx thought that alienation was to be blamed on markets, there are grounds for arguing that the principal factor accounting for the lukewarm support of Marxists for cooperatives is the market orientation of these firms.

In point of fact, behind the unenthusiastic attitude of Marxists towards cooperation we also perceive a political factor associated with the Bolshevik revolution: the widespread belief, throughout the past century, that the essence of socialism lay in Soviet-type centralised planning and the resulting strong stand of Marxists against anyone daring to suggest a different view of the new social order. This may explain why the idea of cooperatives as the cells of a new mode of production and the 'third road' away from capitalism and central planning was widely shared until the advent of fascism and Nazism, whereas following the turbulent Thirties and World War II cooperation lost the support of communist parties and developed into a reformist movement principally endorsed by socialists, Catholics or Protestants inimical to the idea of overthrowing capitalism.[8]

A different explanation for the critical attitude of a great many Marxists towards the idea of democratic firm management as an alternative mode of production is suggested in a book that Walras published in 1865.

Analysing the cooperative firms existing in his day (i.e. Marx's lifetime) in connection with the three sources of wealth considered in economic theory, land, capital and labour, Walras argued that as people strive to secure ever greater amounts of all three types of wealth, they will in due time become owners of estates combining land and capital with the use of labour. In Walras's view, this meant that economic progress could be defined as the road towards a piecemeal, though ever more effective access of every individual to all these categories of wealth and, specifically, as the ultimate path of workers to the ownership of capital (see Walras 1865, p. 14).[9]

This is why Walras emphasised two salient characteristics of cooperatives:

a   in terms of scope, a tendency to create venture capital which is jointly owned by all the members and is therefore indivisible; and
b   in terms of the source of such resources, the fact that this venture capital is accumulated thanks to systematic wage deductions (see Walras, op. cit., pp. 5–6).

In conclusion, Walras defined cooperation as a tool enabling workers to acquire capital through saving (see Walras, op. cit., p. 7).

Walras's own and comparable approaches gained wide acceptance and remained the received opinion for many years to come. In 1947, during the proceedings of the Italian Constituent Assembly the economist Dominedò extolled cooperation as a movement which would pool capital and labour in the same hands (see Constituent Assembly, Proceedings, p. 4000).

Walras's analysis sheds light on still another factor explaining the tepid concern of Marxists with cooperation, and as his line of reasoning is an excellent resume of the views of cooperation in his own and Marx's time, it helps explain why Marx borrowed from Mill the description of cooperatives as firms in which workers were 'their own capitalists'.

To clear the field of this objection, it is worth stressing the far-reaching distinction between labour-managed firm (LMF) and worker-managed firm (WMF) cooperatives introduced by more recent economic cooperation theorists. As LMFs fund their investments solely with loan capital, while WMFs use retained earnings for this purpose, in a system of LMFs the capsized capital-labour relationship is indeed re-reversed, and workers using loan capital do not fit within Mill's characterisation as people who become 'their own capitalists'.

In the estimation of Valerio Castronovo (1987, p. 513), the cooperative movement was always more sensitive to the teachings of Mazzini than those of Marx. For this reason, he argued, supporters of cooperation "prioritised the prospect of pooling capital and labour in the same hands and gave little attention to issues such as class struggle or the emancipation of the proletariat through revolution". From this, he deduced that communists never rated cooperation as a suitable tool for changing society or cooperative firms as the cells of a new economic order expected to operate independently of the mechanisms of capitalism.

However, as soon as it is made clear that a system of genuine LMF-type cooperatives triggers the reversal of the existing relationship between capital and labour, the close links between cooperation and the principles of class struggle and the role that cooperatives may play as the cells of a potentially new social order will appear palpably clear.[10]

Further Marxist criticisms of democratic firm management

Marxists critical of cooperation include those who share Marx and Engels's belief that a system of producer cooperatives was bound to give rise to a form of socialism with conservative or bourgeois traits.

This view appears to be implied in the following passage from the *Manifesto of the Communist Party* (1848, p. 513):

> We may cite Proudhon's *Philosophie de la Misère* as an example of this form. The Socialistic bourgeois want all the advantages of modern social conditions without the struggle and dangers necessarily resulting therefrom. They desire the existing state of society, minus its revolutionary and disintegrating elements. They wish for a bourgeoisie without a proletariat. The bourgeoisie naturally conceives the world in which it is supreme to be the best; and bourgeois socialism develops this comfortable conception into various more or less complete systems.

With reference to this passage, it is worth raising two questions, i.e. whether a worker-controlled firm system is a social order in which the bourgeoisie can exist without the proletariat or the proletariat without the bourgeoisie and whether this passage from the *Manifesto* can be read as a critique of the capitalistic essence of a system of producer cooperatives.

Provided it is true that the distinct characteristics of bourgeois society are capitalistic production relations and a dominant class of masters who own production means, keep workers in subjection and think of «the world ruled by them» as bound to last forever, as soon as it is made clear that the social order created by a cooperative firm system is one where capitalists are stripped of all power, both these questions can be answered in the negative.

The view to which we take exception may seem to be supported by the reflection that the traditional confrontation between competing bourgeois capitalists and mutually supportive workers will draw to an end in the post-revolutionary order, thanks to the fact that the new order will have to be founded on the traditional solidarity relations binding worker to worker, rather than the competitive climate in which capitalists typically operate.

Although this idea is widely shared by Marxists and accounts for their belief that the society to rise from the ashes of capitalism will be founded on organised collective actions, rather than mercantile competition, I do not rate it as fully convincing since the direct effects of the re-reversal of the capsized capital-labour relationship will be an end to capitalism and worker exploitation and, hence, the establishment of a full-fledged socialist order.

At any rate, the opinion to which I take exception may explain why Beatrice Webb, Rodbertus and Bernstein described cooperation as an intermediate form between capitalism and socialism and flatly denied its socialist essence (see Bernstein 1899, pp. 154–55).

In support of my point it is possible to argue that all but few Marxists are fully aware that the precondition for overthrowing capitalism is solving the conflict between capital and labour, rather than the plan-market opposition – as will be explained in more detail in Chapter 8. "To list as the primary factor [...] not class relations but market relations is due... to an error in principle", Bettelheim wrote, because it shifts focus on side-issues and diverts our attention away from the crucial factor: the existence of a class, the 'bourgeoisie', which is inimical to worker power (see Bettelheim 1969; see, also, *inter alia*, Marek 1982, p. 75).[11]

My point is backed up by a wealth of passages from Marx's works, including some of those quoted above. A relevant excerpt from *Capital* runs as follows:

> Capitalist production has itself brought it about that the work of supervision is readily available, quite independent of the ownership of capital. It has therefore become superfluous for this work of supervision to be performed by the capitalist. A musical conductor need in no way be the owner of the instruments in his orchestra, nor does it form part of his function as a conductor that he should have any part in paying the 'wages' of other musicians. Cooperative factories provide the proof that the capitalist has become just as superfluous as a functionary in production as he himself, from his superior vantage-point, finds the large landlord.[12]
>
> (Marx 1894, p. 511)

One more factor explaining the tepid attitude of Marxists towards cooperation is the belief that taking a strong stand against capitalists would not take us very far. Since the system will continue to be governed by the laws of capital as long as capital exists, it is argued, the need to battle for the abolition of capital takes precedence over the need to strip means of production from the hands of their capitalist owners. The extent to which this argument is misleading has been made clear by the reflections developed above.[13]

To account for the negative attitude of Marxists towards cooperation it is also worth considering that after the collapse of the Paris Commune, Marx lost all interest in cooperatives – probably due to the long string of failures the cooperative movement experienced from the mid-seventies of the nineteenth century onward. Indeed, as Marxism has always been described as a form of 'scientific socialism', i.e. a theoretical approach which does not 'preach' the advent of communism, but predicts it as a necessary development,[14] it should not come as a surprise that firms which have not proved able to head towards a major performance are not rated as capable of ushering in communism.

"The cooperative form, Kautsky wrote, can ... only be implemented sporadically and imperfectly and will never become the prevailing form" (Kautsky 1892b, p. 109).

A comparable line of reasoning is developed in a paper by the well-known Italian Marxist thinker E. Leone. The awareness that existing cooperatives were offering positive proof that the capital–labour antagonism could be transcended by turning profit-driven enterprises into firms working towards the advancement of society, he argues, induced Marx to support the cooperative firms in which workers were becoming "their own capitalists», but when, in the 1860s and 1870s, the movement experienced a dramatic string of failures, he resolved to theorise a different transition scenario" (see Leone 1902, p. 287).

Still another explanation for the half-hearted support that cooperation draws from Marxists is the opposition of trade unions to modes of worker protection other than union action.

The idea that trade unions are reluctant to accept democratic firm management was strongly emphasised by Gramsci. According to this author, «trade unionism is evidently nothing but a reflection of capitalist society, not a potential means of transcending capitalist society. It organises workers, not as producers, but as wage-earners, that is as creations of the capitalist system of private property, as sellers of their labour power» (Gramsci 1919–1920, p. 45). Joining together labourers who are active in one and the same trade or industrial sector, use the same tools and give shape to comparable materials – Gramsci wrote (1919–1920) – trade or industry unions prevent labourers from thinking of themselves as producers and make them feel 'commodities' to be priced in accordance with the competition mechanisms prevailing in national or world markets. Accordingly, while Councils are revolutionary entities prepared to endorse the struggle between opposed classes by their very nature, the bureaucratic apparatuses of trade unions strive to stop the class struggle from being unleashed (see Gramsci 1919–1920, p. 133).[15]

Comparable reflections are developed in the *Prison Notebooks*, where trade unionism is described as a child of liberalism, rather than Marxism (see Gramsci 1975, *passim*).[16]

As is well known, few Marxists are prepared to endorse Gramsci's emphasis on the need for 'spontaneous' protests from subaltern classes or his warning that underrating or, worse still, despising such 'spontaneous' movements could have serious consequences in terms of preventing the relevant energies from being put in the service of superior political goals. Not for nothing, Gramsci emphasised, 'spontaneous' movements of the subaltern classes have usually been countered by a reactionary backlash of the Right, the dominant class (see Gramsci 1951, p. 58).

The defence of 'spontaneity' implies endorsing the council movement in the awareness that its ultimate aim is inducing discontented workers to go on strike and battle for higher wages until the masters have no way out but to give their firms over to the workers.[17]

An additional explanation for the critical attitude of Marxists towards co-operation is implied in Oskar Negt's argument that, as workers progress from utter misery and direct oppression to more tolerable conditions, they become more and more willing to accept plans that are palmed off as miraculous solutions to the evils of the world, but are actually nothing but fake social reforms (see Negt 1978, pp. 110–11).

The scant attention that pro–cooperation passages in Marx's works have so far received from Marxists can also be traced to the circumstance that the paper in which Ward made the first attempt to flesh out a full-fledged theory of producer cooperatives was published no earlier than 1958. Until the mid-1970s, it was almost exclusively philosophers that used to concern themselves with Marxist theory. In this connection, Vanek himself (1971a and 1971b) argued that the scant success of the cooperative movement was to be partly blamed on the fact that the creation of a theory of producer cooperatives entered the research agenda of economists comparatively late.

This reflection takes us back to what are probably the two main explanations for the scant attention of Marxists for the cooperative movement: on the one hand, the already mentioned poor record of performance of the movement and, on the other, and perhaps even more importantly, Lenin's argument (as reported in Vacca 1972, p. 162) that Marxism changes and develops at every single step in the advancement of science. With respect to the latter, let me remark that the findings of cooperation theorists highlighted in the literature throughout the fifty and more years since the appearance of Ward's 1958 article and, specifically, the improvements over capitalists afforded by democratic firm management must necessarily affect our understanding of Marxism.

In the light of these reflections, it is possible to argue that the half-hearted support of contemporary Marxists for democratic firm control can be principally blamed on the misinterpretation of Marxism caused by the fact that the version of Marxism that was vulgarised throughout the twentieth century, though marred by conceptual distortions, was officialised irrespective of the dissent of the academic world (Sève 2004, p. 156).

Until 1914, it was the German Social-Democrats that dictated to the world their own, supposedly orthodox approach to Marxist theory. Subsequently, this was replaced by an even more oppressive version of Marxism which the Russians imposed during the period of Soviet hegemony.[18] Later still, the line separating what is truly Marxist from what is not was increasingly blurred. Today, a popular catchphrase runs that Marxism may come in a thousand different versions, but a measure of intolerance is nonetheless seen to persist.

For the sake of completeness, let me mention that Hayek puts part of the blame for the non-supportive attitude of Marxists towards cooperatives on 'intellectuals' of sorts, i.e. on journalists, teachers, artists, actors and other people who are not major scientists, but have made it their profession to popularise ideas (see Hayek 2009, p. 44). More often than not, he argues, these people are not particularly intelligent and have but second-hand knowledge of scientific advancements, but as they are masters in the exposition of a wide array of issues they are able to influence and even shape the public sentiment. Whether or not, and in what way, we shall ever learn of the results of the work of the expert and the original thinker – he concludes – depends mainly on the decisions of all those popularisers of ideas who pass themselves off as 'intellectuals'.

In Hayek's view, these new categories of self-styled 'intellectuals' are an absolute novelty in history, and while it is true that no one looks back with regret to the times when knowledge was the exclusive domain of the affluent classes of society, it is a fact that the transfer of culture from more to less educated groups has far-reaching consequences in terms of the way public opinion is being moulded (op. cit., p. 45).

If this is a correct description of the role of 'intellectuals', it is possible to argue that due to their inadequate cultural backgrounds they have helped circulate an idea which is unsupported by Marx's own writings and was scientifically refuted during the socialist calculation debate of the 1930s: the belief that the centrally planned system established in the Soviet Union had satisfactorily translated all socialist ideals into practice and that this justified consigning to oblivion all revolutionary ambitions.

Peter Marcuse's approach to producer cooperatives

In an article published in the *Monthly Review* in 2015, Peter Marcuse accurately describes the impulse to socialism that may come from a system of producer cooperatives. His line of reasoning deserves a comment.

"!Co-ops in production» or worker-owned enterprises, he argues, are «desirable experimental improvements over standard capitalist practices» which «work in the direction of social welfare» and can be described as «models of socialism within capitalist society» illustrating «politically practicable steps along the road to… a possible alternative society." Although cooperatives have limitations that must be recognised, he argues, their potential is far from exhausted.

In sum, cooperative firms play a positive role because their very existence in capitalistic systems is proof that workers are in a position to run factories by themselves, that democracy in the workplace is possible, and that capitalists are not necessary for the organization of production.

According to Marx, socialism was a radical alternative to capitalistic society whose organisational forms could come in a variety of different forms depending on the context prevailing from time to time. From Mill's perspective, the partners of a cooperative become their own capitalists, take the place of the latter and, consequently, provide ample proof that modern society can do without capitalists. Cooperatives are expected to work towards increasing the well-being of their workers and, consequently, to abate alienation. As a result, their role in today's society is strictly dependent on, and commensurate with, the degree to which they are actually able to achieve the improvements mentioned above.

In this connection, P. Marcuse quotes a passage from *Capital*:

> From Peter Marcuse's perspective, cooperatives can operate effectively in just a few sectors, for instance education, health care, municipal services and the arts, which he rates as exceptions which are "constantly under threat because of the expansion of destructive privatisation processes".

This reflection, combined with Marx's argument that worker co-ops operating in a profit-driven capitalistic market economy could not conduct business independently of that economy, leads him to emphasise their unquestionable limitations and to describe cooperatives operating in capitalistic systems as 'insulated and small defensive towers in a landscape not changed by their presence'.

In his opinion, however, these limitations may produce two antithetical effects. On the one hand, they may generate the impetus required to look forward and attempt to bring about wide-ranging changes; on the other, it cannot be ruled out that the effort entailed in setting up cooperatives intended to vie with capital-managed businesses and the frustration associated with this effort may undermine, rather than increase, the chances for a system change and 'easily pre-empt the impetus to try to expand in more radical directions'.

Further on, P. Marcuse mentions Marx's recommendation that cooperatives were to abstain from relying on state aid in the competitive race against their capitalistic rivals. Such a behaviour, Marx argued, would only provide evidence of the workers' inability to rise to the challenge of change.

Further on in his analysis, Peter Marcuse warns that compared to Marx's day the conditions under which the establishment of cooperatives was expected to generate benefits for society as a whole had greatly worsened. In particular, he argued,

- globalisation, automation and information technology stand in the way of the achievement of radical changes;
- capitalists have acquired even more power;
- the media have become even more influential, and as they are controlled by the masters the role of ideologies is also on the rise;
- thanks to their access to more efficient welfare services, workers are now less hostile to capitalism and there is a growing concern with purely intellectual well-being; and
- the role of the State in the maintenance of the *status quo* has increased.

These changes, he writes, seem to contradict the enthusiastic support that Marx gave to cooperation when the Paris Commune seemed about to supplant capitalism. The memory of the failure of this plan, he argues, is still vivid in the minds of people.

Lastly, he adds that cooperatives are unable to play an appreciable role in combating the escalating influence of finance in today's world.

Summing up the role of cooperatives at the present day, Peter Marcuse argues that «cooperatives are still important as models for alternative modes of production capable of operating in a world without capitalists», but that it is fair to admit that they cannot go much beyond the increasingly limited, if still absolutely vital, role allowed to them within the existing the mode of production.

Conclusion

1. The idea that "those who work in the mills should own them" – that is to say that firms should be run by the workers on their own – was suggested, among others, by the greatest social thinker of the twentieth century, John Dewey, but was shared by Marxists such as Anton Pannekoek, Karl Korsch, Angelo Tasca, Antonio Gramsci, Richard Wolff and Ernesto Screpanti, as well as by socialists including Pierre Proudhon, John Stuart Mill, Karl Polanyi and G.D.H. Cole – to mention just a few.

Ever since John Stuart Mill described a cooperative firm system as "the nearest approach to social justice" and "the most beneficial ordering of industrial affairs for the universal good which it is possible at present to foresee" (Mill 1871, p. 792), economic theorists have concerned themselves closely with worker control of firms and have offered convincing evidence that such a system would not only work efficiently but would even ensure appreciable improvements over capitalism.

Hence, it is possible to endorse both Sartre's claim that such obviously democratic institutions as workers' committees may act as "the founding stones of the future socialist society" (see Sartre 1960, p. 29) and Landauer's description of a cooperative firm system as "the first true step towards a strong stand against capitalism" (quoted in Candela 2014, p. 210).

The Italian patriot Giuseppe Mazzini put the matter in this way: "Acquiring title in the fruits of our labour is the goal that lies ahead", and as "the combination of capital and productive work in the same hands will result in immense advantages not only for workers, but for society at large, it is our duty to work towards its attainment" (Mazzini 1862, p. 233). R. Tawney, for his part, maintained that the preconditions for attaining full freedom are absence of repression and, most importantly, opportunities for self-advancement through the extension of representative institutions to industry (see Tawney 1918, p. 103). In sync with both of them, Marcovic emphasised that no theoretical approach could be rated as truly radical or revolutionary unless it was designed to create conditions under which producers in association would be able to freely dispose of the output of their work (Marcovic 1969, p. 143).[19]

In a paper of 1970 Lucio Magri wrote that workers' councils, though certainly an integral component of Marxist revolutionary theory, had never been materially established since the times were never thought to be ripe for such a move, but that a fresh impetus in this direction was the prerequisite for dismantling the obstacles standing in the way of the emergence of a revolutionary bloc (see Magri 1970, p. 72).

The proposal to have workers run business enterprises on their own is closely associated with the dramatic crisis of capitalism today, with the collapse of the Soviet-type centralised planning model and, even more generally, with the crisis of statism and the evident decline of kingship.

In this connection, Bobbio argued that "the leading actors in political affairs are invariably groups, i.e. organisations such as associations, unions of various trades and professions, as well as political parties propounding a gamut of different ideologies". Consequently – he concluded – "it is groups, rather than individuals, that loom large in the political agenda of a democratic society without a king" (for this argument of Bobbio's, see Bolaffi 2002, p. 156).

The belief that a system of producer cooperatives gives rise to a new mode of production goes hand in hand with the assumption that a well organised system of this kind ensures effective control of production without interfering with free market mechanisms and is true to the traditional socialist and Marxist vision notwithstanding its market orientation.

A preliminary question to be raised at this point is why market-oriented cooperatives should be analysed against the background of Marxian theory – an approach which I rate as essential and therefore adopted in previous studies as well (see Jossa 2012c, 2014, 2015).[20]

From the perspective of those who think that Marx's revolution in social science is comparable to Copernicus' revolution in astronomy (Plechanov 1911, p. 2), that Marxist thought "will never die" (Gramsci 1917, p. 43) or that it takes a revolution to change the current mode of production, cross-references to Marxian thought are not only necessary, but constitute the sole mode of scholarly reflection that any social scientist is expected to adopt.

In this connection, Wright Mills went so far as to contend that no one could think of himself as a modern social thinker if he failed to come to terms with Marx's theoretical approach (see Wright Mills 1962, p. 7), and Bloom remarked that "each great cultural era of the globe seems to be fated to live through an absorbing and usually bitter controversy over the merits and relevance of the doctrines of Karl Marx" (1943, p. 53).[21]

The question arising at this point is: what is socialism?

Before I attempt to answer this question, let me specify that ever since the close of the nineteenth century the ongoing debate over the comparative merits of capitalism versus socialism has always revolved around a form of socialism typified by centralised planning. It is common knowledge that Marx and Engels strongly argued against Bakuninism on account of its failure to acknowledge the State and abstentionism in politics. The call for the suppression of the State – Engels wrote to Cafiero in 1871 – is an old slogan we used to spout as young men, but it would be stupid to include it in our programme for the International (see Engels 1871).

Pareto is one of many academics who emphasised the statist strain running beneath the socialist ideas circulating in Europe. The extent to which this is true is confirmed by his own and Hayek's later argument that any scientific approach to socialism requires a comparative analysis of two antithetical systems, namely free competition versus state-controlled production.

It is well known that Marx always consistently refused to concern himself with what he termed "the cook-shops of the future". In Wright Mills 1962 (p. 90), for instance, we read that Marx thought it beyond our power to predict with certainty what the post-capitalist society would be like and that he dismissed detailed scenarios of this future as nothing but the mental constructs of utopians and dreamers. Just as Marx hated indulging in day-dreams, Wright Mills concluded, so he shrank from going into details about the future.

Although this goes to rule out any conflicts between Marx's approach and the claim that socialism is democratic firm control, rather than statism or social democracy, Marxists tend to be cynical about the prospects of creating a system of worker-controlled firms.

2. For all its major advantages self-management socialism has usually received less attention than it would have deserved. What the reasons accounting for the half-hearted attitude of Marxists towards democratic management?

Marxists are dubious to recognise the importance of cooperation economics because of their strong aversion to markets.[22] This refers us back to the question if Marx and Engels opposed markets to the point of discouraging their retention even during the transition to communism.

Engels believed that the true focus point of volume one of *Capital* was not capitalism proper, but just a pre-capitalist commodity production method. In fact, this view is proved wrong by the Introduction to the *Grundrisse*, where we read that following a review of Hegel's *Logic* Marx dropped his initial plan to commence his exposition with a description of commodities production in a pre-capitalist society and resolved to start with an analysis of capitalism. This was made clear by Bidet in a comparative analysis of the *Grundrisse* and *Capital*, which showed that the distinction between a market economy and a capitalist system emerged much more clearly from the former than the latter. And although this did not justify any direct conclusions about the role of markets in a post-capitalist economy, Bidet concluded, it doubtless rendered "the prospect of basing socialism on the abolition of the market less self-evident" (Bidet 2001, p. 377; see, also, Petrucciani & Russo 2010, p. 12). In fact, nowhere did Marx or Engels ever claim that the instant abolition of markets was a necessary precondition for the success of a revolution.

To account for the unenthusiastic support that cooperatives draw from Marxist is it worth bearing in mind that after the collapse of the Paris Commune, from the mid-seventies of the nineteenth century onward, the cooperative movement experienced a long string of failures. And as Marxism is a form of 'scientific socialism', a theoretical approach which does not 'preach' the advent of communism, but predicts it as a necessary development, it comes as no surprise that firms which had failed to make a success of their business were not rated as capable of ushering in communism. The cooperative form, Kautsky wrote, can only be implemented sporadically and imperfectly and will never become the prevailing form (Kautsky 1892b, p. 109).

The unenthusiastic attitude of Marxists towards cooperation can also be blamed on a political factor associated with the Bolshevik revolution: the widespread belief, throughout the past century, that the essence of socialism lay in Soviet-type centralised planning and the resulting strong stand of Marxists against anyone daring to suggest a different view of the new social order. This may explain why the idea of cooperatives as the cells of a new mode of production and the 'third road' away from capitalism and central planning was widely shared until the advent of Fascism and Nazism, whereas following the turbulent Thirties and World War II cooperation lost the support of communist parties and developed into a reformist movement principally endorsed by socialists, Catholics or Protestants, inimical to the idea of overthrowing capitalism.[23]

An additional explanation for the half-hearted support cooperation draws from Marxists is offered by Fineschi, who draws attention to the fact that in capitalist systems the natural relation between work implements and workers is capsized: it is the human body that has to adapt to such implements and not vice versa, as would be natural. On closer analysis, however, it is worth noting that the re-reversal of the capsized capital-labour relationship expected to be triggered by democratic firm management would actually oblige society to retrace, as it were, its steps and re-adopt the pre-capitalist organisational model. Moreover, having regard to Marx's denial of a 'human nature in general', in strictly scientific terms there is nothing to support the contention that the re-reversed capital-labour relationship would be consistent with human nature. In the words of Fineschi:

> If something as the essence of man did exist and if it were appropriate to read the 'natural' work process from such a perspective, the only way to eradicate estrangement would be restoring this process to its proper status, that is to say re-reversing the capsized subject-object relation typical of the capitalist working mode and, in essence, reverting to individual work, the 'natural' process. But this is not what Marx had in mind.
>
> (Fineschi 2006, p. 101)

To refute this objection, let me emphasise (in departure from Marx's maturer approach) that a human nature in general does exist, though it tends to change over time. A quote from the *Economic-Philosophical Manuscripts of 1844* is clear evidence that the younger Marx did not deny the existence of a human nature in general:

> Industry – he wrote – is the actual, historical relationship of nature, and therefore of natural science, to man. If, therefore, industry is conceived as the exoteric revelation of man's essential powers, we also gain an understanding of the human essence of nature, or the *natural essence of man*.
>
> (Marx 1844, p. 121)

Similarly, in the *Grundrisse* (Marx 1857–1858, p. 121) we read that man originally appears "*as a species-being (Gattungswesen), clan-being, herd animal*" and even in Marx's maturer works, from which the idea of a general human nature has disappeared, we still perceive a persistent element of naturalism: man is no ape.

Leaving Marx's actual thought out of account, there can be little doubt that nothing can prevent a modern Marxist from claiming that a general human nature does exist, though it changes in accordance with the prevailing production mode. Today a man is a man and, as such, different from his ape ancestor.

Specifically, anyone denying the existence of a general human nature may nonetheless believe that within a democratic firm system such typical evils of capitalism as estrangement and alienation would at the very least be alleviated. And there can be little doubt that abating alienation is the precondition for realizing human nature to the full. Although Marx formulated his alienation theory in the *Economic-Philosophical Manuscripts of 1844*, when he did believe in the existence of a general human nature, nowhere in that work did he claim that the precondition for eradicating alienation was restoring the appropriate work process by re-reversing the capsized capital-labour relationship typical of capitalism. As Marx blamed alienation on markets, there are grounds for arguing that the principal factor accounting for the lukewarm support of Marxists for cooperatives is the market orientation of these firms.

For my part, I share the view of the Marxist scholar Callari that Marxists have to wrest themselves free from an anti-market bias which he describes as a form of 'agoraphobia' (Callari 2009, p. 368) and find it hard to believe that this aversion should have led so many Marxists to overlook or altogether dismiss the thesis I am advancing in this book: my belief that the establishment of a democratic firm system would amount to a real and proper revolution against capital and the sole form of revolution feasible today.

Insofar as this is true, the tendency of Marxists to underrate the positive influence of self-management on personality and its potential for improving income distribution is at odds with the emphasis they have traditionally been laying on the alienation-generating effect of capitalism and on its adverse impact on personality and income distribution.

3. The Marxist Tronti thought of self-management as part of the ideology of extreme left-wing socialists and old-style communists (see Tronti 1978, p. 292); Fraenkel dismissed it as a form of reactionary romanticism (see Fraenkel 1972, p. 80),[24] Bettelheim remarked that Marxian passages extolling the major potential of cooperation had been consigned to oblivion, and Adler described workers' councils as the 'forsaken children' of the working class (see Adler 1973, p. 246).[25] Some authors flatly deny that the transfer of corporate management powers from capitalists to workers would give rise to a genuine revolution. According to Sweezy, for instance, to assume that a free market system with state-owned production means and firms run by non-capitalists constitutes a socialist order is to mistake legal relations for production relations, because a system where firms are run by groups of workers set on maximising profits by manufacturing goods and placing them on the market is a near proxy for capitalist production relations (see Sweezy 1968).

As far as I can see, it is principally the market and private profit orientation of cooperative firms that accounts for the non-supportive attitude of

Marxists towards such a system.[26] On this point, Sen has argued that right to this day most Marxists and socialists have refused to accept the idea that being generically against markets is "as odd as being generically against conversation" (Sen 1999, p. 12).[27] In fact, this attitude is also in stark conflict with Lenin's call for a socialist system capable of making the most of "personal incentive, personal interest and business principles" (Lenin 1921, p. 44) and his idea that socialism cannot do without actions designed to promote competition "between practical organisers from among workers and peasants" (Lenin 1919, p. 393).

Notes

1 According to Chomsky, while it is still a matter for debate whether, and to what extent, State tyranny in Russia is to be blamed on the Bolshevik doctrine or the circumstances under which the State arose and grew, it is clear that the contention that the Soviet system is socialist in nature is but a cruel, cruel joke (see Chomsky 1971, p. 79).

2 For a critical review of my earlier writings on the links between democratic firm control and socialism, see Capo (2003), Zagari (2011), Winn (2013), Bellanca (2014) and Marcuse (2015).

3 From Pivetti (2006, p. 82) we learn that Sraffa, aware of the scant regard in which Marx was held by mainstream economists and desirous to arouse the interest that his critique of economic theory deserved, did not as much as mention that the true underpinning of his approach was Marxian theory. Since my target audience is principally formed of Marxists, such an overly cautious attitude is unnecessary in this book. On this point, see, also, Sylos Labini (2006, pp. 34–35).

4 Describing Fraenkel's approach as that of an 'organicist', Marramao highlights in it a line of continuity with the German statist tradition revealed by the fact that cooperative factors making for compromise by far outnumber conflictual factors (see Marramao 1982, pp. 557–58).

5 Marxists rejecting the view of a system of worker-controlled firms as a new mode of production include Labriola (1970, pp. 271–72), Mondolfo (1923, p. 93), Sweezy (1968, 1969), Althusser (1969, 1995, p. 94), as well as Gunn (2006, p. 345).

6 Marxist and non-Marxist intellectuals alike are said to be "romantically clinging to the determination to oppose exchange in principle" (see Solmi 1954, p. xxiii).

7 The Marxist scholar Callari has argued that it is high time for Marxists to wrest themselves free from their anti-market bias, which he describes as a form of 'agoraphobia' (see Callari 2009, p. 368).

8 In fact, several authors have emphasised that the adoption of centralised planning in the Soviet Union triggered a divisive debate within the cooperative movement (see, for example, MacPherson 2008, pp. 635 and 639). I hardly need remind the reader that "the 1917 revolution marks an unbridgeable divide, in the history of capitalism, between the pre- and post-revolutionary periods" (Strada 1982, p. 87).

9 In other words, Walras hoped that "privately-owned worker-run enterprises would steadily increase in number" (Herland 1996, p. 150).

10 Some scholars prefer to link the cooperative movement to Owen, rather than the Rochdale pioneers. "What the Rochdale movement really did – they argue – was to commence the process of *joint-stock shop-keeping*, a very different thing from that which Owen had in mind" (see Clarke 1962, p. 120); and the aim of this process was to help workers become owners of capital (as WMFs are seen to do).

11 According to Marx – Howard and King wrote (2001, p. 794) – the commoditisation of products in capitalistic systems was of lesser consequence than the marketing of inputs, particularly of labour services, for an obvious reason: if markets are not extended to the factors of production, market dependence is necessarily partial.

12 The bourgeoisie is "the class of the big capitalists, who in all advanced countries are in almost exclusive possession of the means of subsistence" (Engels 1847a, p. 100)

13 The idea that the capital-labour relationship should be reversed right within capitalism is rejected by some authors on the assumption that such a move would entail a twist of Marxism towards economism, i.e. "the theoretical reduction of capital to *economics* and understatement of the far-reaching role it played throughout history" (see, for instance, Vacca 1972, p. 90). In contrast, it is perfectly consistent with a genuinely Marxian rationale to theorise the primacy of economics in capitalistic societies.

14 According to Kautsky, scientific socialists think of the struggle between warring classes, the ultimate triumph of the proletariat and the advent of socialism as necessary developments, while Tucker (1961, Introduction) objects that this belief was proved wrong by the publication of the *Economic-Philosophical Manuscripts* (in a Russian version in 1927 and the German original in 1932). All the same, the idea of Marxism as theorising the advent of socialism as a necessary development has remained the received view right to this day (see, *inter alia*, Altvater 1968; Poulantsas 1968; Murgescu 1969, p. 196).

15 According to Menzani, this explains why the 'collateralist policies' of the Italian 'Lega delle Cooperative', that is to say the practice of having unions and cooperatives switch roles, are the wrong approach to this issue (see, *inter alia*, Menzani 2007, pp. 330–32).

16 Much like Gramsci, Bordiga also described trade unionism and reformism as the material expressions of individualism, bourgeois utilitarianism and loss of faith in the final triumph of revolution (see Livorsi 1976).

17 Salvadori (1973) and Maciocchi (1974) are two of the authors who see a line of continuity between Gramsci's defence of spontaneous protests as the workers' path to power (in *Ordine Nuovo*) and his approach in the *Prison Notebooks*, where he called upon the Party to spearhead the revolution of the working class.

18 In my opinion, Gruppi's argument that throughout the period of Soviet hegemony the Party encouraged dissent, rather than suppressing it is barely acceptable (see Gruppi 1962, p. 193).

19 According to Chomsky, while it is still a matter for debate whether, and to what extent, State tyranny in Russia is to be blamed on the Bolshevik doctrine or the circumstances under which the State arose and grew, it is clear that the contention that the Soviet system is socialist in nature is but a cruel joke (see Chomsky 1971, p. 79).

20 For a critical review of my earlier writings on the links between democratic firm control and socialism, see Capo (2003), Zagari (2011), Winn (2013), Bellanca (2014) and Marcuse (2015).

21 From Pivetti (2006, p. 82) we learn that Sraffa, aware of the scant regard in which Marx was held by mainstream economists and desirous to arouse the interest that his critique of economic theory deserved, did not as much as mention that the true underpinning of his approach was Marxian theory. Since my target audience is principally formed of Marxists, such an overly cautious attitude is unnecessary in this book. On this point, see, also, Sylos Labini (2006, pp. 34–35).

22 Marxist authors claiming that a socialist system should promptly do away with markets and inhibit the working of market mechanisms include-to mention just one-the best-known Japanese Marxist, K. Uno, who rates socialism as antithetical to markets capitalism.

23 In fact, several authors have emphasised that the adoption of centralised plan-
    ning in the Soviet Union triggered a divisive debate within the cooperative
    movement.
24 Describing Fraenkel's approach as that of an "organicist", Marramao highlights
    in it a line of continuity with the German statist tradition revealed by the fact that
    cooperative factors making for compromise by far outnumber conflictual factors
    (see Marramao 1982, pp. 557–58).
25 Marxists rejecting the view of a system of worker-controlled firms as a new
    mode of production include Labriola (1970, pp. 271–72), Mondolfo (1923, p. 93),
    Sweezy (1968, 1969), Althusser (1969, 1995, p. 94), as well as Gunn (2006, p. 345).
26 Marxist and non-Marxist intellectuals alike are said to be "romantically clinging
    to the determination to oppose exchange in principle" (see Solmi 1954, p. xxiii).
27 The Marxist scholar Callari has argued that it is high time for Marxists to wrest
    themselves free from their anti-market bias, which he describes as a form of 'ag-
    oraphobia' (see Callari 2009, p. 368).

Bibliography

AA. VV., 1958, *Studi gramsciani*, 2nd edition, Editori Riuniti, Rome, 1973.

AA. VV., 1962, *Fabian Essays*, Allen & Unwin, London.

AA. VV., 1968, *Cent'anni dopo il Capitale*, Samonà e Savelli, Rome, 1970.

AA. VV., 1969a, *Marx vivo*, Mondadori, Milan.

AA. VV., 1969b, *Sviluppo economico e rivoluzione*, De Donato, Bari.

AA. VV., 1970a, *Il controllo operaio*, Samonà e Savelli, Rome.

AA. VV., 1970b, *Marxismo ed etica*, Ital. transl., Feltrinelli, Milan.

AA. VV., 1971, *Anarchici e anarchia nel mondo contemporaneo*, Atti del convegno promosso dalla Fondazione Luigi Einaudi, Einaudi, Turin.

AA. VV., 1974, *Classe, consigli, partito*, Alfani editore, Rome.

AA. VV., 1977, *John Maynard Keynes nel pensiero e nella politica economica*, Feltrinelli, Milan.

AA. VV., 1978–1982, *Storia del marxismo*, Einaudi, Turin.

AA. VV., 1978, *Operaismo e centralità operaia*, Editori Riuniti, Rome.

AA. VV., 1986, *Cooperare e competere*, Feltrinelli, Milan.

AA. VV., 1990, *Gramsci e il marxismo contemporaneo*, ed. by B. Muscatello, Editori Riuniti, Rome.

AA. VV., 2008a, *Lessico marxiano*, manifestolibri, Rome.

AA. VV., 2008b, *Sinistra senza sinistra*, Feltrinelli, Milan.

Abbagnano N., 2006, *Storia della filosofia*, vol. 9, Gruppo editoriale l'Espresso, Rome.

Abendroth W., 1958, Il marxismo è 'superato'? in Abendroth, 1967.

Abendroth W., 1967, *Socialismo e marxismo da Weimar alla Germania Federale*, Ital. transl., La Nuova Italia, Florence, 1978.

Acemoglu D., Johnson S., Robinson J., 2002, Reversal of Fortune: Geography and Development in the Making of Modern World Income Distribution, in *Quarterly Journal of Economics*, vol. 117.

Acton H. B., 1955, *The Illusion of an Epoch*, Cohen & West, London.

Adler M., 1904, Kant e il socialismo, in Agazzi, 1975.

Adler M., 1919, *Democrazia e consigli operai*, Ital. transl., De Donato, Bari, 1970.

Adler M., 1927, Il socialismo di sinistra. Necessarie osservazioni su riformismo e socialismo rivoluzionario, in Marramao 1977.

Adler M., 1974, Il socialismo e gli intellettuali, a cura di L. Paggi, De Donato, Bari.

Adorno T. W., 1951, *Minima Moralia.*, Ital., transl. and introd. by R. Solmi, Einaudi, Turin, 1954.

Adorno T. W., 1969, È superato Marx? In AA. VV., 1969a.

Agazzi E., 1975, *Marxismo ed etica*, Feltrinelli, Milan.

AISSEC, 1993, Proceedings of the *9th Scientific Convention*, MIMEO.

Akerlof G. A., 1982, Labor Contracts as a Partial Gift Exchange, in *Quarterly Journal of Economics*, vol. 96, no. 11.

Albert M., 2003, *L'economia partecipativa*, Datanews, Rome.

Albinati E. 2009, Presentazione di Pasolini, 1962.

Albritton R., Sekine T. T., 1995, *A Japanese Approach to Political Economy*, Palgrave, New York.

Alchian A. A., 1984, Specificity, Specialization, and Coalitions, in *Journal of Economic Theory and Institutions*, vol. 140, no. l, March.

Alchian A. A., Demsetz, H., 1972, Production, Information Costs and Economic Organization, in *American Economic Review*, vol. 62, December.

Althusser L., Balibar E., 1965, *Leggere il Capitale*, Ital. transl., Feltrinelli, Milan, 1968.

Althusser L., 1965a, *Per Marx*, Ital. transl., Editori Riuniti, Rome, 1969.

Althusser L., 1965b, L'oggetto del capitale, in Althusser & Balibar, 1965.

Althusser L., 1969 and 1995, *Sur la reproduction*, Presses universitaires de France, Paris.

Althusser L., 1972, Risposta a John Louis, in Althusser, 2005.

Althusser L., 1973, La critica del culto della personalità, in Althusser, 2005.

Althusser L., 1974, Elements of Self-criticism, in Althusser, 1976.

Althusser L., 1976, *Essays in Self-criticism*, New Left Books, London.

Althusser L., 2005, *I marxisti non parlano mai al vento*, ed. by L. Tomasetta, Mimesis, Milan.

Altvater E., 1968, L'attualità del Capitale, in AA. VV., 1968.

Altvater E., 1982, La teoria del capitalismo monopolistico di Stato e le nuove forme di socializzazione capitalistica, in Hobsbawm *et alii*, 1978–1982, vol. IV.

Amirante C., 2008, *Dalla forma Stato alla forma mercato*, Giappichelli, Turin.

Angel P., 1975, Stato e società borghese nel pensiero di Bernstein, in Istituto Giangiacomo Feltrinelli, Milan, 1975.

Ansart P., 1967, *La sociologia di Proudhon*, Ital. transl., Il Saggiatore, Milan, 1972.

Ansart P., 1969, *Marx e l'anarchismo*, Ital. transl., Il Mulino, Bologna, 1972.

Anweiler O., 1958, *Storia dei soviet, 1905–1921*, Ital. transl., Laterza, Bari, 1972.

ARA, 1977, *Quale socialismo; quale Europa*, Feltrinelli, Milan.

Arena R., Salvadori N., 2004, eds. *Money, Credit and the Role of the State*, Ashgate, Farnham.

Arendt H., 1978, *La vita della mente*, Ital. transl., Il Mulino, Bologna, 2009.

Arienzo A., Borrelli G., 2011, *Emergenze democratiche, ragion di Stato, governance, gouvernementalité*, Giannini editore, Naples.

Arnason J. P., 1982, Prospettive e problemi del marxismo critico nell'Est europeo, in Hobsbawm *et alii*, 1978–1982.

Aron R., 1965, The Impact of Marxism in the Twentieth Century, in Drachkovitch, 1965.

Aron R., 1969, Equivoco e inesauribile, in AA. VV., 1969.

Aron R., 1970, *Marxismi immaginari; da una sacra famiglia all'altra*, Ital. transl., F. Angeli, Milan, 1977.

Arrighi G., 2007, *Adam Smith a Pechino*, Ital. transl., Feltrinelli, Milan, 2008.

Arthur C. J., 2001, Value, Labour and Negativity, in *Capital and Class*, no. 73, Spring.

Arthur C. J., 2009, The Possessive Spirit of Capital: Subsumption/Inversion/ Contradiction, in Bellofiore and Fineschi, 2009.

Aspromourgos T., 2000, Is an Employer-of-Last-Resort Sustainable? A Review Article, *Review of Political Economy*, vol. 12, no. 2.

Assemblea costituente; atti, http: //legislature. camera.it /index.asp.

Atkinson A. B., ed., 1993, *Alternatives to Capitalism; the Economics of Partnership*, Macmillan, London.

Avineri S., 1968, *Il pensiero politico e sociale di Marx*, Ital. transl., Il Mulino, Bologna, 1972.

Backhaus H. G., 1997, *Dialektik der Wertform*, Ça ira, Freiburg.

Backhouse R., 1985, *A History of Modern Economic Analysis*, Blackwell, Oxford.

Badaloni N., 1962, *Marxismo come storicismo*, Feltrinelli, Milan.

Badaloni N., 1972, *Il Marxismo italiano negli anni sessanta*, Editori Riuniti, Rome.

Bagnasco A., 2008, *Ceto medio*, Il Mulino, Bologna.

Bagnoli L., 2010, ed., *La funzione sociale della cooperazione*, Carocci, Rome.

Bahro R., 1977, *Eine Dokumentation*, Europäische Verlagsanstalt, Frankfurt.

Baker G. P., Jensen M. C., & Murphy K. J., 1988, Compensation and Incentives: Practice *vs.* Theory, in *Journal of Finance*, vol. 43, no. 3.

Bakunin M., 1873, *Stato e anarchia*, Ital. transl., Feltrinelli, Milan, 1968.

Balibar E., 1974, *Cinq études du matérialisme historique*, Maspero, Paris.

Balibar E., 1993, *La filosofia di Marx*, Ital. transl., manifestolibri, Rome, 1994.

Ball T., Farr J., 1984, eds, *After Marx*, Cambridge University Press, Cambridge.

Baran P. A., Sweezy P. M., 1966, *Monopoly Capital*, Monthly Review Press, New York.

Bardhan P., Roemer J. E., eds., 1993, *Market Socialism: The Current Debate*, Oxford Economic Press, New York.

Barlett W., Cable J., Estrin S., Derek C., & Smith S., 1992, Labour-Managed versus Private Firms: An Empirical Comparison of Cooperatives and Private Firms in Central Italy, in *Industrial and Labour Relations Review*, vol. 46.

Barone E., 1908, Il Ministro della produzione in uno stato collettivista, in *Giornale degli economisti*, vol. 34.

Barreto T., 2011, Penser l'entreprise cooperative: au delà du réductionisme du *mainstream*, in *Annals of Public and Cooperative Economics*, vol. 82, no. 2.

Barro R. J., 1996, Democracy and Growth, in *Journal of Economic Growth*, vol. 1.

Bascetta M., 2004, *La libertà dei postmoderni*, manifestolibri, Rome.

Basevi P., 1951, Le prime tre lettere di Engels a Carlo Cafiero, in *La società*, December.

Bataille G., 1976, *Il limite dell' utile*, trad. it., Adelphi Edizioni, Milano, 2000.

Bataille G., 1996, *Il limite dell'utile*, Ital. transl., Adelphi Edizioni, Milan, 2000.

Battilani P., Bertagnoni G., 2007, *Competizione e valorizzazione del lavoro*, Il Mulino, Bologna.

Bauer O., 1920, Bolscevismo o socialdemocrazia, in Marramao, 1977.

Bauman Z., 2014, *Il demone della paura*, Laterza, Bari-Rome.

Baumol W., 1953, Firms with Limited Money Capital, in *Kyklos*, vol. 6, no. 2.

Becattini G., 2009, Il *mea culpa* degli economisti, in *Il Ponte*, Ybk LXV, no. 10.

Bell J. R., 1995, Dialectics and Economic Theory, in Albritton & Sekine, 1995.

Bellanca N., 2014, Il socialismo cooperativo di Bruno Jossa, https://sviluppofelice.wordpress.com/2014/11/24.

Bellas C., 1972, *Industrial Democracy and the Worker-Owned Firm: A Study of Twenty-one Plywood Companies in the Pacific Northwest*, Praeger, New York.

Bellofiore R., 1993, *Per una teoria monetaria del valore-lavoro. Problemi aperti nella teoria marxiana, tra radici ricardiane e nuove vie di ricerca*, in Lunghini, 1993.

Bellofiore R., 1998, ed., *Marxian Economics; a Reappraisal*, Palgrave Macmillan, New York.

Bellofiore R., Finelli R., 1998, Capital, Labour and Time: The Marxian Monetary Labour Theory of Value as a Theory of Exploitation, in Bellofiore, 1998.

Bellofiore R., 2007, *Da Marx a Marx?* manifestolibri, Rome.

Bellofiore R., Fineschi R., 2009, *Re-reading Marx: New Perspectives after the Critical Edition*, Palgrave Macmillan, New York.

Ben-Ner A., 1987, Producer Cooperatives: Why Do They Exist in Market Economies? in Powel, 1987.

Ben-Ner A., 1988, The Life-Cycle of Worker-Owned Firms in Market Economies: A Theoretical Analysis, in *Journal of Economic Behavior and Organization*, vol. 10, no. 3.

Ben-Ner A., Hahn T., Jones D. C., 1996, The Productivity Effects of Employee Participation in Control and in Economic Returns: A Review of Empirical Evidence, in Pagano & Rowthorn, 1996.

Bendix R., 1960, *Max Weber; an Intellectual Portrait*, Doubleday & Company, New York.

Benkler Y., 2006, *The Wealth of Networks: How Social Production Transforms Markets and Freedom*, Yale University Press, New Haven.

Bensaïd D., 2002, *Marx for Our Times*, Verso, London.

Berlin I., 1963, *Marx*, Ital. transl., La Nuova Italia, Florence, 1967.

Berman K. V., Berman M. D., 1989, An Empirical Test of the Theory of the Labour-Managed Firm, in *Journal of Comparative Economics*, vol. 13, no. 2.

Berman M. D., 1977, Short Run Efficiency in the Labour-Managed Firm, in *Journal of Comparative Economics*, vol. 1, no. 3.

Bernier B., 1974, Conrad Schmidt e l'inizio della letteratura economica 'marxista', in Istituto Giangiacomo Feltrinelli, 1974.

Bernstein E., 1899, *Evolutionary Socialism. A Criticism and Affirmation*, Shocken Books, New York, 1961.

Bernstein E., 1901, *Zur Geschichte und Theorie des Sozialismus*, Akademischer Verlag für Soziale Wissenschaft, Berlin.

Bernstein E., 1918, *Völkerbund oder Staatenbund*, P. Cassirer, Berlin.

Bertelè A., Cantore A., 1969, *Liberalismo e socialismo*, Vallecchi editore, Florence.

Bettelheim C., 1969, *La transizione all'economia socialista*, Ital. transl., Jaca Books, Milan, 1969.

Bhaskar R., 1991, 'Dialectics' Entry, in Bottomore, 1991.

Bhaskar R., 1993, *Dialectic: The Pulse of Freedom*, Verso, London.

Bidet J., 1990, La teoria del modo di produzione capitalistico, in AA. VV., 1990.

Bidet J., 1998, *Que faire du Capital?* Presses Universitaires de France, Paris.

Bidet J., 2001, New Interpretations of Capital, in Bidet & Kouvelakis, 2001.

Bidet J., Kouvelakis S., 2001, eds, *Critical Companion to Contemporary Marxism*, Brill, Leiden and Boston, 2008.

Birchall J., 2012, The Comparative Advantages of Member-owned Businesses, in *Review of Social Economy*, vol. 70, no. 3, September.

Blejer M. I., Škreb M., 1997, *Macroeconomic Stabilization in Transition Economics*, Cambridge University Press, Cambridge.

Blinder A., 1995, ed., *Paying for Productivity: A Look at the Evidence*, Brookings Institution, Washington, D.C.

Bloch E., 1968, *Karl Marx*, Ital. transl., Il Mulino, Bologna, 1972.

Bloch E., 1970, Marx pensatore della rivoluzione, in Coppellotti, 1972.

Bloom S. F., 1943, Man of His Century: A Reconsideration of the Historical Significance of Karl Marx, in Wood 1988.

Blumberg P., 1968, *Industrial Democracy: The Sociology of Participation*, Constable, London.

Blundell-Wignall A., 1976, On Exposing the Transformation Problem, in *Australian Economic Papers*, vol. 15, no. 27.

Bobbio N., 1958a, La dialettica in Marx, in *Rivista di filosofia*, vol. 49.

Bobbio N., 1958b, Nota sulla dialettica in Gramsci, in AA. VV., 1958.

Bobbio N., 1984, *Il futuro della democrazia*, Einaudi, Turin.

Bobbio N., 1985, *Stato, governo, società; frammenti di un dizionario politico*, 2nd edn, Einaudi, Turin, 1995.

Bobbio N., 1989, A. Massarenti interviewing Bobbio, in *Il Sole-24 ore*, 5 April.

Bodei R., 2013, *Immaginare altre vie; realtà, progetti, desideri*, Feltrinelli, Milan.

Bolaffi A., 2002, *Il crepuscolo della sovranità*, Donzelli editore, Rome.

Bonar J., 1893, *Philosophy and Political Economy in Some of Their Historical Relations*, Sonnenschein, London.

Bonazzi G., 2002, Perché i sociologi italiani del lavoro e dell'organizzazione, pur essendo pro labour, non sono post-bravermaniani e meno ancora foucaultiani, in *Sociologia del lavoro*, vols. II and III, nos. 86–87.

Bonefeld W., 2010, Abstract Labour: Against Its Nature and On Its Time, in *Capital and Class*, vol. 34, no. 2.

Bonefeld W., 2011, Debating Abstract Labour, in *Capital and Class*, vol. 35, no. 3.

Bonin J. P., Putterman L., 1987, *Economics of Cooperation and the Labor-Managed Economy; Fundamentals of Pure and Applied Economics*, no. 4, Harvard Academic Publishing, New York.

Bonin J. P., Jones D. C., & Putterman L., 1993, Theoretical and Empirical Studies of Producer Cooperatives: Will the Twain Ever Meet? in *Journal of Economic Literature*, vol. 31.

Boss E., 1990, *Theories of Surplus and Transfer; Parasites and Producers in Economic Thought*, Unwin Hyman, Boston.

Bottomore T. B., 1991, ed., *A Dictionary of Marxist Thought*, II edit., Blackwell, Oxford.

Bourdet Y., 1974, *Pour l'Autogestion*, Anthropos, Paris.

Bowles S., 1985, The Production Process in a Competitive Economy: Walrasian, Neo-Hobbesian, and Marxian Models, in *American Economic Review*, vol. 75, no. 1, March.

Bowles S., Gintis H., & Gustafsson B., 1993, eds, *Markets and Democracy: Participation, Accountability and Efficiency*, Cambridge University Press, Cambridge.

Bowles S., Gintis H., 1986, *Democracy and Capitalism*, Basic Books, New York.

Bowles S., Gintis H., 1993, Post-Walrasian Political Economy, in Bowles, Gintis & Gustaffson, 1993.

Bowles S., Gintis H., 1996, The Distribution of Wealth and the Viability of the Democratic Firm, in Pagano & Rowthorn, 1996.

Bowles S., Gintis H., 2002, Social Capital and Community Governance, in *Economic Journal*, vol. 112.

Braudel F., 1977, *Afterthoughts on Material Civilization and Capitalism*, Johns Hopkins University Press, Baltimora.

Braverman H., 1974, *Labour and Monopoly Capital*, Monthly Review Press, New York.

Brewer A., 1995, A Minor Post-Ricardian? Marx As An Economist, in *History of Political Economy*, vol. 27, no. 1.

Brewer A., 2002, The Marxist Tradition in the History of Economics, in Weintraub, 2002.

Brewer A. A., Browning M. J., 1982, On the Employment Decision of a Labour-Managed Firm, in *Economica*, vol. 49, no. 194.

Bronfenbrenner M., 1967, Marxian Influences in 'Bourgeois' Economics, in Wood, 1988, vol. III.

Bronfenbrenner M., 1970, The Vicissitudes of Marxian Economics, in Wood, 1988, vol. III.

Bruni L., 2006, *Reciprocità*, B. Mondadori, Milan.

Buchanan A. E., 1982, *Marx and Justice; the Radical Critique of Liberalism*, Rowman & Allanheld, Totowa, New Jersey.

Bulgarelli M., Viviani M., 2006, eds, *La promozione cooperativa; Copfond tra mercato e solidarietà*, Il Mulino, Bologna.

Buonocore V., Jossa B., 2003, eds, *Organizzazioni economiche non capitalistiche*, Il Mulino, Bologna.

Burgio A., 2007, *Dialettica; tradizioni, problemi sviluppi*, Quodlibet Studio, Macerata.

Burke J. P., 1981, The Necessity of Revolution, in Burke, Crocker, Legters, 1981.

Burke J. P., Crocker L., Legters L. H., 1981, eds, *Marxism and the Good Society*, Cambridge University Press, Cambridge.

Burns T., 2010, Capitalism, Modernity and the Nation State: A Critique of Hannes Lacher, in *Capital & Class*, vol. 34, no. 2.

Cacciatore G., 1987, Il Marx di Gramsci. Per una rilettura del nesso etica-teoria politica nel marxismo, in Cacciatore & Lomonaco, 1987.

Cacciatore G., Lomonaco F., 1987, *Marx e i marxisti cent'anni dopo*, Guida Editori, Naples, 1987.

Callari A., 2009, A Methodological Reflection on the 'Thick Socialism' of *Socialism after Hayek,* in *Review of Social Economy*, vol. XVII, no. 3, September.

Campbell M., Reuten G., 2002, eds, *The Culmination of Capital; Essays on Volume III of Marx's Capital*, Palgrave, London.

Candela G., 2014, *Economia, Stato, anarchia*, Elèuthera, Milan.

Capitini A., 1968, Omnicrazia: il potere di tutti, in Capitini, 2016.

Capitini A., 2016, *Attraverso due terzi del secolo; Omnicrazia: il potere di tutti*, Il Ponte Editore, Florence.

Capo G., 2003, Spunti di riflessione da una teoria economica della cooperazione, in Buonocore & Jossa, 2003.

Caracciolo A., Scalia G., 1959, *La città futura*, Feltrinelli, Milan.

Carandini G., 1971, *Lavoro e capitale nella teoria di Marx*, Marsilio, Padua.

Carandini G., 1973, *La struttura economica della società nelle opere di Marx*, Marsilio, Padua.

Carandini G., 2005, *Un altro Marx*, Laterza, Rome.

Carboni C., ed., 1986, *Classi e movimenti in Italia, 1970–1985*, Laterza, Bari-Rome.

Carchedi G., 1984, The Logic of Prices and Values, in *Economy and Society*, vol. 13, no. 4.

Carchedi G., 2011, A Comment on Bonefeld's 'Abstract Labour: Against its Nature and on its Time', in *Capital and Class*, vol. 35, no. 2.

Carroll Glenn R., 1984, Organization Ecology, in *Annual Review of Sociology*, vol. 10.

Carroll Glenn R., Hannan M. T., 1989, Density Dependence in the Evolution of Populations of Newspaper Organizations, in *American Sociological Review*, vol. 54.

Carver T., 1984, Marxism as Method, in Ball & Farr, 1984.

Carver T., Thomas P., 1995, eds, *Rational Choice Marxism*, Macmillan, London.

Cassano F., 1973, *Marxismo e filosofia in Italia, 1958–1971*, De Donato, Bari.

Castronovo V., 1987, Dal dopoguerra ad oggi, in Zangheri, Galasso & Castronovo, 1987.

Catephores G., 1989, *An Introduction to Marxist Economics*, Macmillan, London.

Cattabrini F., 2010, Assemblea costituente: il dibattito sulla cooperazione, in Bagnoli, 2010.

Chaddad F., 2012, Advancing the Theory of Cooperative Organization: The Cooperative as a True Hybrid, in *Annals of Public and Cooperative Economics*, vol. 83, no. 4.

Chattopadhyay P., 2010, The Myth of Twentieth-Century Socialism and the Continuing Relevance of Karl Marx, in *Socialism and Democracy*, vol. 24, no. 3.

Chilosi A., 1992a, ed., *L'economia del periodo di transizione; dal modello di tipo sovietico all'economia di mercato*, Il Mulino, Bologna.

Chilosi A., 1992b, Il socialismo di mercato: modelli e problemi, in Chilosi, 1992a.

Chiodi G., Ditta L., 2008, eds, *Sraffa or an Alternative Economics*, Palgrave Macmillan, London.

Chiodi G., 2008, Beyond Capitalism: Sraffa's Economic Theory, in Chiodi and Ditta, 2008.

Chiodi P., 1973, *Sartre e il marxismo*, Feltrinelli, Milan.

Chomsky N., 1971, *Conoscenza e libertà*, Ital. transl., Il Saggiatore, Milan, 2010.

Chomsky N., 2009, Un mondo ingiusto, in *Internazionale*, ybk 16, no. 816.

Chomsky N., 2013, *I padroni dell'umanità*, Ponte alle grazie, Milan, 2014.

Cingoli M., 2001, *Il primo Marx (1835–1841)*, Edizioni Unicopli, Milan.

Cingoli M., 2005, Marx e il materialismo, in Musto, 2005.

Cinnella E., 2014, *L'altro Marx*, Della Porta, Pisa-Cagliari.

Clarke W., 1962, Industrial, in AA. VV., 1962.

Clayre A., 1980, ed., *The Political Economy of Cooperation and Participation: A Third Sector*, Oxford Economic Press, Oxford.

Coase R., 1960, The Problem of Social Cost, in *Journal of Law and Economics*, vol. 3, no. 1.

Cohen F., 1973, *Bucharin e la rivoluzione bolscevica*, Ital., transl., Feltrinelli, Milan, 1975.

Cohen G. A., 1978 and 2000, *Karl Marx's Theory of History: A Defence*, Clarendon Press, Oxford.

Cohen G. A., 1978, Robert Nozick and Wilt Chamberlain: How Patterns Preserve Liberty, in Arthur & Show, 1978.

Cohen G. A., 1983, Forces and Relations of Production, in Roemer, vol. II.

Cohen G. A., 1995, *Self-Ownership, Freedom, and Equality*, Cambridge University Press, Cambridge.

Cohen G. A., 2000, *If You Are an Egalitarian, How Come You're So Rich?* Harvard University Press, Cambridge, MA.

Cole G. C. H., 1953, *Attempts at General Union*, Macmillan, London.

Cole G. D. H., 1920, *Guild Socialism Re-stated*, Leonard Parsons, London.

Colletti L., 1958, Lettera di Colletti a Gerratana, in Cassano, 1973.

Colletti L., 1968, Bernstein e il marxismo della seconda internazionale, preface to Bernstein, 1899.

Colletti L., 1969, *Il marxismo ed Hegel*, Laterza, Bari.

Colletti L., 1970, *Ideologia e società*, Laterza, Bari.

Colletti L., 1974, *Intervista politico-filosofica*, Laterza, Bari.

Colletti L., 1979, *Tra marxismo e no*, Laterza, Bari.

Colletti L., 1980, *Tramonto dell'ideologia*, Laterza, Bari.

Colombo A., 1994, ed., *Crollo del Comunismo sovietico e ripresa dell'utopia*, Edizioni Dedalo, Bari.

Colonna M., Hagemann H., & Hamouda O., eds, 1994, *Capitalism, Socialism and Knowledge: The Economics of F.A. Hayek*, vol. II, Elgar, Aldershot.

Commons J. R., 1924, *Legal Foundations of Capitalism*, University of Wisconsin Press, Milwaukee, 1968.

Conte M. A., 1982, Participation and Performance in U.S. Labour-managed Firms, in Jones & Svejnar, 1982.

Copeland M. A., 1931, Economic Theory and the Natural Science Point of View, in *American Economic Review*, vol. 21, no. 1, March.

Copeland M. A., 1936, Common's Institutionalism in Relation to the Problem of Social Evolution and Economic Planning, in *Quarterly Journal of Economics*, vol. 50, no. 2, February.

Coppellotti F., 1972, *Marx e la rivoluzione*, Feltrinelli, Milan.

Cornu A., 1948, *Karl Marx e il pensiero moderno*, Ital. transl., Einaudi, Turin, 1949.

Cornu A., 1955, *Marx ed Engels dal liberalismo al comunismo*, Ital. transl., Feltrinelli, Milan, 1962.

Cortesi L., 2010, *Storia del comunismo; da utopia al Termidoro sovietico*, manifesto-libri, Rome.

Craig B., Pencavel I., 1995, Participation and Productivity: A Comparison of Worker Cooperatives and Conventional Firms in the Plywood Industry, in *Brookings Papers: Microeconomics*, vol. I.

Croce B., 1896a, Sulla concezione materialistica della storia, reprinted in Croce, 1968.

Croce B., 1896b, Sulla forma scientifica del materialismo storico, in Croce, 1968.

Croce B., 1899, *Materialismo storico ed economia marxista*, Laterza, Bari, 1968.

Crocker D. A., 1981, Markovic on Social Theory and Human Nature, in Burke, Crocker & Legters, 1981.

Crouch C., 2003, *Postdemocrazia*, Ital. transl., Laterza, Bari, 2005.

Cunow H., 1899, Zur Zusammenbruchsheorie, in *Die neue Zeit*, vol. XVII.

Cuomo G., 2003, La cooperativa di produzione italiana e i modelli teorici di riferimento, in Buonocore, Jossa, 2003.

Cuomo G., 2010, *Microeconomia dell'impresa cooperativa di produzione*, Giappichelli, Turin.

Cuomo, G., 2015, Impresa cooperativa e democrazia economica, in *Studi Economici*, no. 116.

Curi U., 1975, *Sulla 'scientificità' del marxismo*, Feltrinelli, Milan.

Dahl R. A., 1985, *A Preface to Economic Democracy*, Polity Press, Cambridge.

Dahl R. A., 1989, *Democracy and its Critics*, Yale University Press, New Haven.

Dahrendorf R., 1957, *Classi e conflitto di classe nella società industriale*, Ital. transl., Laterza, Bari, 1963.

Dal Pra M., 1972, *La dialettica in Marx*, 2nd edition, Laterza, Bari.

Dalmasso S., 1995, La ricerca di un'altra via. Le 7 tesi sul controllo operaio di Panzieri e Libertini, in *Per il '68'*, no. 7, 1995.

Damjanovic P., 1962, Les conceptions de Marx sur l'autogestion sociale, *Praxis*, no. 1.

Dawkins R., 1989, *Il gene egoista*, Ital. transl., Oscar Mondadori, Milan, 1995.

De Angelis M., 1995, Behond the technological and Social Paradigms: A Political Reading of Abstract Labour as the Substance of Value, in *Capital and Class*, no. 57, Autumn.

De Giovanni B., 1976, *La teoria politica delle classi nel 'Capitale'*, De Donato, Bari.

De Gregory T. R., 2003, Vitalism versus Hamiltonian Matter of Fact Knowledge, in *Journal of Economic Issues*, vol. XXXVII, no. 1.

De Vroey M., 1982, On the Obsolescence of Marxian Theory of Value, in *Capital and Class*, vol. 17, Summer.

Defourny J., 1992, Comparative Measures of Technical Efficiency for 500 French Workers' Cooperatives, in Jones and Svejnar, 1992.

Defourny J., Estrin S., Jones D. C., 1985, The Effects of Workers' Participation on Enterprise Performance, in *International Journal of Industrial Organization*, vol. 3, no. 2.

Della Volpe G., 1964, *Rousseau e Marx*, 4th edition, Editori Riuniti, Rome.

Demsetz H., 1988a, *Ownership, Control and the Firm; the Organization of Economic Activity*, vol. I, Basil Blackwell, Oxford.

Demsetz H., 1988b, The Theory of the Firm Revisited, in Demsetz, 1988a.

Derrida J., 1993, *Spettri di Marx*, Ital. transl., Raffaello Cortina, Milan, 1994.

Deutscher I., 1970, *Lenin; frammento di una vita e altri saggi*, Ital. transl., Laterza, Bari, 1970.

Di Siena G., 1972, Biologia, darwinismo sociale e marxismo, supplement to *Critica marxista*, no. 4, 1972.

Dickinson H. D., 1933, Price Formation in a Socialist Community, in *Economic Journal*, vol. 43, June.

DiQuattro A. R., 1981, Alienation and Justice in the Market, in Burke, Crocker & Legters, 1981.

Dobb M., 1933, Economic Theory and the Problems of a Socialist Economy, reprinted in Dobb, 1955.

Dobb M., 1939a, Gli economisti e la teoria economica del socialismo, reprinted in Dobb, 1955.

Dobb M., 1939b, A Note on Saving and Investment in a Socialist Economy, re-printed in Dobb, 1955.

Dobb M., 1953, Rassegna della discussione riguardante il calcolo economico in un'economia socialista, in reprinted in Dobb, 1955.

Dobb M., 1954a, *Teoria economica e socialismo*, Ital. transl., Editori Riuniti, Rome, 1974.

Dobb M., 1954b, Una conferenza su Marx, in Dobb, 1954a.

Dobb M., 1955, *On Economic Theory and Socialism: Collected Papers*, Routledge & Kegan, London.

Dobb M., 1956, Pianificazione, in Napoleoni, 1956.

Dobb M., 1969, *Welfare Economics and the Economics of Socialism*, Cambridge University Press, Cambridge.

Domar E. D., 1966, The Soviet Collective Farm as a Producer Cooperative, in *American Economic Review*, vol. 56, no. 4.

Donnaruma C., Partyka N., 2012, Challenging the Presumption in Favor of Markets, in *Review of Radical Political Economics*, vol. 44, no. 1.

Doucouliagos C., 1995, Worker Participation and Productivity in Labor-Managed and Participatory Capitalist Firms: A Meta-Analysis, in *Industrial and Labour Relations Review*, vol. 49, no. 1.

Dow G., 1993a, Democracy versus Appropriability. Can Labour-managed Firms Flourish in a Capitalist World? in Bowles, Gintis, Gustafsson, 1993.

Dow G., 1993b, Why Capital Hires Labor: A Bargaining Perspective, in *American Economic Review*, vol. 83, no. 1

Dow G., 1998, Review of Jossa & Cuomo, 1997, *Journal of Economic Literature*, vol. 36, no. 2.

Dow G., 2003, *Governing the Firm; Workers' Control in Theory and Practice*, Cambridge University Press, Cambridge.

Dow G., 2018, The Theory of The Labor-Managed Firm: Past, Present, and Future, in *Annals of Public and Cooperative Economics*, vol. 89, no. 3.

Dow G., Putterman L., 1996, Why Capital (Usually) Hires Labour: A Review and Assessment of Some Proposed Explanations, MIMEO.

Drachkovitch M. M., 1965, ed., *Marxism in the Modern World*, Oxford University Press, London.

Dreyfus M., 2012, La cooperazione di produzione in Francia dalle origini alla Grande guerra, in *Il Ponte*, a. 68, no. 5–6.

Drèze J. H., 1976, Some Theory of Labour Management and Participation, in *Econometrica*, vol. 44, no. 6.

Drèze J. H., 1989, *Labour-Management, Contracts and Capital Markets. A General Equilibrium Approach*, Basil Blackwell, Oxford.

Drèze J. H., 1993, Self-Management and Economic Theory: Efficiency, Funding and Employment, in Bardhan & Roemer, 1993.

Dubravcic D., 1970, Labour as an Entrepreneurial Input; an Essay on the Theory of the Producer Cooperative Economy, *Economica*, vol. 37, no. 147.

Duffield J., 1970, The Value Concept in Capital in Light of Recent Criticism, reprinted in Wood, 1988.

Dugger W. M., 2003, David Hamilton: A Radical Institutionalist, in *Journal of Economic Issues*, vol. XXXVII, no. 1, March.

Duménil G., Lévy D., 2001, Old Theories and New Capitalism: The Actuality of Marzxian Economics, in Bidet & Kouvelakis, 2008.

Dunayewskaya R., 1988, *Marxism and Freedom: From 1776 until Today*, Columbia University Press, New York.

Dunlap L. A., 1979, Social Production in Karl Marx, in *Review of Social Economy*, vol. 37, no. 3.

Dussel E., 1999, *Un Marx sconosciuto*, Manifestolibri, Rome.

Dworkin R., 2006, *La democrazia possibile*, Ital. transl., Feltrinelli, Milan, 2007.

Edwards R. C., 1979, *Contested Terrain*, Basic Books, New York.

Einaudi L., 1920, *Partecipazione degli operai alla gestione e socializzazione*, in Einaudi, 1966.

Einaudi L., 1966, *Cronache economiche e politiche di un trentennio*, vol. V, 1919–1920, Einaudi, Turin.

Eldret M., Hanlon M., 1981, Reconstructing the Value-Form Analysis, in *Capital & Class*, vol. 13.

Elster J., 1978, *Logic and Society: Contradictory and Possible Worlds*, Wiley & Sons, Chichester.

Elster J., 1984, Historical Materialism and Economic Backwardness, in Ball & Farr, 1984.

Elster J., 1985, *Making Sense of Marx*, Cambridge University Press, Cambridge.

Elster J., Moene K. O., 1989, *Alternatives to Capitalism,* Cambridge University Press, Cambridge.

Engels F., 1844, *La sacra famiglia*, Ital. transl., Editori Riuniti, Rome, 1969.

Engels F., 1845, Due discorsi a Eberfeld, in Marx & Engels, *Opere complete*, vol. 4.

Engels F., 1847, Lettera del 23–24 November, in Marx & Engels, *Opere complete*, vol. 38.

Engels F., 1847a, *Principles of Communism*, in Marx & Engels, *Collected Works*, vol. 6.

Engels F., 1847b, Draft of a Communist Confession of Faith, in Marx & Engels, *Collected Works*, vol. 6.

Engels F., 1847c, Lettera del 23–24 novembre, in Marx & Engels, *Opere complete*, vol. 38.

Engels F., 1859a, Review of *Per la critica dell'economia politica*, in Marx, 1859.

Engels F., 1859b, Letter to Marx of 12 December, in Marx-Engels, 1972.

Engels F., 1871, Lettera a Cafiero del 1–3 luglio, in Basevi, 1951.

Engels F., 1872, Letter to C. Terzaghi of Jan. 14, in Marx & Engels, *Collected Works*, vol. 44.

Engels F., 1878, *Antidühring*, Ital. transl., Editori Riuniti, Rome, 1968.

Engels F., 1882, *Socialism, Utopian and Scientific*, Foreign Languages Publishing House, Moskow, 1976.

Engels F., 1884, Prefazione a Marx, 1847.

Engels F., 1885, Per la storia della Lega dei comunisti, in Marx-Engels, 1966.

Engels F., 1890–91, In the Case of Brentano versus Marx. Regarding Alleged Falsification of Quotation, in Marx & Engels, *Collected Works*, vol. 27.

Engels F., 1890, Farewell Letter to the Readers of the *Sozialdemokrat*, in Marx & Engels, *Collected Works*, vol. 27.

Engels F., 1891a, Introduction to Marx, 1849.

Engels F., 1891b, A Critique of the Draft Social-Democratic Programme of 1891, in Marx & Engels, *Collected Works*, vol. 27.

Engels F., 1891c, Socialism: Utopian and Scientific, in Marx & Engels, *Collected Works*, vol. 25.

Engels F., 1892, Lettera a Lafargue, 12 / XI, in Marx & Engels, *Collected Works*, vol. 38.

Engels F., 1894a, On Authority, reprinted in Engels, 1959.

Engels F., 1894b, Prefazione to the III vol. of *Capitale*, in Marx, 1894.

Engels F., 1895a, Introduction to Karl Marx's *The Class Struggle in France, 1848 to 1850*, in Marx & Engels, *Collected Works*, vol. 27.

Engels F., 1895b, Letter to K. Kautsky of April 1st, in Marx & Engels, *Collected Works*, vol. 27.

Engels F., 1959, *Basic Writings in Political and Philosophy*, ed. by L. Feuer, Doubleday, Garden City, New York.

Erlich A., 1978, Dobb and the Marx-Feldman Model: A Problem in the Soviet Economic Strategy, *Cambridge Journal of Economics*, vol. 15, no. 2, June.

Estrin S., 1983, *Self-Management: Economic Theory and Yugoslav Practice*, Cambridge University Press, Cambridge.

Estrin S., 1991, Some Reflections on Self-Management, Social Choice and Reform in Eastern Europe, in *Journal of Comparative Economics*, vol. 15, no. 2.

Estrin S., Jones D. C., 1992, The Viability of Employee-Owned Firms: Evidence from France, in *Industrial and Labor Relations Review*, vol. 45, no. 2.

Estrin S., Jones D. C., 1995, Worker Participation, Employee Ownership and Productivity: Results from French Producer Cooperatives, in Derek & Jones, 1995.

Estrin S., Jones D. C., & Svejnar J., 1987, The Productivity Effects of Worker Participation: Producer Cooperatives in Western Europe, in *Journal of Comparative Economics*, vol. 11, no. 1.

Eswaran M., Kotwal A., 1989, Why Are Capitalists the Bosses? in *Economic Journal*, vol. 99, March.

Etzioni A., 1990, Concorrenza incapsulata, in Magatti, 1990.

Faccioli D., Fiorentini G., 1998, Un'analisi di efficienza comparata tra imprese cooperative e for profit, in Fiorentini & Scarpa, 1998.

Fanelli R., 1997, Introduzione. Una soggettività immaginaria, in Althusser, 1969 and 1995.

Fausto D., Pica F., eds, 2000, *Teoria e fatti del federalismo fiscale*, Il Mulino, Bologna.

Favilli P., 2001, Socialismo e marginalismo. La 'battaglia delle idee': una lettura, in Guidi & Michelini, 2001.

Ferrajoli L., 1978, Esiste una democrazia rappresentativa? in Ferrajoli & Zolo, 1978.

Ferrajoli L., Zolo D., 1978, *Democrazia autoritaria e capitalismo maturo*, Feltrinelli, Milan.

Fine B., 2001, The Marx–Hegel Relationship: Revisionist Interpretations, in *Capital & Class*, special issue, no. 75, Autumn.

Fine B., Jeon H., & Gimm G. H., 2010, Value Is as Value Does: Twixt Knowledge and the World Economy, in *Capital & Class*, vol. 34, no. 1.

Finelli R., 2007, Un marxismo 'senza Capitale', in Bellofiore, 2007.

Fineschi R., 2005a, ed., *Karl Marx: Rivisitazioni e prospettive*, Mimesis, Milan.

Fineschi R., 2005b, Teoria della storia e alienazione in Marx, in Fineschi, 2005a.

Fineschi R., 2006, *Marx e Hegel; contributi ad una rilettura*, Carocci.

Fineschi R., 2007, Attualità e praticabilità di una teoria dialettica del 'Capitale' (ovvero: Marx è un ferro vecchio?), in Burgio, 2007.

Finocchiaro M. A., 1988, *Gramsci and the History of Dialectical Thought*, Cambridge University Press, Cambridge.

Fiorentini G., Scarpa, C., eds, 1998, *Cooperative e mercato*, Carocci, Rome.

Fistetti F., 1977, Democrazia e transizione. La II internazionale, Lenin e il rapporto con la tradizione teorico-politica del movimento operaio, in AA. VV., 1977.

Fitoussi J. P., 1995, *Le débat interdit*, Arléa, Paris.

Fitzroy F. R., Kraft K., 1987, Cooperation, Productivity and Profit Sharing, in *Quarterly Journal of Economics*, vol. 102, no. 1.

Fleetwood S., 2006, Rethinking Labour Markets: A Critical–Realist–Socioeconomic Perspective, in *Capital & Class*, vol. 89, Summer.

Fleischer H., 1969, *Marxismo e storia*, Il Mulino, Bologna.

Forgacs D., 1995, Gramsci in Gran Bretagna, in Hobsbawm, 1995.

Foucault M., 2008, *Il governo di sé e degli altri*, Ital. transl., Feltrinelli, Milan, 2009.

Fougeyrollas P., 1959, *Le marxisme en question*, Èditions du Soeil, Paris.

Fraenkel E., 1972, Rätemythos und soziale Selbstbehauptung, in Saladin & Wildhaber, 1972.

Frančevič V., Uvalic M., 2000, eds, *Equality, Participation, Transition*, Macmillan, London.

Freeman A., 2010, Marxism without Marx: A Note towards a Critique, in *Capital & Class*, vol. 34, no. 1, February.

Freeman A., Carchedi G., 1995, *Marx and Non-Equilibrium Economics*, Elgar, Cheltenham.

Freeman A., Kliman A., & Wells J., 2004, eds, *The New Value Controversy and the Foundations of Economics*, E. Elgar, Cheltenham.

Freni G. *et alii*, 2016, *Economic Theory and its History*, Routledge, London.

Fromm E., 1961, *Marx's Concept of Man*, Frederick Ungar, New York.

Fromm E., 1962, *Marx e Freud*, Ital. transl., Il Saggiatore, Milan, 1968.

Fromm E., 1976, *Avere o essere?* Ital. transl., Mondadori, Milan, 1977.

Frowen S. F., 1997, ed., *Hayek: Economist and Social Philosopher*, MacMillan, London.

Fukuyama F., 1989, The End of History? in *The National Interest*, Summer.

Fukuyama F., 1992, *La fine della storia e l'ultimo uomo*, Ital. transl., Rizzoli, Milan, 1992.

Furubotn E. G., 1976, The Long-run Analysis of the Labor-managed Firm: An Alternative Interpretation, in *American Economic Review*, vol. 66, no. 1.

Furubotn E. G., 1980, The Socialist Labor-managed Firm and Bank-financed Investment: Some Theoretical Issues, in *Journal of Comparative Economics*, vol. 4, no. 2.

Furubotn E. G., Pejovich S., 1970, Tax Policy and Investment Decision of the Yugoslav Firm, in *National Tax Journal*, vol. 23, no. 3.

Furubotn E. G., Pejovich S., 1973, Property Rights, Economic Decentralization and the Evolution of the Yugoslav Firm, 1965–72, in *Journal of Law and Economics*, vol. 16, October.

Galasso G., 2013, *Liberalismo e democrazia*, Salerno editrice, Rome.

Galli C., 2010, *Perché ancora destra e sinistra*, Laterza, Bari.

Gallino L., 1987, Su alcuni fraintendimenti di Marx e intorno a Marx in tema di evoluzione della società, in Cacciatore & Lomonaco, 1987.

Garaudy R., 1969, Il concetto di struttura in Marx e le concezioni alienate della struttura, in AA. VV., 1969.

Garaudy R., s. d., *L'alternativa; cambiare il mondo e la vita*, Ital. transl., Cittadella editrice, Assisi, 1972.

Garegnani P., & Petri F., 1982, Marxismo e teoria economica d'oggi, in AA. VV., 1982.

Garegnani P., 1981, *Marx e gli economisti classici*, Einaudi, Turin.

Garin E., 1969, Politica e cultura in Gramsci, in AA. VV., 1969.

Garson G. D., 1973, Beyond Collective Bargaining, in Hunnius, Garson, Case, 1973.

Geary R. J., 1974, Difesa e deformazione del marxismo in Kautsky, in Istituto Giangiacomo Feltrinelli, 1974.

Gentile G., 1974, *La filosofia di Marx*, Sansoni, Florence.

Gibbons R. 1998, Incentives in Organizations, in *Journal of Economic Perspectives*, vol. 12.

Gibson-Graham J. K., 2003, Enabling Ethical Economies: Cooperativism and Class, in *Critical Sociology*, Summer.

Giddens A., 1981, *A Contemporary Critique of Historical Materialism*, University of California Press, Berkeley.

Gilbert A., 1984, Marx's Moral Realism: Eudaimonism and Moral Progress, in Ball & Farr, 1984.

Gintis H., 1976, The Nature of Labor Exchange and the Theory of Capitalistic Production, in *Review of Radical Political Economics*, vol. 8, no. 2.

Gintis H., 1989, Financial Markets and the Political Structure of the Enterprise, in *Journal of Economic Behavior and Organization*, vol. 11, no. 2.

Gintis H., Bowles S., 1981, Structure and Practice in the Labour Theory of Value, in *Review of Radical Political Economics*, vol. 12, no. 4, Winter.

Gobetti P., 1924, *La rivoluzione liberale*, Einaudi, Turin, 1965.

Gobetti P., 1929, Rassegna di questioni politiche, reprinted in Gobetti, 1969.

Gobetti P., 1969, *Scritti politici*, Einaudi, Turin.

Godelier M., 1966, Sistema, struttura e contraddizione nel *Capitale*, Ital. transl., in Godelier & Seve, 1970.

Godelier M., 1982, Il marxismo e le scienze dell'uomo, in Hobsbawm *et alii*, 1978–1982, vol. IV.

Godelier M., Sève L., 1970, *Marxismo e strutturalismo*, Einaudi.

Goldstein W. S., 2006, ed., *Marx, Critical Theory and Religion*, Leiden, Brill.

Gonnard R., 1930, *Histoire des doctrines économiques*, Valois, Paris.

Gordon D. M., 1976, Capitalist Efficiency and Socialist Efficiency, in *Monthly Review*, vol. 24.

Gould C. C., 1985, *Rethinking Democracy*, Cambridge University Press, Cambridge.

Gramsci A., 1914–18, *Scritti giovanili*, Einaudi, Turin, 1972.

Gramsci A., 1917, La rivoluzione contro il «Capitale», in *L'Avanti!*, 24 December, reprinted in Gramsci 1914–18.

Gramsci A., 1918, Individualismo e collettivismo, in Gramsci, 1958.

Gramsci A., 1919–1920, *L'Ordine nuovo*, Einaudi, Turin, 1954.

Gramsci A., 1921–22, *Socialismo e fascismo; l'Ordine Nuovo*, Einaudi, Turin, 1955.

Gramsci A., 1951, *Passato e presente*, Einaudi, Turin.

Gramsci A., 1975, *Quaderni del carcere*, ed. by V. Gerratana, Einaudi, Turin.

Gramsci A., 1984, *Il nostro Marx, 1918–1919*, ed. by S. Caprioglio, Einaudi, Turin.

Gramsci A., 1994, *Scritti di economia politica*, Boringhieri, Turin.

Grossman H., 1940, *Marx, l'economia politica classica e il problema della dinamica*, Ital. transl., Laterza, Bari, 1971.

Grossman S. J., Hart O. D., 1986, The Costs and Benefits of Ownership: A Theory of Vertical and Lateral Integration, in *Journal of Political Economy*, vol. 94, no. 4.

Gruppi L., 1962, Contro l'impoverimento della dialettica marxista, in Cassano, 1973.

Gruppi L., 1972, *Il concetto di egemonia in Gramsci*, Editori Riuniti, Rome.

Gui B., 1982, Imprese gestite dal lavoro e diritti patrimoniali dei membri: una trattazione economica, in *Ricerche economiche*, vol. 36, no. 3.

Gui B., 1985 Limits to External Financing: A Model and an Application to Labour-Managed Firm, in Jones & Svejnar, 1985.

Gui B., 1993, The Chances for Success of Worker Managed Firm Organization: An Overview, in A.I.S.S.E.C., 1993.

Gui B., 1996, Is there a Chance for the Worker-managed Form of Organization? in Pagano & Rowthorn, 1996.

Guidi M. E. L., Michelini L., 2001, *Socialismo e marginalismo nell'Italia liberale*, 1870–1925, Feltrinelli, Milan.

Gunn C. E., 2006, Cooperatives and Market Failure: Workers' Cooperatives and System Mismatch, in *Review of Radical Political Economics*, vol. 38, no. 3.

Gunn C. E., 2011, Workers' Participation in Management, Workers' Control in Production, in *Review of Radical Political Economics*, vol. 43, no. 3.

Gurvitch G., 1962, *Dialectique et sociology*, Flammarion, Paris.

Gustafsson Bo, 1974, Capitalismo e socialismo nel pensiero di Bernstein, in Istituto Giangiacomo Fertrinelli, Milano, 1974.

Habermas J., 1963, *Teoria e prassi nella società tecnologica*, Ital. transl., Laterza, Bari, 1969.

Habermas J., 1969, La tecnica e la scienza come ideologie, in AA. VV., 1969.

Hahn F. H., 1993, Il futuro del capitalismo: segni premonitori, in *Rivista milanese di economia*, no. 46, April–June.

Hall R., Jones C., 1999, Why Do Some Countries Produce so Much More Output for Worker than Others, in *Quarterly Journal of Economics*, vol. 64, no. 1.

Hamilton D., 1999, *Evolutionary Economics: A Study of Change in Economic Thought*, Transaction Pubblishers, New Brunswick.

Hamilton D., 2003, Technology Is Not Ancillary: The Dramatic and Prosaic in Economic Theory, in *Journal of Economic Issues*, vol. XXXVII, no. 1, March.

Hansmann H., 1996, *The Ownership of Enterprise*, Harvard University Press, Cambridge, MA.

Harman C., 1977, Gramsci versus Eurocommunism, Part 2. International Socialism 1(99), www.marxists. anu.edu.au.

Hart O., 1989, An Economist's Perspective on the Theory of the Firm, in *Columbia Law Review*, vol. 89, no. 7.

Hart O., 1995, *Firms, Contracts and Financial Structures*, Clarendon Press, Oxford.

Hart O., Moore J., 1990, Property Rights and the Nature of the Firm, in *Journal of Political Economy*, vol. 98, no. 6.

Hart O., Moore J., 1996, The Governance of Exchanges: Members' Cooperatives versus Outside Ownership, *working paper*, http//ssrn.com/abstract=60039.

Haug F. W., 2005, Sul processo di apprendimento di Marx: dai *Grundrisse* alla traduzione francese del primo libro del *Capitale*, in Musto, 2005.

Haupt G., 1978a, *L'internazionale socialista dalla Comune a Lenin*, Einaudi, Turin.

Haupt G., 1978b, Marx e il marxismo, in Hobsbawm *et alii* 1978–82, vol. I.

Hayek F. A., 1960, *The Constitution of Liberty*, University of Chicago Press, London.

Hayek F. A., 1982, *Legge, legislazione e libertà*, Ital. transl., Il Saggiatore, Milan, 1986.

Hayek F. A., 2009, *Tra realismo e utopia liberale: scritti 1949–1956*, ed. by M. Gregori, Mimesis, Milan.

Hegel G. W. F., 1831, *Scienza della logica*, II ediz., Ital. transl., Laterza, Bari, 1974.

Heilbroner R. L., 1980, *Marxismo pro e contro*, Armando, Rome, 1982.

Heller A., 1969, Il posto dell'etica nel marxismo, in AA. VV., 1969.

Heller A., 1976, *The Theory of Need in Marx*, St Martin's Press, New York.

Heller A., 1980, *Per cambiare la vita*; an interview by Ferdinando Adornato, Editori Riuniti, Rome.

Heller A., 1987, Marx, giustizia, libertà: il profeta libertario, in Cacciatore & Lomonaco, 1987.

Henderson W. O., 1977, *The Life of Friedrich Engels*, Cass, London.

Herland M., 1996, Three French Socialist Economists: Leroux, Proudhon, Walras, in *Journal of the History of Economic Thought*, vol. 18, Spring.

Hicks J. R., 1969, *A Theory of Economic History*, Oxford University Press, Oxford.

Hinden R., 1964, ed., *The Radical Tradition*, Pantheon Books, New York.

Hirsch F., 1976, *The Social Limits to Growth*, Harvard University Press, Cambridge, MA.

Hirschman A. O., 1982, Rival Interpretations of Market Society: Civilizing, Destructive or Feeble? in *Journal of Economic Literature*, vol. 20, December.

Hobsbawm E. J., 1982, Il marxismo, oggi: un bilancio aperto, in Hobsbawm *et alii*, 1978–1982, vol. IV.

Hobsbawm E. J., 1995, ed., *Gramsci in Europa e in America*, Laterza, Bari.

Hobsbawm E. J., 2011, *Come cambiare il mondo*, trad. Ital., Rizzoli, Milano, 2012.

Hobsbawm E. J., 2012, *Come cambiare il mondo*, Ital. transl., Bur, Milan, 2012.

Hobsbawm E. J., Haupt G., Marek F., Ragionieri E., Strada V., & Vivanti C., 1978–1982, eds, *Storia del marxismo*, 5 vols, Einaudi, Turin.

Hodges D. C., 1965, The Value Judgement in *Capital*, reprinted in Wood, 1988.

Hodges D. C., 1970, Marx's Concept of Value and Critique of Value Fetishism, reprinted in Wood, 1988.

Hodges D., Gandy R., 1982, Marx and Economic Determinism, in *Review of Radical Political Economics*, vol. 14, no. 1, Spring.

Hodgson G. M., 1982, Marx without the Labor Theory of Value, reprinted in Wood, 1988, vol. II.

Hodgson G. M., 1999, *Economics and Utopia*, Routledge, London.

Hodgson G. M., 2000, What Is the Essence of Istitutional Economics? in *Journal of Economic Issues*, vol. 34, no. 2.

Hodgson G. M., 2003, Darwinism and Institutional Economics, in *Journal of Economic Issues*, vol. 37, no. 1, March.

Hofmann W., 1971, *Da Babeuf a Marcuse*, Ital. transl., Mondadori, Milan.

Hollas D., Stansell S., 1988, An Examination of the Effect of Ownership Form on Price Efficiency: Proprietary, Cooperative, and Municipal Electric Utilities, in *Southern Economic Journal*, vol. 50.

Holloway J., 2002, *Change the World Without Taking Power: The Meaning of Revolution Today*, Pluto Press, London.

Honneth A., 2015, *L'idea di socialismo*, Ital. transl., Feltrinelli, Milan, 2016.

Horkheimer M., 1972, *Studi di filosofia della società*, Ital. transl., Einaudi, Turin, 1981.

Horvat B., 1969, *An Essay on Yugoslav Society*, International Arts and Science Press, New York.

Horvat B., 1975, On the Theory of the Labor-managed Firm, reprinted in Prychitko and Vanek, 1996.

Howard M. C., King J. E., 1975, *L'economia politica di Marx*, Ital. transl., Liguori, Naples, 1980.

Howard M. C., King J. E., 2001, Where Marx Was Right Toward a More Secure Foundation for Heterodox Economics, in *Cambridge Journal of Economics*, vol. 25, no. 6, November.

Howard M. C., King J. E., 1989, *A History of Marxian Economics*, vol. I, 1883–1929, Macmillan, London.

Huberman L., Sweezy P. M., 1968, *Introduzione al socialismo*, Ital. transl., Savelli, Rome, 1978.

Hudis P., 2000, The Dialectical Structure of Marx's Concept of 'Revolution in Permanence', in *Capital & Class*, no. 70, Spring.

Hudis P., 2013, *Marx's Concept of the Alternative to Capitalism*, Haymarket Books, Chicago.

Hume D., 1877a, *Essays*, Macmillan, London.

Hume D., 1877b, Enquiry Concerning the Principles of Morals, in *Essays*, vol. 2.

Hunnius G., Garson G. D., Case J., 1973, eds, *Workers Control: A Reader or Labor and Social Change*, Vintage Books, New York.

Hutchison T. W., 1978, Friedrich Engels and Marxist Economic Theory, in Wood, 1988.

Hyppolite J., 1969, Lo «scientifico» e l'«ideologico» in una prospettiva marxista, in AA. VV., 1969.

Ilyenkov E. V., 1960, *La dialettica dell'astratto e del concreto nel* Capitale *di Marx*, Ital. transl., Feltrinelli, Milan, 1961.

Ireland N. J., Law P. J. 1981, Efficiency, Incentives, and Individual Labor Supply in the Labor-managed Firm, *Journal of Comparative Economics*, vol. 5, no.1.

Ishibashi S., 1995, The Demonstration of the Law of Value and the Uno-Sekine Approach, in Albritton and Sekine, 1995.

Istituto Giangiacomo Feltrinelli, 1974, *Storia del marxismo contemporaneo*, Feltrinelli, Milan.

Istituto Gramsci, 1972, *Il marxismo italiano degli anni sessanta e la formazione teorico-politica delle nuove generazioni*, Editori Riuniti, Rome.

Jacobsson F., Johannesson M., Borgquist L, 2007, Is Altruism Paternalistic? in *Economic Journal*, vol. 117.

Jahn W., Noske D., 1980, Ist das Aufsteigen vom Abstrakten zum Konkreten die wissenschaftlich richtige Methode? in *Arbeitsblätter zur Marx-Engels-Forschung*, vol. II.

Jay P., 1980, The Workers' Cooperative Economy, in Clayre, 1980.

Jensen M. C., Meckling, W. J., 1979, Rights and Production Functions: An Applications to Labor-managed Firms and Codetermination, in *Journal of Business*, vol. 52, no. 4.

Johnstone M., 1980, Lenin e la rivoluzione, in Hobsbawm *et alii*, 1978–1982.

Jones D. C., Backus D. K., 1977, British Producer Cooperatives in the Footwear Industry: An Empirical Evaluation of the Theory of Financing, in *Economic Journal*, vol. 87, no. 9.

Jones D. C., Pliskin J., 1991, The Effects of Worker Participation, Employee Ownership and Profit Sharing on Economic Performance: A Partial Review, in Russel & Rus, 1991.

Jones D. C., Svejnar J., eds, 1985, *Advances in the Economic Analysis of Participatory and Labor-Managed Firms*, JAI Press, Greenwich.

Jones D. C., Svejnar J., eds, 1995, *Advances in the Economic Analysis of Participatory and Labor-Managed Firms*, vol. IV, JAI Press, Greenwich.

Jossa B., 1979, Introduzione all'autogestione, in *Rassegna economica*, no. 6.

Jossa B., 1980, Socialismo, pluralismo ed autogestione, in *Rassegna economica*, no. 1.

Jossa B., 1981, L'equilibrio di breve periodo in un'impresa autogestita in *Rassegna economica*, luglio-agosto.

Jossa B., 1982, La teoria economica delle cooperative di produzione: un'analisi introduttiva, in *Rivista della cooperazione*, aprile-giugno.

Jossa B., 1985, Due opinioni sulla teoria dell'impresa cooperativa; con una conclusione sulla definizione del socialismo, in *Rivista Internazionale di Scienze Sociali*, no. 1.

Jossa B., 1986a, Autogestione e proprietà delle imprese, in *Politica ed Economia*, April.

Jossa B., 1986b, Considerazioni su un 'tipo ideale' di cooperative di produzione, in *Studi economici*, no. 28.

Jossa B., 1987, Intervento, in Cacciatore e Lomonaco, 1987.

Jossa B., 1988, Sul problema del sottoinvestimento delle imprese gestite dai lavoratori, in AISSEC, *V Convegno Scientifico annuale*, Pavia.

Jossa B., 1989a, Socialismo e autogestione, in Jossa, 1989b.

Jossa B., 1989b, *Teoria dei sistemi economici*, UTET, Turin.

Jossa B., 1990, Sulla transizione dall'economia di comando al socialismo di mercato, in *Note economiche*, no. 2.

Jossa B., 1992, Socialismo di mercato e distribuzione del reddito, in Chilosi, 1992.

Jossa B., 1993, The Problem of Under-investment in Firms Managed by Workers (in collaboration with P. Casavola), in Atkinson, 1993.

Jossa B., 1994a, Ordine spontaneo e liberismo secondo Hayek, in Jossa, 1994b.

Jossa B., 1994b, ed., *Il neoliberismo: teoria e politica economica*, F. Angeli, Milan.

Jossa B., 1994c, Hayek and Market Socialism, in Colonna, Hagemann & Hamouda, 1994.

Jossa B., 1997, *The Economic Theory of Socialism and the Labour managed Firm* (with G. Cuomo), E. Elgar, Cheltenham.

Jossa B., 1998, *Mercato, socialismo e autogestione*, Carocci, Rome.

Jossa B., 1999, *La democrazia nell'impresa*, Editoriale scientifica, Naples.

Jossa B., 2001, L'impresa gestita dai lavoratori e la disoccupazione classica e keynesi-ana, *Rivista italiana degli economisti*, no. 1, April.

Jossa B., 2002, Il marxismo e le imprese gestite dai lavoratori, in *Economia Politica*, a. XIX, no. 3.

Jossa B., 2004, The Democratic Firm as a Public Good, in Arena & Salvadori, 2004.

Jossa B., 2005a, Marx, Marxism and the Cooperative Movement, in *Cambridge Journal of Economics*, no. 1.

Jossa B., 2005b, *La teoria economica delle cooperative di produzione e la possibile fine del capitalismo*, Giappichelli, Turin.

Jossa B., 2006, L'economia politica della rivoluzione democratica, in *Economia Politica*, vol. XXII, no. 3.

Jossa B., 2008a, How Cooperative Firms Should be Organised from the Perspective of Today's Economic Theory, in *Politica Economica*, no. 3.

Jossa B., 2008b, *L'impresa democratica*, Carocci, Rome.

Jossa B., 2009, Unemployment in a System of Labour-Managed Firms, in Salvadori & Opocher, 2009.

Jossa B., 2010a, A Few Advantages of Cooperative Firms, in *Studi Economici*, no. 65.

Jossa B., 2010b, *Esiste un'alternativa al capitalismo?* manifestolibri, Rome.

Jossa B., 2011, L'impresa democratica come nuova prospettiva per il marxismo, in *Economia politica*, no. 1.

Jossa B., 2012a, A System of Self-managed Firms as a New Perspective on Marxism, in *Cambridge Journal of Economics*, vol. 36, no. 4.

Jossa B., 2012b, Cooperative Firms as a New Production Mode, in *Review of Political Economy*, vol. 24, no. 3.

Jossa B., 2012c, Alienation and the Self-Managed Firm System, in *The Review of Radical Political Economics*, 2013, vol. 46, no. 2.

Jossa B., 2012d, *Il marxismo e le sfide della globalizzazione*, manifestolibri, Rome.

Jossa B., 2014, *A System of Cooperative Firms as a New Production Mode*, Routledge, London.

Jossa B., 2015, *Un socialismo possibile*, Il Mulino, Bologna.

Jossa B., 2016, Self-management and Socialism, in Freni *et alii*, 2016.

Jossa B., 2017, *Labour Managed Firms and Post-Capitalism*, Routledge, London.

Jossa B., 2018, *A New Model of Socialism*, E. Elgar, Cheltenham.

Jossa B., Casavola P., 1993, The Problem of Under-Investment in Firms Managed by Workers, in Atkinson, 1993.

Jossa B., Cuomo G., 1997, *The Economic Theory of Socialism and the Labour–Managed Firm*, E. Elgar, Cheltenham.

Jossa B., Lunghini G., 2006, eds., *Marxismo oggi*, Il Ponte Editore, Florence.

Kaldor N., 1972, The Irrelevance of Equilibrium Economics, in *Economic Journal*, vol. 82, December.

Kalecki M., 1937, The Principle of Increasing Risk, in *Economica*, vol. 3, November.

Kalmi P., 2000, Employment Share Trade under Employee Share Ownership: An Application to Transition Economies, in *Economic Analysis*, vol. 3, no. 1.

Kant I., 1784, Idea per una storia universale dal punto di vista cosmopolitico, in Kant, 1965.

Kant I., 1787, *Critica della ragion pura*, Ital. transl., Laterza, Bari, 1966.

Kant I., 1798, Se il genere umano sia in costante progresso verso il meglio, in Kant, 1956.

Kant I., 1965, *Scritti politici e di filosofia della storia e del diritto*, UTET, Turin.

Karsz S., 1974, *Teoria e politica: Louis Althusser*, Ital. transl., Dedalo libri, Bari, 1976.

Kautsky K., 1892a, *Il Programma di Erfurt*, Ital. transl., Samonà e Savelli, Rome, 1971.

Kautsky K., 1892b, *Introduzione al pensiero economico di Marx*, Ital. transl., Laterza, Bari, 1972.

Kautsky K., 1899, *Bernstein und das sozialdemokratische Program. Eine Antikritik*, Dietz, Stuttgart.

Kautsky K., 1902, Che cosa è una rivoluzione sociale, in Mills, 1962.

Kautsky K., 1906, *Etica e concezione materialistica della storia*, Ital. transl., Feltrinelli, Milan, 1975.

Kautsky K., 1909a, *Der Weg zur Macht*, Buchhandlung Vorwärts, Berlin.

Kautsky K., 1909b, *The Social Revolution*, C. Kerr & Co London.

Kautsky K., 1960, *Erinnerungen und Erörterungen*, Gravenhage, Berlin.

Kellner D., 1995, The Obsolescence of Marxism? in Magnus & Cullenberg, 1995.

Keynes J. M., 1926a, *Laissez-Faire and Communism*, New Republic, Inc., New York.

Keynes J. M., 1926b, La fine del *laissez-faire*, in Keynes, 1926a.

Keynes J. M., 1979, *The Collected Writings of John Maynard Keynes*, vol. XXIX; *The General Theory and After: A Supplement*, Macmillan, London.

Keynes J. M., various years, *The Collected Writings of John Maynard Keynes*, vol. XIV, Mac-millan, London.

Khalil E. L., Boulding K. E., 1996, eds, *Evolution, Order and Complexity*, Routledge, London.

Kicillof A., Starosta G., 2007, Value Form and Class Struggle: A Critique of the Autonomist Theory of Value, in *Capital and Class*, no. 92, Summer.

Kicillof A., Starosta G., 2011, On Value and Abstract Labour: A Reply to Werner Bonefeld, in *Capital and Class*, vol. 35, no. 2.

Kihlstrom R., Laffont J. J., 1979, A General Equilibrium Entrepreneurial Theory of Firm Formation Based on Risk Aversion, in *Journal of Political Economy*, vol. 87, no. 4, August.

Kincaid J., 2001, The New Dialectic, in Bidet & Kouvelakis, 2001.

Kirchgassner G., 1989, On the Political Economy of Economic Policy, in *Economia delle scelte pubbliche*, a. VII, no. 1–2.

Kleiner D., 2010, *The Telecommunist Manifesto*, Institute of Network Cultures, Amsterdam.

Kliman A. J., 1998, Value, Exchange Value and the Internal Consistency of Volume III of Capital: A Refutation of Refutations, in Bellofiore, 1998.

Kliman A. J., 2010, The Disintegration of the Marxian School, in *Capital & Class*, vol. 34, no. 1.

Kolakowsky L., 1976–77, *Nascita, sviluppo, dissoluzione del marxismo*, Ital. transl., SogarCo, Milan, 1980.

Kornai J., 1980, *Economics of Shortage*, North-Holland, Amsterdam.

Kornai J., 1992, *The Socialist System: The Political Economy of Communism*, Princeton University Press, Princeton.

Kornai J., 1994, *Overcentralization in Economic Administration*, 2nd edition, Oxford University Press, Oxford.

Korsch K., 1891, *Il programma di Erfurt*, Ital. transl., Samonà e Savelli, Rome, 1971.

Korsch K., 1922, *Consigli di fabbrica e socializzazione*, Ital. transl., Laterza, Bari, 1970.

Korsch K., 1923, *Marxismo e filosofia*, Ital. transl., Sugar editore, Milan, 1966.

Kouvelakis S., 2005, Marx e la critica della politica, in Musto, 2005.

Krassò N., Mandel E., & Johnstone M., 1970, *Il marxismo di Trockij*, Ital. transl., De Donato, Bari.

Krugman P., 2009, How Did Economists Get It So Wrong? http://www. nytimes. com/2009/09/06 /magazine/ 06Economic-t.html?pagewanted= all&_r=0.

Kundera M., 1973, *La vita è altrove*, Ital. transl., Adelphi, Milan, 1987.

Labriola A., 1895, In memoria del Manifesto dei Comunisti, in Labriola, 1965.

Labriola A., 1902, *Discorrendo di socialismo e di filosofia*, Edizioni Millennium, Bologna, 2006.

Labriola A., 1942, *La concezione materialistica della storia*, Laterza, Bari.

Labriola A., 1970, *Scritti politici*, ed. by V. Gerratana, Laterza, Bari.

Lacan J., 1955, La cosa freudiana, in Lacan, 1972.

Lacan J., 1972, *La cosa freudiana e altri scritti*, Einaudi, Turin.

Laibman D., 2006, The Future Within the Present: Seven Theses for a Robust Twenty-First-Century Socialism, in *Review of Radical Political Economics*, vol. 18, no. 3, Summer.

Laibman D., 2007, *Deep History*, State of New York Press, New York.

Laibman D., 2013, Market Socialism: Design, Prerequisites, Transition, in *Review of Radical Political Economics*, vol. 45, no. 4.

Landauer G., 1985, *Ein Weg zur Befreiung der Arbeiterklasse*, Verlag von Adolf Marreck, Berlin.

Lange O., 1935, Marxian Economics and Modern Economic Theory, in *Review of Economic Studies*, vol. 2, no. 3, June.

Lange O., 1936–37, On the Economic Theory of Socialism, in *The Review of Economic Studies*, vol. 4, nos. 1 and 2, reprinted with changes in Lippincott, 1938.

Lange O., 1957, Alcuni problemi riguardanti la via polacca al socialismo, in Lange, 1966.

Lange O., 1966, *Socialismo ed economia socialista*, Ital. transl., La Nuova Italia, Florence.

Lasch C., 1995, *La rivolta delle élite*, Ital. transl., Neri Pozza, Vicenza, 2017.

Laski H. J., 1947, *Le origini del liberalismo europeo*, Ital. transl., La Nuova Italia, Florence, 1962.

Latouche S., 1999, *La sfida di Minerva, razionalità occidentale e ragione mediterranea*, Ital. transl., Bollati Boringhieri, Turin, 2000.

Lawler J., 1994, Marx's Theory of Socialism: Nihilistic and Dialectical, in Patsouras, 1994.

Lazonick W., 1978, The Subjection of Labour to Capital: The Rise of the Capitalist System, in *Review of Radical Political Economics*, vol. 10, no. 1.

Lefebvre H., 1968, Bilancio di un secolo e di due mezzi secoli (1867–1917–1967), in AA. VV., 1968.

Lehning A., 1969, Anarchisme et bolscevisme, in AA. VV., 1971.

Lenin V. I., 1913, Tre fonti e tre parti integranti del marxismo, in Lenin, 1965.

Lenin V. I., 1917, *L'imperialismo, fase suprema del capitalismo*, Ital. transl., Editori Riuniti, Rome, 1969.

Lenin V. I., 1918, La rivoluzione proletaria e il rinnegato Kautsky, in Lenin, *Opere complete*, vol. XXVIII.

Lenin V. I., 1919, Come organizzare l'emulazione? in Lenin, *Opere complete*, vol. XXVI.

Lenin V. I., 1920, L'estremiamo, malattia infantile del comunismo, in

Lenin V. I., 1921, *La nuova politica economica*, in Lenin, 1972.

Lenin V. I., 1923, Sulla cooperazione, in Lenin, 1965.

Lenin V. I., 1957–70, *Opere complete*, Editori Riuniti, Rome.

Lenin V. I., 1965, *Opere scelte*, Editori Riuniti, Rome.

Lenin V. I., 1972, *La costruzione del socialismo*, Editori Riuniti, Rome.

Leone E., 1902, Sul principio di cooperazione nei suoi rapporti con il socialismo, in *Critica sociale*, vol. XII, no. 18.

Lepage H., 1978, *Autogestion et capitalisme*, Masson, Paris.

Lerner A. P., 1938. Theory and Practice in Socialist Economics, in *Review of Economic Studies*, vol. 6, no. 1.

Leube K. R., 1988, Social Policy: Hayek and Schmoller Compared, in *International Journal of Social Economics*, nos 9–10–11.

Levine D. J., Tyson L., 1990, Participation, Productivity and the Firm's Environment, in Blinder, 1990.

Levine D. J., 1995, *Reinventing the Workplace. How Business and Employees Can Both Win*, Brookings Institution, Washington D.C.

Levine D. J., 1998, The Structure of Marx's Argument in *Capital*, in Bellofiore, 1998.

Lichtheim G., 1965, *Marxism: An Historical and Critical Study*, F. A. Praeger, New York.

Lindenberg D., 1975, *Il marxismo introvabile*, Ital. transl., Einaudi, Turin, 1978.

Lipietz A., 1982, The So-Called 'Transformation Problem' Rivisited, in *Journal of Economic Theory*, vol. L, no. 26.

Lippi M., 1976, *Marx; il valore come costo sociale reale*, Etas Libri, Milan.

Lippincott B. E., 1938, ed., *On the Economic Theory of Socialism*, University of Minnesota Press, Philadelphia.

Liss S. B., 1984, *Marxist Thought in Latin America*, University of California Press, Berkeley and Los Angeles.

Livorsi F., 1976, *Amadeo Bordiga*, Editori Riuniti, Rome.

Livorsi F., 2009, Il mistero del comunismo nella storia, in *Il Ponte*, a. LXV, no. 9.

Longxi Z., 1995, Marxism: From Scientific to Utopian, in Magnus & Cullenberg, 1995.

Lorenz R., 1974, La costruzione del socialismo in Lenin, in Istituto Giangiacomo Feltrinelli, 1974.

Losurdo D., 2005, Marxismo, globalizzazione e bilancio storico del socialismo, in Musto, 2005.

Lowit T., 1962, Marx et le mouvement cooperatif, in *Cahiers de l'institut de science èconomique appliquée*, no. 129, September.

Lukàcs G., 1920–21, *Kommunismus, 1920–1921*, Ital. transl., Marsilio Editore, Padua, 1972.

Lukàcs G., 1923, *Storia e coscienza di classe*, Ital. transl., Sugarco Edizioni, 1974, Milan.

Lukàcs G., 1924, *Lenin*, Ital. transl., Einaudi, Turin, 1970.

Lukàcs G., 1956, La lotta tra progresso e reazione nella cultura d'oggi, in Lukàcs, 1968.

Lukàcs G., 1968a, *Scritti politici giovanili, 1919–1928*, Laterza, Bari.

Lukàcs G., 1968b, *Marxismo e politica culturale*, Einaudi, Turin.

Lukàcs G., 1971, Vecchia kultur e nuova kultur, in *Quaderni Piacentini*, vol. 43, no. 4.

Lukàcs G., 1972, *L'uomo e la rivoluzione*, Ital. transl., Editori Riuniti, Rome, 1973.

Lukàcs G., 1976, *Ontologia dell'essere sociale*, vol. I, Editori Riuniti, Rome.

Lunghini G., 1993, ed., *Valori e prezzi*, UTET, Turin.

Luporini C., 1966, Realtà e storicità: economia e dialettica nel marxismo, in Luporini, 1974.
Luporini C., 1974, *Dialettica e materialismo*, Editori Riuniti, Rome.
Luxemburg R., 1899, Riforme sociali o rivoluzione, in Luxemburg, 1967.
Luxemburg R., 1913, *L'accumulazione del capitale*, Ital. transl., Einaudi, Turin, 1960.
Luxemburg R., 1918, Discorso sul programma, in Luxemburg, 1967.
Luxemburg R., 1948, La rivoluzione russa, in Luxemburg, 1967.
Luxemburg R., 1967, *Scritti politici*, ed. by L. Basso, Editori Riuniti, Rome, 1967.
Macciocchi M. A., 1974, *Per Gramsci*, Il Mulino, Bologna.
MacGregor D., 1984, *The Communist Ideal in Hegel and Marx*, University of Toronto Press, Toronto.
MacPherson I., 2004, Democracy: Utopian and Scientific, in Ball & Farr, 2004.
MacPherson I., 2008, The Cooperative Movement and the Social Economy Traditions: Reflections on the Mingling of Broad Visions, in *Annals of Public and Cooperative Economics*, vol. 79, nos 3–4.
Magatti M., 1990, ed., *Azione economica come azione sociale*, F. Angeli, Milan.
Magnus B., Cullenberg S., 1995, *Whither Marxism?* Routledge, New York.
Magri L., 1970, 'Via italiana' e strategia consiliare, reprinted in AA. VV., 1974.
Maitan L., 1995, La crisi attuale, in Colombo, 1994.
Major G., 1996, Solving the Underinvestment and Degeneration Problem of Workers' Cooperatives: Non-Voting and Vote-Weighted Value-Added Residual Shares, in *Annals of Public and Cooperative Economy*, vol. 67, no. 4.
Makoto I., 2006, Marx's Economic Theory and the Prospect for Socialism, in Uchida, 2006.
Mandel E., 1967, *La formation de la pensée économique de Karl Marx*, Maspero, Paris.
Mandel E., 1973, The Debate on Workers' Control, in Hunnius, Garson & Case, 1973.
Mann T., 1918, *Considerazioni di un impolitico*, Adelphi, Milan.
Marcovic M., 1969, Marx e il pensiero critico-scientifico, in AA. VV., 1969.
Marcuse H., 1954, *Ragione e rivoluzione*, Ital. transl., Il Mulino, Bologna, 1966.
Marcuse H., 1969, Un riesame del concetto di rivoluzione, in AA. VV., 1969.
Marcuse P., 2015, Cooperatives on the Path to Socialism? in *Monthly Review*, vol. 66, February.
Marek F., 1982, Teorie della rivoluzione e fasi della transizione, in AA. VV, 1978–82.
Marga A., 1995, The Modern World and the Individuals, in Magnus & Cullenberg, 1995.
Marglin S. A., 1974, What Do Bosses Do? in *Review of Radical Political Economics*, vol. 6, no. 2.
Marković M., 1969, Marx e il pensiero critico-scientifico, in AA. VV., 1969.
Markus G., 1966, *Marxismo e antropologia*, Ital. transl., Liguori Editore, Naples, 1978.
Marramao G., 1977, *Austromarxismo e socialismo di sinistra tra le due guerre*, La Pietra, Milan.
Marramao G., 1980, Tra bolscevismo e socialdemocrazia: Otto Bauer e la cultura politica dell'austromarxismo, in Hobsbawm *et alii*, 1978–82.
Marramao G., 1982, Politica e complessità: lo Stato tardo-capitalistico come categoria e come problema teorico, in Hobsbawm *et alii*, 1978–1982, vol. IV.
Marshall A., 1873, The Future of the Working Classes, in Marshall, 1925.
Marshall A., 1889, Cooperation, in Marshall, 1925.
Marshall A., 1890, *Principles of Economics*, Macmillan, London.

Marshall A., 1897, The Old Generation of Economists and the New, in Marshall, 1925.

Marshall A., 1925, *Memorials of Alfred Marshall*, ed. by A. C. Pigou, Macmillan, London.

Marx K., 1841, Difference between the Democritean and Epicurean Philosophy of Nature, in Marx & Engels, *Collected Works*, vol. I.

Marx K., 1843, Critica della filosofia hegeliana del diritto pubblico, in Marx & Engels, 1966.

Marx K., 1844a, *Manoscritti economico-filosofici del 1844*, Einaudi, Turin, 1968.

Marx K., 1844b, *On the Jewish Question*, in Marx & Engels, 1975–2001, vol. III.

Marx K., 1845, Tesi su Feuerbach, in Marx & Engels, *Opere Complete*, vol. V.

Marx K., 1847, *Miseria della filosofia*, Ital. transl., Editori Riuniti, Rome, 1969.

Marx K., 1849, *Lavoro salariato e capitale*, Ital. transl., Editori Riuniti, Rome, 1971.

Marx K., 1852a, *The Eighteenth Brumaire of Louis Bonaparte*, in Marx & Engels, 1975–2001, vol. 11.

Marx K., 1852b, New York Times article of August 25th.

Marx K., 1857–58, *Lineamenti fondamentali della critica dell'economia politica*, La Nuova Italia, Florence, 1970.

Marx K., 1857, Introduzione a *Per la critica dell'economia politica*, in Marx, 1859.

Marx K., 1858, Letter to Engels, dated 14 January, Ital. transl., in Marx & Engels, 1972.

Marx K., 1859, Outline of the Critique of Political Economy, in Marx & Engels, *Collected Works*, vol. 29.

Marx K., 1860, Letter to Engels of 19 December, in Marx & Engels, 1972, vol. III.

Marx K., 1861–63, Economic Manuscript of 1861–63, in Marx & Engels, 1975–2001, vols. 30–34.

Marx K., 1861, Letter to Lassalle of 16 January, in Marx & Engels, 1975–2001, vol. 30.

Marx K., 1863–66, *Il Capitale: libro I, capitolo VI inedito*, La Nuova Italia, 1969, Florence.

Marx K., 1864, Indirizzo inaugurale e statuti provvisori dell'Associazione internazionale degli operai, Ital. transl., in Marx & Engels, 1966.

Marx K., 1867a, *Capital*, vol. I, Penguin Books, Harmondsworth, 1986.

Marx K., 1867b, Letter to Engels of 7 December in Marx-Engels, 1972, vol. V.

Marx K., 1868a, Letter to Engels of 30 April, in Marx-Engels, 1972.

Marx K., 1868b, Lettera a Kugelmann del 6 marzo, in Marx-Engels, 1971.

Marx K., 1869, Letter to Laura and Paul Lafargue of 15 February, in Marx-Engels, 1975–2001.

Marx K., 1871, The Civil War in France, in Marx & Engels, *Collected Works*, vol. 22.

Marx K., 1873, Poscritto alla seconda edizione del *Capitale*, in Marx, 1867.

Marx K., 1875a, *Critique of the Gotha Programme*, in Marx & Engels, 1975–2001, vol. 24.

Marx K., 1875b, Letter to Peter Lavrov del 12–17 November, in Marx-Engels, 1975–2001.

Marx K., 1877, Letter of end 1877 to the editor's office dell'*Otecestvennye Zapinski*, in Marx-Engels, 1965.

Marx K., 1894, *Capital*, vol. III, Penguin Books, Harmondsworth, 1981.

Marx K., 1895, *The Class Struggles in France*, in Marx & Engels, 1975–2001, vol. 10.

Marx K., Engels F., 1845–1846, *L'ideologia tedesca*, Ital. transl., 3rd edition, Editori Riuniti, Rome, 1969.

Marx K., Engels F., 1848, *Manifesto del partito comunista*, in Marx & Engels, 1966.

Marx K., Engels F., 1850, Indirizzo al Comitato centrale della Lega dei comunisti del marzo 1850, in Marx-Engels, 1978.

Marx K., Engels F., 1942, *Selected Correspondence, 1846–95*, International Publisher, New York.

Marx K., Engels F., 1965, *India, Cina, Russia*, Ital. transl., Il Saggiatore, Milan.

Marx K., Engels F., 1966, *Opere scelte*, Editori Riuniti, Rome.

Marx K., Engels F., 1971, *Lettere sul Capitale*, Editori Laterza, Bari.

Marx K., Engels F., 1972, *Carteggio Marx-Engels* (1857–1860), Editori Riuniti, Rome.

Marx K., Engels F., 1975–2001, *Collected Works*, voll. 1–49, Lawrence and Wishart, London.

Marx K., Engels F., 1978, *Proletariato e comunismo*, ed. by G. M. Bravo, Editori Riuniti, Rome.

Marx K., Engels F., 1944–1951, *Opere complete*, Editori Riuniti, Rome.

Marzano F., 1997, Complementarietà di piano e mercato, in Schiavone, 1997.

Matthias E., 1957, *Kautsky e il kautskismo*, Ital. transl., De Donato editore, Bari, 1971.

Mattick P., 2002, Class, Capital and Crisis, in Campbell & Reuten, 2002.

Matyaszovsky V., 1986, Nota introduttiva a Liska, in AA. VV., 1986.

Mavroudeas S. D., 2004, Forms of Existence of Abstract Labour and Value-Form, in Freeman, Kliman & Wells, 2004.

Mayer T., 1994, *Analytical Marxism*, Sage Publications, London.

Mazzini G., 1862, *Il socialismo e la democrazia*, in Mazzini, undated.

Mazzini G., undated, *Politica ed Economia*, Sonzogno, Milan.

Mazzoli E., Zamagni S., eds, 2005, *Verso una nuova teoria economica della cooperazione*, Il Mulino, Bologna.

Mc Glone T., Kliman A., 1996, One System Or Two? The Transformation of Values into Prices of Production versus the Transformation Problem, in Freeman & Carchedi, 1996.

McCain R. A., 1977, On the Optimal Financing Environment for Worker Cooperatives, in *Zeitschrift für Nationalökonomie*, vol. 37, nos. 3–4.

McCain R. A., 1992, Transaction Costs, Labor Management, and Co-determination, in Jones & Svejnar, 1992.

McMurtry J. J., 2004, Social Economy as a Social Practice, in *International Journal of Social Economics*, vol. 31, nos. 9 and 10.

McQuarie D., Amburgey T., 1978, Marx and Modern System Theory, in Wood, 1988, vol. IV.

Meade J. E., 1972, The Theory of Labour-managed Firms and of Profit Sharing, *Economic Journal*, vol. 82, March, Supplement.

Meade J. E., 1979, The Adjustment Processes of Labor Cooperatives with Constant Returns to Scale and Perfect Competition, in *Economic Journal*, vol. 89, December.

Meade J. E., 1989, *Agathotopia*, Ital. transl., Feltrinelli, Milan, 1989.

Meek R., 1956, *Saggi sulla teoria del valore-lavoro*, Ital. transl., Feltrinelli, Milan, 1973.

Mehring F., 1918, *Vita di Marx*, Ital. transl., Editori Riuniti, Rome, 1966.

Menard C., 2007, The Economics of Hybrid Organizations? in *Journal of Institutional and Theoretical Economics*, vol. 160, no. 3.

Menzani T., 2007, Le cooperative associate al CNS, in Battilani & Bertagnoni, 2007.

Merleau-Ponty M., 1948, *Le avventure della dialettica*, Ital. transl., Sugar, Milan, 1965.

Mészàros I., 1995, *Behond Capital*, Merlin Press, London.

Meyer A. G., 1957, *Il leninismo*, Ital. transl., Edizioni di Comunità, Milan, 1965.

Meyer T., 1994, *Analytical Marxism*, vol. I, Sage Publications, London.

Miconi B., 1981, Valori e prezzi nell'analisi marxiana e nella letteratura economica, in Panizza and Vicarelli, 1981.

Mill J. S., 1871, *Principles of Political Economy*, ed. by Ashley, Longmans, Green and Co., 1909.

Miller D., 1989, *Market, States and Community*, Clarendon Press, Oxford.

Miller E. S., 2002, Economics in a Public Interest: Remark upon Receiving the Veblen-Commons Award, in *Journal of Economic Issues*, vol. XXXVI, no. 2, June.

Miller E. S., 2003, Evolution and Stasis: The Institutional Economics of David Hamilton, in *Journal of Economic Issues*, vol. XXXVII, no. 1, March.

Miller R. W., 1984, Producing Change: Work, Technology, and Power in Marx's Theory of History, in Ball and Farr, 1984.

Mills C. W., 1948, *The New Man of Power*, Harcourt Brace, New York.

Mills C. W., 1959, *The Sociological Imagination*, Oxford University Press, New York.

Mills C. W., 1962, *I marxisti*, Ital. transl., Feltrinelli, Milan, 1969.

Mises L. von, 1932 and 1951, *Socialism; an Economic and Sociological Analysis*, Engl. Transl., Yale University Press, New Haven, 1981.

Miyazaki H., Neary H. N., 1983, The Illyrian Firm Revisited, in *Bell Journal of Economics,* vol. 14, no. 1.

Mohun S., 1991, Abstract Labour, in Bottomore, 1991.

Mondolfo R., 1909, Feuerbach e Marx, in Mondolfo, 1968.

Mondolfo R., 1923, *Sulle orme di Marx*, Cappelli, Bologna.

Mondolfo R., 1952, *Il materialismo storico in Federico Engels*, La Nuova Italia, FlorencD., 1998e.

Mondolfo R., 1962, La concezione dell'uomo in Marx, in Mondolfo, 1968.

Mondolfo R., 1968, *Umanismo di Marx. Studi filosofici, 1908–1966*, Einaudi, Turin.

Montaldi D., 1975, *Korsch e i comunisti italiani*, Savelli, Rome, 1975.

Montias J. M., 1976, *The Structure of Economics Systems*, Yale University Press, New Haven.

Morishima M., 1973, *La teoria economica di Marx*, Ital. transl., ISEDI, Milan, 1974.

Morris J., 1966, Commodity Fetishism and the Value Concept: Some Contrasting Point of View, reprinted in Wood, 1988.

Moseley F., 1982, The 'New Solution' to the Transformation Problem: A Sympathetic Critique, in *Review of Radical Political Economics*, vol. 32, no. 2.

Moseley F., 1993a, ed., *Marx's Method in 'Capital': A Reexamination*, Humanities Press, Atlantic Highlands.

Moseley F., 1993b, Marx's Logical Method and the Transformation Problem, in Moseley, 1993a.

Moseley F., 1998, Marx's Logic in *Capital* and the 'Transformation Problem', in Bellofiore, 1998.

Murgescu C., 1969, Alcune riflessioni sommarie in occasione di un anniversario, in AA. VV., 1969a.

Murray P., 2002, The Illusion of Economic: The Trinity Formula and the 'Religion of Everyday Life', in Campbell & Reuten, 2002.

Musgrave R. A., 1958, On Merit Goods, in Musgrave, 1986, vol. I.

Musgrave R. A., 1986, *Public Finance in a Democratic Society*; Collected Papers of Richard A. Musgrave, vol. I. Wheatsheaf Books, Brighton.

Musto M., 2005a, ed., *Sulle tracce di un fantasma*, manifestolibri, Rome.

Musto M., 2005b, Marx a Paris: la critica del 1844, in Musto, 2005a.

Musto M., 2011, *Ripensare Marx e i marxismi*, Carocci, Rome.

Mygind N., 1997, Employee Ownership in Baltic Countries, in Uvalic & Vaugham-Whitehead, 1997.

Napoleoni C., 1956, ed., *Dizionario di economia politica*, Ed. Comunità, Milan.

Napoleoni C., 1962a, Squilibri economici e pianificazione in Italia, *La Rivista Trimestrale*, no. 2, June.

Napoleoni C., 1962b, ed., Mercato, pianificazione e imprenditorialità, *La Rivista trimestrale*, no. 3, September.

Napoleoni C., 1970, Su alcuni problemi del marxismo, in Sweezy *et alii*, 1970.

Napoleoni C., 1972, *Lezioni sul Capitolo sesto inedito di Marx*, Boringhieri, Turin.

Napoleoni C., 1985, *Discorso sull'economia politica*, Boringhieri, Turin.

Nassisi A. M., 1987, ed., *Marx e il mondo contemporaneo*, Editori Riuniti, Rome.

Naville P., 1948, *Psychologie, Marxisme, Matérialisme. Essais critiques*, Rivière, Paris.

Negri A., 1977, Keynes e la teoria dello Stato capitalistico, oggi, in AA. VV., 1977.

Negri A., 1998, *Marx oltre Marx*, manifestolibri, Rome.

Negt O., 1978, L'ultimo Engels, in Hobsbawm *et alii*, 1978–82.

Negt O., 1979, Il marxismo e la teoria della rivoluzione nell'ultimo Engels, in AA. VV., 1978–1982, vol. II.

Nisbet R. A., 1977, *Storia e cambiamento sociale. Il concetto di sviluppo nella tradizione occidentale*, Ibl Libri, Milan.

Nordhal R. A., 1982, Marx on the Use of History in the Analysis of Capitalism, in Wood, 1988, vol. I.

Nove A., Thatcher I. D., 1994, eds, *Markets and Socialism*, Elgar, Aldershot.

Nozick R., 1974, *Anarchy, State and Utopia*, Basil Blackwell, Oxford.

Nuti D. M., 1978, Investment, Interest and Degree of Centralization in Maurice Dobb's Theory of Socialist Economy, *Cambridge Journal of Economics*, vol. 3, no. 2.

Nuti D. M., 1992, Il socialismo di mercato. Il modello che avrebbe potuto esserci, ma che non c'è mai stato, in Chilosi, 1992a.

Nuti D. M., 1997, Employeism: Corporate Governance and Employee Share Ownership in Transitional Economies, in Blejer, Škreb, 1997.

Nuti D. M., 2000, Employee Participation in Enterprise Control and Returns: Patterns, Gaps and Discontinuities, in Frančevič, Uvalic, 2000.

Nutzinger H. G., 1975, Investment and Financing in a Labour-managed Firm and Its Social Implications, in *Economic Analysis and Workers' Management*, vol. 9, nos. 3–4.

O'Boyle B., 2013, Reproducing the Social Structure: A Marxist Critique of Anthony Giddens's Structuration Methodology, in *Cambridge Journal of Economics*, vol. 17, no. 5.

Offe C., 1977, *Lo stato nel capitalismo maturo*, Ital. translation of eight articles from German, Etas Libri, Milan, 1977.

Ojzerman T. I., 1969, Il materialismo storico di Marx e alcuni problemi dello sviluppo sociale contemporaneo, in AA. VV., 1969, vol. I.

Ollman B., 1976, *Alienation; Marx's Conception of Man in Capitalistic Society*, 2nd edition, Cambridge University Press, Cambridge.

Ollman B., 1998, ed., *Market Socialism; the Debate among Socialists*, Routledge, London.

Ollman B., 2003, *Dance of the Dialectic; Steps in Marx's Method*, University of Illinois Press, Chicago.

Orfei R., 1970, *Marxismo e umanismo*, Coines Edizioni, Rome.

Pagano U., 2006, Marx fra autoritarismo e democrazia economica, in Jossa & Lunghini, 2006.

Pagano U., Rowthorn R., 1996, eds, *Democracy and Efficiency in Economic Enterprise*, Routledge, London.

Panaccione A., 1974, L'analisi del capitalismo in Kautsky, in Istituto Giangiacomo Feltrinelli, 1974.

Panizza R., Vicarelli S., 1981, eds, *Valori e prezzi nella teoria di Marx*, Einaudi, Turin.

Panzieri R., 1957, Capitalismo contemporaneo e controllo operaio, in *Mondo operaio*, no. 12, December.

Panzieri R., 1967, Lotte operaie nello sviluppo capitalistico, in Panzieri, 1975.

Panzieri R., 1975, *La ripresa del marxismo leninismo in Italia*, Sapere edizioni, Milan.

Pareto V., 1902, *I sistemi socialisti*, Unione tipografica, Editrice Torinese, Turin, 1951.

Pasolini P. P., 1962, *Il sogno di una cosa*, Garzanti, Milan, 2009.

Pasolini P. P., 1964, Marxismo e cristianesimo, in Pasolini, 1995.

Pasolini P. P., 1975, *Scritti corsari*, Garzanti, Milan.

Pasolini P. P., 1995, *Interviste corsare*, Atlantide editoriale, Rome.

Patsouras, 1994, ed., *Debating Marx*, Lewiston, New York.

Pejovich S., 1982, Karl Marx, Property Rights and the Process of Social Change, in *Kyklos*, vol. 35, no. 3, reprinted in Wood, 1988.

Pelikan J., 1977, Il socialismo e l'Europa orientale, in ARA, 1977.

Pellicani L., 1976, Socialismo e pluralismo, in *Mondoperaio*, 1976.

Pellicani L., 1987, La dialettica marxiana: scienza o gnosi? in Cacciatore & Lomonaco, 1987.

Pérotin V., 2004, Early Cooperative Survival: The Liability of Adolescence, in *Advances in Economic Analysis of Participatory and Labour-managed Firms*, vol. 8, no. 1.

Pérotin V., 2006, Entry, Exit, and the Business Cycle: Are Cooperatives Different? in *Journal of Cooperative Economics*, vol. 34, no. 2.

Perri S., 1998, *Prodotto netto e sovrappiù*, Turin, UTET.

Petrović G., 1975, *Socialismo e filosofia*, Ital. transl., ed. by Gabriella Fusi, Feltrinelli, Milan, 1976.

Petrucciani S., Russo M., 2010, Presentazione. Leggere il *Capitale* per comprendere la modernità, in Bidet, 2004.

Petruccioli C., 1972, Su alcuni aspetti del rapporto tra stratificazione sociale e orientamenti ideologici, in Istituto Gramsci, 1972.

Pica F., 2000, Per un federalismo municipalista (I principi: il federalismo e la costituzione italiana), in Fausto & Pica, 2000.

Piff P., et al., 2012, Reply to Francis in *Proceedings of the National Academy of Sciences*, vol. 109, no. 25.

Pittatore S., Turati G., 2000, A Map of Property Rights in Italy and the Case of Cooperatives: An Empirical Analysis of Hansmann's Theory, in *Economic Analysis*, vol. 3, no. 1.

Pivetti M., 2006, *Marx e lo sviluppo dell'economia critica*, in Jossa & Lunghini, 2006.

Plamenatz J., 1963, *Man and Society*, McGraw-Hill, New York.

Plechanov G. V., 1895, *La concezione materialistica della storia*, Samonà e Savelli, La Nuova sinistra, Rome, 1970.

Plechanov G. V., 1911, *Anarchismo e socialismo*, 3rd edition, Ital. transl., Samonà e Savelli, Rome, 1971.

Plekhanov G., 1976, *Selected Philosophical Works*, vol. II, Progress Publishers, Moscow.

Polanyi K., 1987, *La libertà in una società complessa*, Ital. transl., Bollati Boringhieri, Turin, 1987.

Pompeo Faracovi O., 1972, *Il marxismo francese contemporaneo fra dialettica e struttura*, Feltrinelli, Milan.

Poulantsas N., 1968, Brevi note sull'oggetto del Capitale, in AA. VV., 1968.

Powel W., ed., 1987, *The Non-Profit Sector: A Research Handbook*, Yale University, New Haven, CT.

Prandergast C., 1999, The Provisions of Incentives on Firms, in *Journal of Economic Literature*, vol. 37.

Prestipino G., 1973, *Natura e società*, Editori Riuniti, Rome.

Proudhon J. P., 1846, *Système des contradictions économiques*, Rivière, Paris, 1923.

Prychitko D. L., Vanek J, eds, 1996, *Producer Cooperatives and Labor-managed Systems*, E. Elgar, Cheltenham.

Przeworski A., 1995, Class, Production and Politics: A Reply to Burawoy, in Carver & Thomas, 1995.

Pugliese E., 2008, Le trasformazioni delle classi sociali in Italia negli ultimi decenni, in *Economia italiana*, no. 3.

Putterman L., 1982, Some Behavioural Perspectives on the Dominance of Hierarchical Over Democratic Forms of Enterprise, in *Journal of Economic Behaviour and Organization*, vol. III, nos. 2–3.

Putterman L., 1993, After the Employment Relation: Problem on the Road to Industrial Democracy, in Bowles, Gintis and Gustafsson, 1993.

Putterman L., Roemer J. E., & Silvestre J., 1998, Does Egalitarianism Have a Future? in *Journal of Economic Literature*, vol. 36, no. 2.

Quadrio Curzio A., Marseguerra G., 2008, eds, *Democracy, Institutions and Social Justice*, Libri Scheiwiller, Milan.

Quarter J., 1992, *Canada's Social Economy*, J. Lorimer & Co, Toronto.

Rabbeno U., 1889, Le società cooperative di produzione. Contributo allo studio della questione operaia, in *La rivista della cooperazione*, no. 1, Rome.

Radnitzky G., 1999, *La filosofia politica di Friedrich von Hayek*, Rubettino, Soveria Mannelli.

Ragionieri E., 1965, Il marxismo e la Prima Internazionale, in Ragionieri, 1968.

Ragionieri E., 1968, *Il marxismo e l'Internazionale*, Editori Riuniti, Rome.

Ramos-Martinez A., Rodriguez-Herrera A., 1996, *The Transformation of Values into Prices of Production: A Different Reading of Marx's Text*, in Freeman & Carchedi, 1996.

Rapone L., 2011, *Cinque anni che paiono secoli; Antonio Gramsci dal socialismo al comunismo (1914–1919)*, Carocci Editore, Rome.

Ratner C., 2013, *Cooperation, Community, and Co-Ops in a Global Era*, Springer Publishers, New York.

Rawls J., 1971, *A Theory of Justice*, Harvard Economic Press, Cambridge, MA.

Rawls J., 2000, *Lezioni di storia della filosofia morale*, Ital. transl., Feltrinelli, Milan, 2004.

Reito F., 2008, Moral Hazard and Labour-Managed Firms in Italy after the Law 142/2001, in *Annals of Public and Cooperative Economics*, vol. 79, no. 2.

Resnick S., Wolff R. D., 1982, Classes in Marxian Theory, in *Review of Radical Political Economics*, vol. 13, no. 4.

Rifkin J., 2009, *Civiltà ed empatia*, Ital. transl., Mondadori, Milan, 2011.

Rifkin J., 2014, *La società a costo marginale zero*, Ital. transl., Mondadori, Milan, 2014.

Rigi J., 2013, Peer Production and Marxian Communism: Contours of a New Emerging Mode of Production, in *Capital & Class*, vol. 37, no. 3.

Riguzzi B., Porcari R., 1925, *La cooperazione operaia*, Piero Gobetti editore, Turin.

Roberts W. C., 2006, The Origin of Political Economy and the Descent of Marx, in Goldstein, 2006.

Robinson J., 1942, *Marx e la scienza economica*, Ital. transl., La Nuova Italia, Florence, 1951.

Robinson J., Eatwell, 1973, *Economia Politica*, Ital. transl., Etas Libri, Milan, 1974.

Rockmore T., 2005, Lukàcs tra Marx e il marxismo, in Fineschi, 2005.

Rodinson M., 1969, Sociologia marxista e ideologia marxista, in AA. VV., 1969.

Rodrik D., Subramanian A., Trebbi F., 2002, Institutions Rule: The Primacy of Institutions Over Geography and Integration in Economic Development, NBER, no. 9305, November.

Roemer J. E., 1982, *A General Theory of Exploitation and Class*, Harvard University Press, Cambridge.

Roemer J. E., 1988, *Free to Lose: An Introduction to Marxist Economic Philosophy*, Harvard University Press, Cambridge, MA.

Roemer J. E., 1992, The Morality and Efficiency of Market Socialism, *Ethics*, vol. 102, re-printed in Roemer, 1994a.

Roemer J. E., 1993, Can there Be Socialism after Communism? in Bardhan & Roemer, 1993,

Roemer J. E., 1994a, *Foundations of Analytical Marxism*, E. Elgar, Aldershot.

Roemer J. E., 1994b, On Public Ownership, in Roemer, 1994a.

Roemer J. E., 1994c, *Un futuro per il socialismo*, Ital. transl., Feltrinelli, Milan, 1996.

Roemer J. E., 1994d, *Egalitarian Perspectives; Essays in Philosophical Economics*, Cambridge Economic Press, Cambridge.

Roemer J. E., 2008, Socialism vs. Social Democracy as Income-Equalizing Institutions, in *Eastern Economic Journal*, vol. 34, no. 1.

Roncaglia A., 2008, Il socialismo liberale di Paolo Sylos Labini, in Roncaglia, Rossi, Salvadori, 2008.

Roncaglia A., Rossi P., Salvadori M., 2008, *Libertà. giustizia, laicità; in ricordo di Paolo Sylos Labini*, Laterza, Bari.

Rosdolsky R., 1955, *Genesi e struttura del 'Capitale' di Marx*, Ital. transl., Laterza, Bari, 1971.

Rosenthal J. 1998, *The Myth of Dialectics: Reinterpreting the Marx-Hegel Relation*, Macmillan, London.

Rosselli C., 1930, *Socialismo liberale*, Einaudi, Turin, 1973.

Rothschild K. W., 1986, Capitalist and Entrepreneurs: Prototypes and Roles, in Wagener & Drukker, 1986.

Rovatti P. A., 1973, *Critica e scientificità in Marx*, Feltrinelli, Milan.

Rubel M., 1974a, La légende de Marx ou Engels fondateur, in Rubel, 1974b.

Rubel M., 1974b, *Marx critique du marxisme. Essais*, Payot, Paris.

Rubin I. I., 1928, *Saggi sulla teoria del valore di Marx*, Ital. transl., Feltrinelli, Milan, 1976.

Rusconi G. E., 1968, *La teoria critica della società*, Il Mulino, Bologna.

Russel B., 1935, *Storia delle idee del secolo XIX*, Ital. transl., Mondadori, Milan, 1970.

Russel R., Rus V., eds, 1991, in *International Handbook of Participation in Organizations*, Oxford University Press, Oxford.

Sabattini G., 2014, *Stato, democrazia e socialismo nel dibattito risorgimentale*, Tema, Cagliari.

Sabine G. H., 1937, *Storia del pensiero politico*, Ital. transl., Edizioni di Comunità, Milan, 1962.

Saladin P., Willhaber L., 1972, *Der Staat als Aufgabe*, Helbing & Lientenhahn, Basel-Stuttgart.

Salvadori M. L., 1973, *Gramsci e il problema storico della democrazia*, 2nd edition, Einaudi, Turin.

Salvadori N., Opocher A., 2009, *Long-run Growth, Social Institution and Living Standard*, Edward Elgar, Cheltenham.

Sandkühler H. J., 1970, Kant, il socialismo neokantiano e il revisionismo. Per le origini dell'ideologia del socialismo democratico, in Agazzi, 1975.

Sapelli G., 2006, *Coop: il futuro dell'impresa cooperativa*, Einaudi, Turin.

Sartori G., 1969, *Democrazia e definizioni*, 3rd edition, Il Mulino, Bologna.

Sartori G., 2015, *La corsa verso il nulla*, Mondadori, Milan.

Sartre J. P., 1960, *Critica della ragione dialettica*, Ital. transl., Il Saggiatore, Milan, 1963.

Scalfari E., 1995, Alla ricerca della morale perduta, in Scalfari, 2012.

Scalfari E., 2008, L'uomo che non credeva in Dio, in Scalfari, 2012.

Scalfari E., 2012, *La passione dell'etica; scritti 1963–2012*, Mondadori, Milan.

Scalfari E., 2013, La fragile armonia di una politica ambigua, in *La Repubblica*, 27 ottobre.

Schaff A., Séve L., 1975, *Marxismo e umanesimo*, Dedalo libri, Bari.

Schaff A., 1971, Sulla traduzione francese della VI tesi di Marx su Feuerbach, Ital. transl., in Schaff & Séve, 1975.

Schaff A., 1974, *Marxismo, strutturalismo e il metodo della scienza*, Ital. transl., Feltrinelli, Milan, 1976.

Schiavone G., 1997, ed., *La democrazia diretta*, ediz. Dedalo, Bari.

Schlicht E., von Weizsäcker C. C., 1977, Risk Financing in Labour Managed Economies: The Commitment Problem, in *Zeitschrift für die Gesamte Staats-wissenschaft*, special number.

Schmidt C., 1900, Il socialismo e l'etica, in Agazzi, 1975.

Schumpeter J. A., 1941, An Economic Interpretation of Our Time: The Lowell Lecturer, in Schumpeter, 1991.

Schumpeter J. A., 1954a, *Capitalismo, socialismo e democrazia*, Ital. transl., Edizioni di comunità, 1964.

Schumpeter J. A., 1954b, *Storia dell'analisi economica*, Ital. transl., Einaudi, Turin, 1959.

Schumpeter J. A., 1991, *The Economics and Sociology of Capitalism*, ed. by R. Swedberg, Princeton University Press, Princeton.

Schweickart D., 1993, *Against Capitalism*, Cambridge University Press, Cambridge.

Schweickart D., 1998, Market Socialism: A Defense, in Ollman, 1998.

Schweickart D., 2002, *After Capitalism*, Rowman & Littlefield Publishers, Inc., Lanham.

Schweickart D., 2005, Marx's Democratic Critique of Capitalism, and Its Implications for China's Development Strategy, in *Teaching and Research*, no. 10.

Screpanti E., 2004, Il capitalismo. Ieri, oggi, domani, *mimeo*, Siena.

Screpanti E., 2007a, *Comunismo libertario*, manifestolibri, Rome.

Screpanti E., 2007b, Democrazia redicale e lotta di classe: alcune precisazioni, in *Il Ponte*, ybk. LXIII, no. 8.

Screpanti E., 2013, *Marx dalla libertà alla moltitudine (1841–1843)*, seconda edizione riveduta e corretta, editrice Petit plaisance, Pistoia.

Sekine T. T., 1995a, A Uno School Seminar on the Theory of Value, in Albritton & Sekine, 1995.

Sekine T. T., 1995b, The Necessity of the Law of Value, Its Demonstration and Significance, in Albritton & Sekine, 1995.

Sen A. K., 1999, *Lo sviluppo è libertà*, Ital. transl., Mondadori, Milan, 2000.

Sen A. K., 2015, *La libertà individuale come impegno sociale*, Laterza, Bari.

Sertel M. R., 1982, *Workers and Incentives*, North-Holland, Amsterdam.

Settembrini D., 1973, *Due ipotesi per il socialismo in Marx ed Engels*, Laterza, Bari.

Settembrini D., 1975, *Il labirinto marxista*, Rizzoli, Milan.

Sève L., 2004, *Penser avec Marx aujourd'hui*, Tome I, *Marx et nous*, La Dispute, Paris.

Severino E., 1978, *Gli abitatori del tempo. Cristianesimo, marxismo, tecnica*, Armando, Rome.

Severino E., 2012, *Capitalismo senza futuro*, Rizzoli, Milan.

Shaw W. H., 1984, Marxism, Revolution, and Rationality, in Ball & Farr, 1984.

Sherman H., 1995, *Reinventing Marxism*, Johns Hopkins University Press, London.

Sichirollo L., 1973, *Dialettica*, ISEDI, Milan.

Sidoti F., 1987, Parlamento e governo in Marx. Alcune 'verità sociologiche' di un centenario, in Nassisi, 1987.

Singer P., 1980, *Marx*, Oxford University Press, London.

Sinha A., 1982, The Transformation Problem: Is the Standard Commodity a Solution? in *Review of Radical Political Economics*, vol. 32, no. 2.

Skillman G. L., 2013, The Puzzle of Marx's Missing 'Results': A Tale of Two Theories, in *History of Political Economy*, vol. 48, no. 3.

Smith A., 1790, *Teoria dei sentimenti morali*, VI edition, Ital. transl., Rizzoli, Milan, 2001.

Smith S. C., Ye M. H., 1987, The Behavior of Labor-managed Firms under Uncertainty. In *Annals of Public and Cooperative Economics*, vol. 57, March.

Sofri A., 2008, I Penultimi, in AA. VV., 2008.

Solari S., 2012, The 'Practical Reason' of Reformers: Proudhon vs. Institutionalism, in *Journal of Economic Issues*, vol. XLVI, no. 1.

Solmi R., 1954, Introduzione a Adorno, 1954.

Sombart W., 1894, Zur Kritik des oekonomischen Systems von Karl Marx, in *Archiv für Soziale Gesetzgebung und Statistik*, vol. VII, no. 4.

Southworth G., 1972, Samuelson on Marx: A Note, in *Review of Radical Political Economics*, vol. 4, no. 5, Autumn.

Sowell T., 1967, Marx's *Capital* One Hundred Years Later, reprinted in Wood, 1988.

Sowell T., 1985, *Marxism; Philosophy and Economics*, Quill William Morris, New York.

Spinella M., 1969, ed., *Marx Vivo*, Mondadori, Milan.

Sraffa P., 1960, *Produzione di merci a mezzo di merci*, Einaudi, Turin.

Srinivasan R., Phansalkar S. J, 2003, Residual Claims in Cooperatives: Design Issues, in *Annals of Public and Cooperative Economics*, vol. 74, no. 3, September.

Stauber L. G. 1987, Capitalism and Socialism: Some General Issues and the Relevance of Austrian Experience, reprinted in Nove & Thatcher, 1994.

Stauber L. G., 1989, Age-dependence and Historical Effects on the Failure Rates of Worker Cooperatives. An Event-history Analysis. *Economic and Industrial Democracy*, vol. 10, no. 1.

Stawar A., 1961, *Liberi saggi marxisti*, transl. from Polish, La Nuova Italia, Florence, 1973.

Stedman Jones G., 1978, Ritratto di Engels, in AA. VV., 1978–82, vol. I.

Steedman I., 1977, *Marx after Sraffa*, New Left Books, London.

Steinherr A., 1975, Profit-maximizing vs. Labor-managed Firms: A Comparison of Market Structure and Firm Behavior, in *Journal of Industrial Economics*, vol. 24. no. 1.

Steinherr A., Thiesse J. F., 1979a, Are Labour-managers Really Perverse? in *Economic Letters*, vol. 2, no. 2.

Steinherr A., Thisse J. F., 1979b, Is There a Negatively-sloped Supply Curve in the Labour-managed Firm? in *Economic Analysis and Workers' Management*, vol. 13, no. 35.

Stephen F. H., 1984, The Economic Analysis of Producers' Cooperatives, Macmillan, London.

Sterner T., 1990, Ownership, Technology and Efficiency: An Empirical Study of Cooperatives, Multinationals, and Domestic Enterprises in the Mexican Cement Industry, in *Journal of Comparative Economics*, vol. 14, no. 2.

Stiglitz J. E., 1969, A Re-examination of the Modigliani-Miller Theorem, in *American Economic Review*, vol. 59, December.

Stiglitz J. E., 1993, Market Socialism and Neoclassical Economic, in Bardhan and Roemer, 1993.

Stiglitz J. E., 1994, *Whither Socialism?* MIT Press, Cambridge, MA.

Stiglitz J. E., 2012, *Il prezzo della diseguaglianza*, Ital. transl., Einaudi, Turin, 2013.

Stone B., 1998, Why Marxism Isn't Dead (Because Capitalism Isn't Dead): The Case for Cooperative Socialism, 20th World Congress of Philosophy, Boston, in *Paideia Archiv, Social Philosophy*, 1999.

Strada V., 1982, Marxismo e post-marxismo, in Hobsbawm *et alii*, 1982.

Streit M. E., 1997, Constitutional Ignorance, Spontaneous Order and Rule-Orientation: Hayekian Paradigms from a Policy Perspective, in Frowen, 1997.

Struve P., 1899, La théorie marxienne de l'évolution sociale, reprinted in *Cahiers de l'Institut de science économique appliquée*, 129, September, 1962.

Sweezy P. M., 1942, Teoria dello sviluppo capitalistico, in Sweezy *et alii*, 1970.

Sweezy P. M., 1968, Cecoslovacchia, capitalismo e socialismo, *Monthly Review*, November.

Sweezy P. M., 1969, A Reply to Bettelheim, *Monthly Review*, March–April.

Sweezy P. M., 1971, Sulla teoria del capitalismo monopolistico, in Sweezy, 1972.

Sweezy P. M., 1972, *Il capitalismo moderno*, Ital. transl., Liguori, Naples, 1975.

Sweezy P. M. *et alii*, 1970, *Teoria dello sviluppo capitalistico*, ed. by C. Napoleoni, Boringhieri, Turin.

Sylos Labini P., 1978, *Saggio sulle classi sociali*, Laterza, Bari.

Sylos Labini P., 1984, *Le classi sociali negli anni '80*, Laterza, Bari.

Sylos Labini P., 1987, Osservazioni sull'analisi economica di Marx, in Cacciatore & Lomonaco, 1987.

Sylos Labini P., 2006, Perché gli economisti debbono fare i conti con Marx, in Jossa & Lunghini, 2006.

Tamburrano G., 1959, Fasi di sviluppo nel pensiero politico di Gramsci, in Caracciolo e Scalia, 1959.

Tarrit F., 2006, A Brief History, Scope and Peculiarities of 'Analytical Marxism', in *Review of Radical Political Economics*, vol. 38, no. 4.

Tawney R. H., 1918, *The Conditions of Economic Liberty*, in Hinden, 1964.

Therborn G., 1971, *Critica e rivoluzione; la Scuola di Francoforte*, Ital. transl., Laterza, Bari, 1972.

Thomas A., 1990, Financing Worker Cooperatives in EC Countries, in *Annals of Public and Cooperative Economics*, vol. 61, June.

Thomas H., Defourny J., 1990, Financing Workers' Cooperatives and Self-managed Enterprises, in *Annals of Public and Cooperative Economics*, vol. 61, June.

Thomas H., Logan C., 1982, *Mondragon, an Economic Analysis*, George Allen and Unwin, London.

Thomas P., 1984, Alien Politics: A Marxian Perspective on Citizenship and Democracy, in Ball and Farr, 1984.

Togliatti P., 1920, Cooperative o schiavitù, reprinted in Togliatti, 1967.

Togliatti P., 1967, *Opere*, a cura di Ernesto Ragionieri, Editori Riuniti, Rome.

Tonini V., 1967, *Cosa ha detto veramente Lenin*, Ubaldini, Rome.

Tornquist D., 1973, Workers' Management: The Intrinsic Issues, in Hunnius, Garson & Case, 1973.

Tortia E. 2008, *Le determinanti dello sforzo lavorativo nelle imprese sociali*, University of Trient, Trient.

Tosel A. 2007, Teleologia, dialettica, biforcazione. Quale dialettica oggi? in Burgio, 2007.

Tosel A., 1996, *Études sur Marx (et Engels). Vers un communisme de la finitude*, Kimé, Paris.

Tronti M., 1977, *Sull'autonomia del politico*, Feltrinelli, Milan.

Tronti M., 1978, Operaismo e centralità operaia, in AA. VV., 1978.

Trotsky L., 1940a, Letter to James P. Cannon, in Trotsky, 1969.

Trotsky L., 1940b, Open letter to Comrad Burnham, in Trotsky, 1969.

Trotsky L., 1969, *In difesa del marxismo*, Samonà e Savelli, Rome.

Trotsky L., 1971, *Il giovane Lenin*, trad. it., Mondadori, Milan, 1971.

Trower C., 1973, Collective Bargaining and Industrial Democracy, in Hunnius, Garson and Case, 1973.

Tseo G. K. Y., Hou Gui Sheng, Zhang Peng-Zhu, Zang Libain, 2004, Employee Ownership and Profit Sharing as Positive Factors in the Reform of Chinese State-Owned Enterprises, in *Economic and Industrial Democracy*, vol. 25, no. 1.

Tsuru S., 1969, Marx e l'analisi del capitalismo. Un nuovo studio della contraddizione fondamentale? in AA. VV., 1969.

Tucidide, inizio iv secolo a. C., *La guerra del Peloponneso*, Ital. transl., Garzanti, Milan, 2003.

Tucker R. C., 1961, *Philosophy and Myth in Karl Marx*, Cambridge University Press, Cambridge.

Turati F., 1897, Il miraggio delle cooperative, in *Critica sociale*, 1° August, 16 August e 1° September.

Uchida H., 2006, ed., *Marx for the 21st Century*, Routledge, London.

Ureña E. M., 1977, Marx and Darwin, in Wood, 1988.

Uvalic M., Vaughan-Whitehead, eds, 1997, Privatisation Surprises in Transition Economics: Employee Ownership in Central and Eastern Europe, Elgar, Cheltenham.

Vacatello M., 1972, *Th. W. Adorno: il rinvio della prassi*, La Nuova Italia, Florence.

Vacca G., 1972, Politica e teoria del marxismo italiano degli anni sessanta, in Istituto Gramsci, 1972.

Valenti G., 1901, Contributo alla teoria economica della cooperazione, con un'appendice intorno alla legislazione sulle società cooperative, in *Archivio giuridico «Filippo Serafini»*, nuova serie, Mucchi, Modena.

Valentinov V., Fritzsch J., 2007, Are Cooperatives Hybrid Organizations? An Alternative Viewpoint, in *Journal of Rural Cooperation*, vol. 35, no. 2.

Van Parijs P., 1993a, *Marxism Recycled*, Cambridge University Press, Cambridge.

Van Parijs P., 1993b, Envoi: The Greening of Marx, in Van Parijs, 1993a.

Van Parijs P., van der Veen R. J., 1986, A Capitalist Road to Communism, in Van Parijs, 1993.

Vanek J., 1972, *The Economics of Workers' Management: A Jugoslav Case Study*, Allen & Unwin, London, January.

Vanek J. (Jaroslav), 1970, *The General Theory of Labour-Managed Market Economies*, Cornell University Press, Ithaca.

Vanek J., 1971a, Some Fundamental Considerations on Financing and the Form of Ownership under Labor Management, reprinted in Vanek 1977.

Vanek J., 1971b, The Basic Theory of Financing of Participatory Firms. Reprinted in. Vanek 1977.

Vanek J., 1971c, *The Participatory Economy: An Evolutionary Hypothesis on a Strategy for Development*, Cornell University Press, Ithaca.

Vanek J., 1977a, *The Labor Managed Economy: Essays by J. Vanek*, Cornell University Press, Ithaca.

Vanek J., 1977b, Educazione alla pratica dell'autogestione, in Vanek, 1985.

Vanek J., 1985, *Imprese senza padrone nelle economie di mercato*, Edizioni Lavoro, Rome.

Vanek J., 1993, From Partnership with Paper to Partnership among Human Beings, in Atkinson, 1993.

Veblen T. B., 1964, *What Veblen Thought*, Augustus M. Kelley, New York.

Vercelli A., 1973, *Teoria della struttura economica capitalistica*, Einaudi, Turin.

Vergnanini A., 1914, *Marxismo e cooperativistmo. Le due grandi vie della rivoluzione economica*, Biblioteca della cooperazione e della previdenza, Milan.

Vidoni F., 2007, Sulla presenza della dialettica nell'epistemologia recente, in Burgio, 2007.

Vinci P., 2008, Astrazione determinata, in AA. VV., 2008.

Virno P., 2008, Forza lavoro, in AA. VV., 2008.

Vorländer C, 1911, Kant e Marx, in AA. VV., 1970.

Vranicki P., 1971, *Storia del marxismo*, Ital. transl., Editori Riuniti, Rome, 1971.

Vygodskij V. S., 1967, *Introduzione ai "Grundisse" di Marx*, Ital. transl., La Nuova Italia, Florence, 1974.

Waldmann R. J., Smith S. C., 1999, Investment and Supply Effects of Industry-Indexed Bonds: Tthe Labor Managed Firm, in *Economic Systems*, vol. 23, no. 3.

Wallerstein I., 2002, New Revolts against the System, in *New Left Review*, November-December.

Wallerstein I., 2006, *Comprendere il mondo*, Asterios editore, Trieste.

Walras L., 1865, *Les Associations Populaires de Consommation, de Production et de Credit*, Dentu, Paris.

Walras L., 1987, *Oeuvres économiques complètes*, ed. by C. Hebert and J. P. Potier, Economica, Paris.

Walras L., 1990a, Socialisme et libéralisme. Lettres à M., ed. Scherer, in Walras, 1990b.

Walras L., 1990b, *Etudes d'économie sociale. Théorie de la répartition de la richesse sociale. Œuvres économiques complètes d'Auguste et Léon Walras*, vol. IX, Economica, 1990 [1866–1867].

Ward B. N., 1958, The Firm in Illyria; Market Syndicalism, in *American Economic Review*, vol. 48, no. 4, September.

Watkins W. P., 1986, *Cooperative Principles Today and Tomorrow*, Holyoake Books, Manchester.

Weber Marianne, 1984, *Max Weber, una biografia*, Ital. transl., Il Mulino, Bologna, 1995.

Weil S., 1955, *Riflessioni sulle cause della libertà e dell'oppressione sociale*, Ital. transl., Corriere della Sera, Milan, 2010.

Weil S., 1959, *Lezioni di filosofia*, Ital. transl., Adelphi, 2012.

Weintraub E. R., ed., *The Future of the History of Economics*, Duke University Press, Durham and London.

Weitzman M., Kruse D. L., 1990, Profit Sharing and Productivity, in Blinder, 1990.

Wennerlind C., 2002, The Labor Theory of Value and the Strategic Role of Alienation, in *Capital and Class*, no. 77, Spring.

Westra R., 2002, Marxian Economic Theory and an Ontology of Socialism: A Japanese Intervention, in *Capital and Class*, no. 78, Autumn.

Wetter G. A., 1948, *Il materialismo dialettico sovietico*, Einaudi, Turin.

Williamson O. E., 1980, The Organization of Work: A Comparative Institutional Assessment, in *Journal of Economic Behavior and Organization*, vol. 1, no. 1.

Williamson O. E., 1985, *The Economic Institutions of Capitalism: Firm, Markets, Relational Contracting*, Free Press, New York.

Williamson O. E., 1986, *Economic Organizations: Firm, Market and Policy Control*, Harvester Wheatsheaf, New York.

Wilson E. O., 1998, *L'armonia meravigliosa*, Ital. transl., Mondadori, Milan, 1999.

Winn J., 2013, Notes towards a Critique of 'Labour Managed Firms', http://josswinn.org/2013/07.

Wolff R., 1970, *In difesa dell'anarchia*, Ital. transl., ISEDI, Milan, 1973.

Wolff R., 2012, *Democracy at Work; a Cure for Capitalism*, Haymarket Books, Chicago.

Wolff R., Callari A., & Roberts B., 1982, Marx's (not Ricardo's) Transformation Problem: A Radical Reconceptualization, in *History of Political Economy*, vol. 14, no. 4.

Wolff R., Callari A., & Roberts B., 1984, A Marxian Alternative to the Traditional Transformation Problem, in *Review of Radical Political Economics*, vol. 16, nos. 2–3.

Wolff R., Callari A., & Roberts B., 1998, *The Transformation Trinity: Value, Value Form and Price*, in Bellofiore, 1998.

Wolfstetter E., Brown M., Meran G., 1984, Optimal Employment and Risk Sharing in Illyria: The Labour Managed Firm Reconsidered, in *Journal of Institutional and Theoretical Economics*, vol. 140.

Woltmann L., 1900, La fondazione della morale, in Agazzi, 1975.

Wood J. C., 1988, ed., *Karl Marx's Economics: Critical Assessments*, Croom Helm, New South Wales.

Wright E. O. *et alii*, 1989, *The Debate on Classes*, Verso, London.

Wright E. O., 1995, What Is Analytical Marxism? in Carver & Thomas, 1995.

Xie F., Li A., Li Z., 2013, Can the Socialist Market Economy in China Adhere to Socialism? in *Review of Radical Political Economics*, vol. 45, no. 4.

Zafiris N., 1986, The Sharing of the Firm's Risks between Capital and Labour, in *Annals of Public and Cooperative Economics*, vol. 57, no. 1.

Zagari E., 2011, Nota sull'alternativa al capitalismo proposta da Bruno Jossa, in *Studi economici*, fasc. 104.

Zamagni S., 2005, Per una teoria economico-civile dell'impresa cooperativa, in Mazzoli & Zamagni, 2005.

Zamagni S., 2006, Promozione cooperativa e civilizzazione del mercato, in Bulgarelli & Viviani, 2006.

Zamagni S., 2008, Sul nesso causale tra economia e sviluppo economico, in Quadrio Curzio & Marseguerra, 2008.

Zangheri R., 1987, Nascita e primi sviluppi, in Zangheri, Galasso & Castronovo, 1987.

Zangheri R., Galasso G., Castronovo V., 1987, *Storia del movimento cooperativo in Italia*, Einaudi, Turin.

Zanone V., 2002, Il liberalismo di Franco Romani, in *Biblioteca della libertà*, nos. 164–165, May–August.

Zolo D., 1974, *La teoria comunista dell'estinzione dello Stato*, De Donato, Bari.

Index

Note: Page numbers followed by "n" denote endnotes.

Acton, H. B. 29
Adam Smith at Peking (Arrighi) 11n1
Adler, Max 20, 41, 92, 169, 183
affective knowledge 18
Agathotopia 99
'agoraphobia' 183, 184n7, 186n27
Alchian, A. A. 156
Alchian and Demsetz (AD) 14–15;
    agency theory 17; entrepreneur/
    employee relationship 17; theory of
    the firm 15–17
alienation 9, 10, 82, 86; cause of 8, 79;
    Feuerbachian theory of 9; Hegelian
    core idea of 9–10, 79
all-cooperatives system 3–4
Althusser, L. 29, 34, 36, 64, 111, 123,
    133n7, 184n5; on modes of production
    86; structuralist approach 29
Anti-Dühring (Engels) 81, 113
Anweiler, O. 23, 37
Aristotle 122
Aron, R. 28
Article 3 of Italian Constitution 139

Badaloni, N. 112
Bakunin, M. 98
Bakuninism 169
bankruptcy 96–7, 163
bankruptcy risks: in capitalistic and
    employee-managed firms 68; and
    cooperatives 71n24; in democratic
    firms 68–9
Barone, E. 24
basic contradiction of capitalism: defining
    113–15; from perspective of orthodox
    Marxists 115–17
Bataille, G. 98, 124
Bauer, Otto 92

Benjamin, Walter 60
Ben-Ner, A. 102, 157–8
Bensaïd, D. 23
Berman, M. D. 154
Bernstein, E. 14, 97, 132n2, 170, 173
Bettelheim, C. 169, 174, 183
Bhaskar, R. 117n2
Bidet, J. 62–3, 108, 117n2, 181
Bloom, S. F. 168, 180
Bobbio, Norberto 19, 112, 168, 179; on
    modern democracy 61
Bodei, Remo 60
Bolshevik revolution 70n3, 131, 171, 181
Bordiga, Amadeo 185n16
bourgeoisie 4, 21–2, 185n12
bourgeois society 94n16
bourgeois utilitarianism 185n16
Bowles, S. 67, 134n16, 134n17
Bretton Woods system 147
Brewer, A. 154
British Marxists 13n26, 94n15
Browning, M. J. 154
Bukharin, Nikolai 4–7
Burke, J. P. 43–4
Burns, T. 84

Cafiero, Carlo 169, 180
Callari, A. 183, 186n27
capital: inverse relation with labour 82;
    power of 19–22
Capital (Marx) 3, 4, 10, 49–50, 109–10,
    113, 116, 174, 181
capital goods 136, 141, 152, 155–6
capitalism 1; defining the basic
    contradiction of 113–15; Gramsci on
    99; Gramsci on corrupting power of
    52–3; and Hegelian matrix of Marxism
    81–2; liberal 54; Marx description

of 82; and technology 54; transition
to democratic firms 37–9; Wolff
on 150–1
capitalistic societies 21; unequal
distribution of political power 21
capitalist systems 182; and brisk firm
creation 157; and competition 69;
investors in 164; *vs.* market economy
181; profit-sharing agreements 161;
wage and salary earners 126
capital-labour contradiction 39–43; and
socialist system 73
capital mobility 142
capital-owned enterprises 151, 153, 155,
157, 161, 165
Capitini A. 66
cash nexus 59n6
Castronovo, Valerio 172
Catholics 171, 182
causality, linear notion of 29
'challenge of Condorcet' 62–3
'challenge of Minerva': self-management
and 103–5
Chomsky, Noam 20, 184n1, 185n19
The Civil War in France (Marx) 10, 80
class consciousness 59n5; of bourgeoisie
21; of workers 42
class relationships 62
closed-membership firms 96
Coase, Ronald 17
coercion 38, 67
Cohen, G. A. 28–9
Cole, G. D. H. 57, 58, 167, 179
Colletti, Lucio 32, 82
Commons, J. R. 127
communism 4–5, 107, 117, 131, 174,
181; philosophical 9–10; Stein's
definition of 80
competition: and capitalist systems 69;
in democratic firm system 96–106; as
economic health indicator 72n25
consumer goods 135
*Contribution to the Critique of Hegel's
Philosophy of Right* (Marx) 9, 79–81, 89,
116, 123
*A Contribution to the Critique of Political
Economy* (Marx) 8, 78–9, 121, 123
cooperation: and character building 52;
and socialism 6–7; *see also* cooperatives
cooperative firm 101–3, 117, 151, 155–8,
161, 164–5, 165n1, 167, 171–3, 177
cooperative movement 51–2
cooperatives 17, 26n6; advantages of
51; categorised as merit goods 75–6;

Gramsci on 53; and human nature
51; and social benefits 76; *see also*
cooperation
Copernicus 168, 180
Cornu, A. 122, 131
Critique of Political Economy (Marx)
59n4, 97
Critique of the Gotha Programme (Marx)
118n4
Croce, B. 15, 22, 46n1, 109, 128
Crouch, C. 1
Cuomo, Gaetano 154, 166n12

Dal Pra, M. 112, 117n2
Darwin, Charles 35–6, 120, 127,
134n18
Darwinian evolutionism 119
Darwinism 35–6, 127
Dawkins, R. 120–2, 130
democracy: industrial 20; political 20;
representative 19; social 20
democratically managed firms: risk
diversification in 163–4
democratic firm management: early
Marxist criticisms of 169–72; further
Marxist criticisms of 173–7; Marxist
criticisms of 167–86; overview 167–9;
Peter Marcuse's approach to producer
cooperatives 177–8
democratic firms 37–9; ESOPs on 70n14;
remote bankruptcy risks in 68–9; *see
also* socialism
democratic firm system: competition
in 96–106; income distribution in
market socialism 100–3; Marshall's
idea of cooperation as character-
moulding agent 100; self-management
and 'challenge of Minerva' 103–5;
solidarity in system of 97–9
Demsetz, H. 156
Descartes, René 104
determinism: described 29; economic
29, 111; technological 29 Dewey, John
167, 179
dialectics: as analysis of a totality with
real oppositions 110–12; introductory
notes on 108–10; as method and
system of thought 112–13
direct cause-effect relations 36
Dobb, Maurice 137–8, 148n1
Domar, E. D. 154
Donnaruma, C. 133n11
Dow, G. 154, 165n1
Drèze, J. H. 159, 161, 166n6

economic democracy: 'classical'
  unemployment in 144; Schweickart's
  approach to 135–49
economic determinism 29, 111
economic fatalism 112
Economic-Philosophical Manuscripts of 1844
  (Marx) 34, 113, 170–1, 182–3, 185n14
economic systems: materialistic analysis
  of human nature in different 123–5;
  self-management and 125
Eibl-Eibesfeldt, Irenäus 120
The Eighteenth Brumaire of Louis Bonaparte
  (Marx) 89
Einaudi, Luigi 106n1
Elster, J. 31
employee-managed system 15
Engels, Friedrich 14, 28, 30–1, 75, 81,
  113, 115, 117, 118n4; on Bakuninism
  169, 180; on communist society 130;
  on human nature 121–2
entrepreneurial risks 18–19
entrepreneurs 16
equity financing 160–3
Ethic (Spinoza) 15
European socialism 97

'fair share' principle 140
fascism 171, 182
Ferguson, Adam 106n2
Feuerbach, Ludwig 8–9, 79, 121–2, 131
'financing agreements' 161
Fine, B. 117n2
Finelli, R. 65, 103, 128
Fineschi, Roberto 82, 112, 116, 170, 182
firms: defined 16; profit 16; risk
  diversification in democratically
  managed 163–4
Fordism 39
Fraenkel, E. 169, 183
Freud, Sigmund 19, 103
Fromm, Erich 15, 18, 99, 123
fundamentalist thesis 29
funding difficulties: of LMFs 159–60; of
  producer cooperatives 159
Furubotn-Pejovich effect 155

Garaudy, R. 109
general equilibrium theory 24
Gentile, Giovanni 22, 117n2
The German Ideology (Marx and Engels)
  30–1, 33–4, 121
German Social-Democrats 176
Gintis, H. 67, 134n16, 134n17
globalisation 107, 117, 178

goods: capital 136, 141, 152, 155–6;
  consumer 135
Gramsci, Antonio 2, 31, 45, 99, 131, 167,
  179; on corrupting power of capitalism
  52–3; on importance of cooperatives
  53; theory of factory councils 52–3
The Great Transformation (Polanyi) 55–6
Grundrisse 109, 171, 181, 182
'guild socialism' 57; *see also* socialism
Gustafsson, B. 133n13

Habermas, J. 106n2
Hahn, F. H. 98, 124
Hansmann, H. 154, 157, 162
Harman C. 68
Hayek, F. A. 7, 38, 67, 169, 176
Hegel, G. W. F. 2, 15, 31, 67, 104, 108–10,
  112–13, 117n2; alienation notion 9, 10
Hegelian dialectics 107
Hegelianism 9, 79, 108
Hegelian matrix of Marxism: and
  capitalism 81–2
Heller, Agnes 11n14, 47n6, 83
Hess, Moses 8–10, 79; on Stein's
  communism definition 80
Hilferding, Rudolf 92
historical materialism 15, 46n1, 69,
  123; and Marxists 28; and material
  production 34; and modes of
  production 34; one-directional
  approach to 48n22; and productive
  forces 31
History and Class Consciousness
  (Lukàcs) 110
'history-as-totality' conception 2
Hobsbawm, E. J. 18
Hodgson, G. M. 32, 107, 127–8; on self-
  management 40
Honneth, A. 1
Horkheimer, M. 32
Horvat, B. 154
Huberman, L. 20
Hudis, P. 112
human capital 40
human nature: Engels on 121–2; Marx on
  121–2; materialistic analysis in different
  economic systems 123–5
'human sciences' 123
Hume, D. 132n4
Hyppolite, J. 109

*An Idea for a Universal History from a
  Cosmopolitan Perspective* (Kant) 47n3
ideological selectivity 90

The Impending Catastrophe and How to Combat It (Lenin) 5
Inaugural Address (Marx) 2–3, 118n4
income distribution, in market socialism 100–3
individualism 59n4, 99–100, 115, 125–6
industrial democracy 20, 58, 155
Industrial Revolution 56
intellectual knowledge 18
investment control, and publicly owned means of production 140–1
investment fund management method: per capita allocation as efficient 141–3
Italian Civil Code 163
Italian Constituent Assembly 172
Italian Constitution: Article 3 of 139

Jensen, M. C. 156–7
Jewish-Christian ethic 98, 124
Jones, Stedman 86

Kalecki, M. 159
Kant, Immanuel 31, 104, 132n4
Karsz, Saul 41, 123
Kautsky, K. 29, 109, 170, 174, 181, 185n14
Keynes, J. M. 105, 125
Kincaid, J. 117n2
Korsch, Karl 102, 167, 179
Kouvelakis, S. 63
Kundera, Milan 12n16

Labini, Sylos 68, 93n4, 109, 184n3
labour-managed firm (LMF) 65, 67, 73, 83, 93n1, 154; possible solutions to funding problems of 159–60; reflections on financing difficulties of 164–5
labour management 41, 136
labour-modified firm (LMF) 114
labour time 24
Labriola, Antonio 14, 25n2, 133n9
laissez faire 55
Lange, Oskar 2, 23, 24, 62
Lange-Lerner model of socialism 24–5
Lasch, Christopher 1, 125
Latouche, Serge 103
Lefebvre, H. 40, 118n6
Leibniz, Gottfried Wilhelm 104
Lenin, V. I. 4–6, 14, 40, 82, 111, 117; on cooperation and socialism 6–7; death 62; on materialistic conception of history 28; reformism 94n13
Leone, E. 174

Lerner, A. P. 24
liberal capitalism 54–7
Lichtheim, G. 10, 80
Life Is Elsewhere (Kundera) 12n16
Logic (Hegel) 109, 181
Lorenz, R. 120
Lukàcs, G. 2, 21, 31, 66, 110; history of *Kultur* 35; scientific Marxism 43
Luporini, C. 87
Luxemburg, Rosa 39, 44, 82–4

Magri, Lucio 168, 179
Major, G. 117n2, 162, 166n11
Manifesto mensile 168
Manifesto of the Communist Party (Marx) 10, 75, 80, 118n4, 173
Marcuse, Peter 177; approach to producer cooperatives 177–8
market economy 1, 4, 51, 54, 148, 181
markets, and planning 152–3
market socialism: income distribution in 100–3; Kornai on 149n2
Marshall, Alfred 51–2, 59n2, 100; idea of cooperation as character-moulding agent 100
Marx, Karl 1; on absolute control 31; on all-cooperatives system 3–4; criticism of conception of history 32; on Darwin and Darwinism 35–6; on Darwinian logic 134n18; on distinction between socialism and communism 107; and historical materialism 28; 'history-as-totality' conception 2; history description 30; on human nature 121–2; on modes of production 84, 86–7; notion of history 33–7, 85; notion of revolution 7–8; and producer cooperatives 49–51; revolutionary vision 78–81; socialism and worker management 75
Marxism 7–8, 10, 12n15, 62, 107–9, 113, 115, 123, 133n10, 170, 174–6, 181, 185n13; and centralised planning 30; collapse of 62, 69n2; and Engels's post-capitalistic mode of production view 61; and materialistic conception of history 14, 28; notion of history 33–7; as theory of revolution 12n18
materialistic analysis of human nature 123–5
materialistic conception of history: described 14; importance of 22; and Marxism 14, 28; theory of the firm 15–17

material production 31; and historical process 34
Mazzini, Giuseppe 128, 132n3, 167, 172, 179
Meade, J. E. 99, 154, 157, 161
Meckling, W. J. 156–7
Mémoires sur l'instruction publique 63
Mészàros, I. 64–5
method, dialectics as 112–13
Mill, John Stuart 99, 167, 179
Millar, John 106n2
Miller, R. W. 29
Mills, Charles Wright 19–20, 91, 99, 168–9, 180–1
Miyazaki, H. 154
modes of production: capitalistic 42; Marx on 84, 86–7; new, as realistic assumption 62–4; notion of 87–9; socialism as 22–3
Monthly Review (2015) 177

'natural rate of growth' 147
Nazism 171, 182
Neary, H. N. 154
Negt, Oskar 110, 175
Newtonian rational mechanics model 105
non-distributable reserves 163
non-voting equities 160–2

October Revolution 40, 93n7
Offe, C. 89–91
On Cooperation 6
'Open Marxism' movement 95n30
orthodox Marxists: basic contradiction of capitalism from perspective of 115–17
Owen, Robert 56
ownership rights 152–3

Pannekoek, Anton 66, 167, 179
Panzieri, Raniero 20, 73, 98
Pareto, V. 24, 104, 169, 180
Parijs, P. van 44
Paris Commune 118n4, 174, 178, 181
Partyka, N. 133n11
Pasolini, Pierpaolo 35, 118n10
Pejovich, S. 19
Pellicani, L. 117n3
Pencavel, I. 154, 165n1
per capita allocation: as efficient investment fund management method 141–3
Petrovic, G. 96
Petruccioli, C. 41–2

'philosophical communism' 9–10, 80
Pivetti, M. 184n3, 185n21
Plamenatz, J. 29
planning, and markets 152–3
Plechanov, G. V. 98
Polanyi, Karl 167, 179; on liberal capitalism 54; model of socialism 57–9; on separation of economy from social relations 53–5; on technology and capitalism 54; theory of economic influence on human feelings 55–7
'political democracy' 20
political power 95n28; unequal distribution of 21
politics, and community life 63
'Praxis Group' of Marxists 48n21
Principles of Economics (Marshall) 51
Prison Notebooks 175, 185n17
private saving 136, 141, 144, 146
producer cooperatives 49–51; funding difficulties of 159; as new production mode 64–6; obstacles to establishment of 157–8; Peter Marcuse's approach to 177–8; and socialist revolution 66
producer cooperative theory 65
production: investment control and 140–1; publicly owned means of 140–1
productive activity 8–9, 79
The Proletarian Revolution and the Renegade Kautsky (Lenin) 89
proletariat 5, 9–10, 21, 75, 78–81, 92, 97, 173
Protestants 171, 182
Proudhon, J. P. 68, 79, 167, 179
public interest 1–2
public investment funding 137–9
publicly owned means of production: investment control and 140–1
public savings 136, 143–4, 147

Radnitzky, G. 7
Ragionieri, E. 69n3
Rawls, J. 104, 123, 132n4
reformism 94n13, 185n16; criticisms of 89–92; democracy and 48n14; *vs.* revolution 12n16; socialist 78
reification of human relations 58–9
remote bankruptcy risks: in democratic firms 68–9; and oppressive market mechanisms 69; and risks of dismissal 69
Renner, Karl 92
revolt of elites 125; against backdrop of self-management theory 125–7

revolution 7–8, 12n16, 13n21
risk diversification: in democratically managed firms 163–4
Rizzi, Bruno 7
Rockmore, T. 117n2
Roemer, J. E. 24
Rohentwurf 109
Roosevelt, Franklin D. 150
Rosenthal, J. 108
Rosselli, C. 67
Rovatti, P. A. 110
Rusconi, G. E. 110
Russian socialism 6

Sabine, G. H. 9
Salvadori, M. L. 185n17
Scalfari, Eugenio 45, 60, 129
Schaff, A. 133n7
Schmidt, Conrad 117n2
Schumpeter, J. A. 108
Schweickart, David 135
Schweickart's model: approach to economic democracy 135–49; investment control and publicly owned means of production 140–1; more criticisms of 145–7; per capita allocation as investment fund management method 141–3; public investment funding 137–9; unemployment issue 143–5; workable form of socialism 135–7
scientific socialism 28, 67
Screpanti, Ernesto 23, 167, 179
second-level cooperatives 164
Second Reform Act 10
Second Reform Bill 80
selfish gene theory: relevance to socialism 129–32; socialism and 120–1
self-managed firms 37; and corporate insolvency 38; and production model 58; workers living standards in 40
self-management 24–5, 40; and the 'challenge of Minerva' 103–5; socialism 57, 124, 156, 181 (*see also* socialism)
self-management theory: equity financing 160–3; financing difficulties of LMFs 164–5; funding difficulties of producer cooperatives 159; non-distributable reserves 163; obstacles to establishment of producer cooperatives 157–8; overview 154–7; revolt of elites against backdrop of 125–7; risk diversification in democratically managed firms

163–4; solutions to funding problems of LMFs 159–60
Sen, Amartya 97, 169, 184
Sertel, M. R. 154
Settembrini, D. 117n1, 118n9
Sève, L. 62, 81
Severino, Emanuele 37–8
Singer, P. 134n19
Smith, Adam 106n2
social capital 40
Social Darwinism 119–20, 127–9
Social Darwinists 128
'social democracy' 20
social evolution 74; Struve's idea of 76–8
'social formation' 84
socialisation 44
socialism 4–5; and cooperation 6–7; and employee management 75; evolution of 23–5; Friedrich von Hayek on 7; Marx and Engels on human nature 121–2; materialistic analysis of human nature in economic systems 123–5; as new mode of production 22–3; overview 119–20; Polanyi's model of 57–9; relevance of the selfish gene theory to 129–32; revolt of elites against backdrop of self-management theory 125–7; scientific core of 66–8; selfish gene 120–1; social Darwinism 127–9; and substitution of worker control 74–6; transition to 19–22, 43–5; workable form of 135–7; and worker management 75
Socialism, Utopian and Scientific (Engels) 61
socialist economy 57–8
socialist enclaves 97
socialist reformism 78
social production relations 2
social psychology 123
'social sciences' 123
solidarity: inter-worker 130; mutual 106n3, 130; in a system of democratic firms 97–9
Sorel, Georges 97
Soviet-type centralised planning model 168, 171, 179
Sowell, T. 29, 32, 44; on Marx's dialectical method 36
Spinoza, Baruch 15, 104
State, and economy 64
State and Revolution (Lenin) 89
State-controlled investment 137, 141
state monopoly capitalism 29
'state socialism' 27n19

Steinherr, A. 154
Stein, Lorenz von 9–10, 79–80; on communism 80
Stiglitz, J. E. 42
structural selectivity 90
Struve, Peter 73–4, 82–6; idea of social evolution 74, 76–8; on Marxists 87; on piecemeal reformist process 88; on reform differentiation 83–4; on socialism 78
surplus value 14
Sweezy, P. M. 64, 169, 183
system of thought: dialectics as 112–13

Tasca, Angelo 167, 179
Tawney, R. H. 23, 37, 167
Taylorism 39
technological determinism 29
technology and capitalism 54
'theories of influence' 91
theory of the firm 15–17
theory of value 14
Therborn, G. 34
Theses on the Philosophy of History (Benjamin) 60
Thesis on Feuerbach (Marx) 121
Thisse, J. F. 154
To Have or to Be (Fromm) 99
Tornquist, D. 155
Tosel, A. 118n6
totalitarian integralism 20
trade unionism 185n16

Tronti, M. 169, 183
Tucker, R. C. 8–9, 78–80

unemployment 136–7; high-wage 137; Keynesian 137, 144; Schweickart's model 143–5; structural 143–4

Valenti, G. 100
van der Veen, R. J. 44
Vanek, J. 37–8, 114, 147–8, 158, 159, 176
Veblen, T. B. 127
voting-equity financing 161
Vygodskij, V. S. 14

Wallerstein, Immanuel 118n5
Walras, L. 171–2, 184n9
Ward, B. N. 25, 101, 124, 147, 154, 176
Webb, Beatrice 173
Weber, Max 26n3, 103
Weil, Simone 60
Western culture 125
Wolff, Richard 135, 167, 179; ownership rights, markets and planning 152–3; WSDE 150–2
worker-managed-firms (WMFs) 65, 155
working class: educational levels of 40, 67; higher income for 67; and living standards 67
WSDE 150–1; working of 151–2

Zamagni, S. 40, 67
Zasulich, Vera 33

.

Printed in Great Britain
by Amazon

65363362R00138